MEMORIES OF
WINTER BALL

MEMORIES OF WINTER BALL

Interviews with Players in the Latin American Winter Leagues of the 1950s

Lou Hernández

McFarland & Company, Inc., Publishers
Jefferson, North Carolina, and London

LIBRARY OF CONGRESS CATALOGUING-IN-PUBLICATION DATA

Hernández, Lou, 1958–
    Memories of winter ball : interviews with players in the
    Latin American Winter League / Lou Hernández.
        p.   cm.
    Includes bibliographical references and index.

    ISBN 978-0-7864-7141-6
    softcover : acid free paper ∞

    1. Baseball players—Latin America—Interviews.
    2. Baseball—Latin America—History.   3. Baseball—History.
    I. Title.
    GV865.A1H477 2013
    796.357098—dc23   2013010965

BRITISH LIBRARY CATALOGUING DATA ARE AVAILABLE

Front cover: Sam Jones and Herman Franks of the Santurce
Crabbers, c. 1954 (National Baseball Hall of Fame Library,
Cooperstown, NY); baseball graphic © 2013 Shutterstock

Manufactured in the United States of America

McFarland & Company, Inc., Publishers
  Box 611, Jefferson, North Carolina 28640
  www.mcfarlandpub.com

For my mother Martha,
who gave me life,
who gave me love.

ACKNOWLEDGMENTS

I would like to express my thanks to all the former ballplayers who provided their time and personal period photos.

Special thanks to Fred Kipp and Don and Isabel Lenhardt. Mr. Kipp took the time to reproduce and share with me enlarged team photos of his former Escogido clubs. Those teams boasted many recognizable future major league standouts. Mrs. Lenhardt took it upon herself to have numerous scrapbook photos reproduced for my use.

A deeply heart-felt degree of gratitude is afforded to the late Charles Monfort, who provided valuable images from his own personal collection.

Special thanks as well to Angel Colón for his photo images, and for the kindness he extended to me during my too brief stay in Puerto Rico.

I appreciate Jim Stocchero's cooperation in arranging an interview with his client Minnie Miñoso. I am grateful to Stan Williams, who helped facilitate a conversation with a former winter league teammate of his, Ed Roebuck. Another player, George Freese, intervened enough for me to secure an interchange with his brother Gene.

On a final, personal note, I would like to recognize and thank Dan Dobbek, who gave me as a gift an official *Liga de Baseball Profesional Cubana* baseball, horsehide cover and all!

TABLE OF CONTENTS

The Venezuelan Winter League

Passing of an Era: Don Leppert 245

PREFACE

The "golden era" of baseball is as elevated and as ennobled in Latin America as anywhere in North America. This is an oral history of players who lived that *época dorada,* playing in the spirited 1950s Pan American winter leagues of Mexico, Nicaragua, Panama, Venezuela, Cuba, the Dominican Republic and Puerto Rico. The consequential Mexican summer league is also included.

I contacted approximately 140 surviving players from the era through mass mailings, requesting their participation in this book. I tried each player twice, if I did not receive an initial response. I managed to speak to a total of 51 players.

The taped interviews—the majority of which were conducted over the phone—followed the same blueprint. I culled background and family information from each interviewee. Especially interesting was learning what ballplayers these future pros admired while they were growing up. From the signing of their first professional contracts, I led these mostly Depression-era babies as young men to their rendezvous in the Latin American leagues. Once there, I asked the former athletes a similar array of questions, ranging from residency, marital situation, diet, entertainment, recreation, stadiums and fans. I was also curious to hear each man's opinion on good players and pitchers they saw or knew. I tried to jog the players' memories on certain teammates and opposing players. When I clicked with a player in this regard, it was quite fulfilling to hear a chuckle, signaling an interesting anecdote was about to come forth. Of course, I cannot take all of the credit. The players dutifully volunteered a vast amount of information that I could not have begun to solicit.

It was great to get various views on the same combustible incident as a different narrator added some additional gem of information that wonderfully rounded out the particular story. The Frank Howard vs. Bill Sneathen Incident in the Dominican Republic and the Rubén Gómez/Orlando Cepeda vs. Mayagüez Fans Incident are two stellar examples.

I was amazed, so often, at the recall of these aged men. Monte Irvin spoke about his time in Mexico—nearly seventy years ago—with remarkable clarity. Eighty-three-year-old Charlie Gorin could name the hotels and casino and San Juan neighborhood he lived in more than half a century ago without hesitation. It was a vastly enjoyable period of their lives, which, no doubt, has kept pleasant and proud memories from completely fading. But I also surmised, in listening to the men, that one big reason for the sustaining recollections was the genuine love for the game that all the players clearly possessed.

I could not help but think about the treatment afforded to the North American players by their interim foreign owners. In addition to receiving higher salaries than the native competitors, all living expenses were paid for the visiting players and their wives and families, if the players chose to bring them. The living conditions and amenities provided to many players, especially in Havana and San Juan, were high-end vacation grade. What a shameful contrast to the inhospitable reception Hispanic players received during the same period in the United States, especially dark-skinned Hispanics. (Although black players from the U.S. might not have received the same upscale accommodations as their Caucasian counterparts, those black players' living conditions and general treatment were levels above what they encountered at home.)

I was marvelously struck by the number of enduring marriages these long-retired warriors of the diamond maintained. At the top of the list of longest unions were Luis and Emma Olmo, fostering 71 years of matrimony, and Cot and Katie Deal, with 67 years of wedded bliss.

Luis Olmo, left, the first Hispanic player to hit a home run in the World Series, and the author in San Juan, Puerto Rico, July 2011 (photograph taken by Jorge López).

I traveled to Puerto Rico during the creative process of this work to attend a ceremony honoring Nino Escalera. The homage to Escalera was conducted by the Puerto Rican chapter of the Society for American Baseball Research. The two-hour event was held at Sixto Escobar Stadium, the historic park of the Puerto Rican Winter League for nearly a quarter century. The front of the park, today, delivers a colorfully attractive welcome. A white brick walkway leads up to a cream-colored façade with arched windows set in a row framed by twin cupolas with Spanish tile. A bronze, pugilistic statue of the stadium's namesake is proudly stationed on a cylindrical perch about 50 feet from the main door. Occupying the usable space inside is the Puerto Rican Sports Hall of Fame and Museum. The 1960-61 league championship trophy presented to Bob Leith and his San Juan Senators team is prominently displayed and most caught my eye during a walk through. (Leith was present at the Escalera ceremony. He was an engaging speaker and showed great affection for Escalera. The former *capitalinos'* owner was quite energetic and spry for a man in his late eighties.)

Located in an idyllic setting — a short walk from the ocean — I tried to imagine *Estadio* Sixto Escobar in its heyday as I strolled around it and peeked through the gated apertures along its concrete perimeter. From the far end of the stadium, I surveyed the long grassy field, the grandstands on either side, and the enclave situated behind what used to be home plate that offered the stadium's best seating. A rust-encrusted chain link fence curved around the far end of the field — the outfield. Certainly not part of the original fencing that signaled loud cheers for any ballplayer who hit balls beyond it during the scores of mild winter nights of six decades past. The stadium's bleachers and large scoreboard that once loomed over that fencing are gone. The athletic track, a long oval cut of burnt orange, stands out the most now. The stadium is no longer in regular use. I was told the park is utilized by the local youth for track and field and soccer practices.

Right across from the ballpark is the old Normandie Hotel. Once a famous vacation stop for the affluent traveler from all over Latin America and the United States, the unique seven-story structure, architecturally designed in the shape of the ocean liner of the same name, stands abandoned with broken windows dotting its exterior. The subject of past restoration efforts due to its national landmark designation by the U.S. government, the hotel was where most visiting players stayed during trips to San Juan. It was the hotel that catered to the visiting national teams that participated in the three Caribbean Series played at Escobar Stadium.

I met several former players at the Escalera function, including the guest of honor. I was later able to speak to Nino as well as standout hurlers Pantalones Santiago and Julio Navarro. They all proved to be great gentlemen, in particular Santiago, with whom I had recurrent phone contact. (Sadly, several months after our meeting, Santiago called me with the news of his wife's passing, practically in his arms, he said.)

I closed every conversation with each player with a request for an autograph on a souvenir baseball. All the players said that they would be happy to accommodate me. It took three balls for me to obtain everyone's signature. I sent the balls to each of the players I did not meet personally, and was thrilled upon their return each time.

The interviews are arranged alphabetically under the leagues in which the players played. Often times, players participated in more than one winter circuit. In those instances, the league in which the player spent the most time or excelled the most was usually the determining placement factor.

Don Leppert is placed as the final interview because his winter league excursions bridged a direct passing of one era into the next — the era depicted in this book into the one that followed. Leppert played winter ball in the 1950s in Mexico and Venezuela, and then one final season in 1962 in Puerto Rico. Leppert was one of the players on one of the teams that inaugurated Hiram Bithorn Stadium in San Juan. The stadium, at a cost of $7 million, was built as the new home of the San Juan Senators and Santurce Crabbers. Its grand opening in October 1962 left Sixto Escobar Stadium, the former home of the Senators and Crabbers, to antiquated status. Sixto Escobar Stadium, the place where so many legendary players performed and the site of many historic episodes in the Puerto Rican Winter League, was, sadly for many, shuttered in deference to progress and the procession of time.

And so, allow me to present the players, all now in the winters of their lives, as they recount their own personal and wistful remembrances of the winters of their youth.

THE CUBAN WINTER LEAGUE

George Altman

George Altman, 78 years young when I interviewed him, was active in a personal empowerment organization and residing in Missouri. He came across as a thoughtful, soft-spoken individual.

Altman earned his trip to the elite Cuban Winter League of 1959 months before the season began, through his own initiative and by having had a standout spring camp with the Chicago Cubs. (Altman credits his playing in Panama the previous winter for paving the way.) The Cubs' rookie played on perhaps the best Cuban baseball team of all time. Altman's Cienfuegos Elefantes club set a record for wins and was the only Cuban League team to boast three 10-game winners. Altman remembered his fellow starters perfectly.

Though fighting ankle problems toward the end of the '59-60 winter season, Altman was still able to lead the league in runs (41). A left-handed slugger, Altman trailed only Panchón Herrera for most four-baggers in the league (15 to 14). Although he stated that his playing time was curtailed in the Caribbean Series of 1960 because of the same ankle problems, Altman managed to hit .438 (7 for 16) and ended up tied for most walks received (6) in the tournament held in Panama City. (One of the free passes he received forced in the winning run in one of the games.)

Altman was a former Negro Leaguer who crossed over to the major leagues in 1959. In his first at-bat in his debut game, Altman was welcomed to the Show by being drilled by a pitch from Don Drysdale. (Altman singled in his second time up against Drysdale, his first official AB.) A nine-year major league player and two-time all-star, the outfielder/first baseman became the first hitter to crack two home runs against Sandy Koufax in one game (August 4, 1961). The former Kansas City Monarchs player also excelled in Japan, slugging 205 home runs during an eight-year, post–big league encampment.

Where are you from?

I am an only child from Goldsboro, North Carolina.

How did you get started in baseball?

My elementary school had a small team and that is how I started, playing around the sandlots.

Who were your baseball heroes?

Jackie Robinson, of course. Willie Mays and Monte Irvin. The year Bobby Thomson hit that home run, that was great.

Tell me about your early experiences playing as a professional.

I was with the Chicago Cubs as a rookie in 1959, and I had not had much experience, because I had played Class A ball. I went to spring training with a Triple A contract, and I found out they needed a centerfielder in Cuba for the next winter season. I never played centerfield, but I told them I did. I had a good spring with the Cubs, because I had played in Panama the prior winter. I knew there were great players in Cuba, major league players. I thought it would be a great experience and it was.

In Cuba, you played on a powerhouse team. What are your recollections of your manager and teammates?

[Mgr.] Antonio Castaño was a good guy. What I most remember about him was his credo: "Today we lose — tomorrow we fight, again." I liked playing for Tony. We had a great team. We had great pitching, good offense, good defense. We had several major leaguers. That was just a fun time to play. That was a great league, with a lot of great players. Camilo

In Cuba, George Altman led the league in runs scored and finished second in home runs for the powerhouse Cienfuegos Elefantes of 1959-60 (courtesy Charles Monfort).

Pascual was a great pitcher. Great curveball. A consummate pro. Pedro [Ramos] was a fun guy. A fun-loving guy. Pistol Pete we called him. He had a good fastball and slider, and was a good teammate. Raúl Sánchez had a ... I do not know if it was a spitball or not, but it was a good sinker. He was accused, let us say. Oswaldo Alvarez and Cookie Rojas were both good fielders, good baseball guys. Both had good speed. Young Chico [Cárdenas]. He was a young guy at the time. I do not know if he had made the Reds yet. Gritty, wiry, thin guy, but with great wrists. I felt Chico was going to be a major league shortstop someday. Don Eaddy was a Cub prospect. He had played college ball in Michigan. Good defender, a real nice guy. [Román] Mejías. Yeah, went on to play with the Pittsburgh Pirates and Houston, I believe. Good power. Tony González. Great outfielder. Real strong arm. Good bat. Could run pretty good. Dan Dobbek, Washington Senators. Dan was our right fielder. Real strong pull hitter. Had good power. Borrego [Alvarez] played some first base for us. He got caught up in the visa thing when he came to the states. I guess some of the guys told him not to go back to Cuba. That was after '59. I think Borrego lost a few years there. I do not know if he was ever able to come back to the states. I think he would have been a real good major leaguer. He had great power. I played mostly first base and some out-field. Tony González was our centerfielder. I played right. I was leading the league in home runs, up until the time I hurt my ankle. I missed a lot of the last month of the season.

What about recollections away from the ball yard?

I remember walking down the street; it was festive, there was music going on all the time, all day long and half the night. Also after the games, at these outdoor parks, there was dancing and, it was just a great, fun time, looking like Mardi Gras every day.

Talk about the stadium in which you played.

It was a pretty big park [Gran Stadium]. A great place to play. I remember, before going to the park, Castro was making his public radio broadcast, and we would go and play the game. We would come back and Castro was still talking. [Laughs.] The same speech!

Did the political situation in Cuba affect you?

Castro had not declared himself at the time. But what I do remember, which was kind of scary, was, once, some of the exiles flew over Havana and dropped leaflets, declaring Castro was communist. I do not know who was involved, but evidently there were some skirmishes inside Havana. Grenades went off. Anyway, next day in the paper there were photos of people lying in the street and the headline in the paper said, UNITED STATES BOMBS

CUBA. It was all propaganda. But it is kind of scary when you see photos like that. We were afraid to go outside for a few days.

Do you remember any important figures that were baseball fans?

General [Camilo] Cienfuegos used to come to the park all the time. I guess he was second-in-command to Castro. He was probably just as popular as Castro, even more so. Maybe that was a problem. Cienfuegos died in a suspicious plane crash. I was saddened by that. He seemed to be a really nice fellow. I never met him personally, but he came to the ballpark.

Where did you live in Cuba?

I lived close to one of the casinos. I cannot say that there was discrimination, or anything like that. There may have been some subtle things going on. I went to the beach a couple of times. For some reason or another, I did not feel that welcomed. I cannot remember what beach that was. I usually hung around the hotel quite a bit, except for these outdoor festivities with the dancing, after the games. I was not the nightclubbing type. My wife came down for maybe six weeks. She did not like it that much. My wife became pregnant, and she went back to the States.

Who, in your opinion, was the best player?

Hard to say who was the best player. The guys on my team. Tony González. The best pitcher I saw down there — Camilo Pascual. Raúl Sánchez was not too far behind. He was a surly, nasty type on the mound. I remember a little skirmish Sánchez and Bob Allison had. Allison was hit by a pitch thrown by Raúl, and Allison was mouthing off to Raúl all the

A commander of the Cuban Revolutionary Army, the popular Camilo Cienfuegos — in his recreational uniform. A pre–Marxist Fidel Castro is in the background. A few months after this photograph was taken, Cienfuegos was killed in an unexplained plane crash over Cuba (Getty Images).

way down to first base. And on the next pitch, Raúl took his wind up and whirled and threw the ball right at Allison at first base. You know what happened next. Everybody is grabbing everybody else, pushing and shoving.

What about the 1960 Caribbean Series in Panama City? What stands out for you?

I did not play that much in the [1960] Caribbean Series, because, as I said, I hurt my ankle. I still had trouble with the ankle the following spring with the Cubs. I was probably so excited to be back in Panama, to see some of my Panamanian friends, that I do not seem to remember too much of the Series. After we won the Series, I came back to Cuba with the team. I do not recall the celebrations. There may have been. I do not remember participating in any. It was probably old hat for them.

You mentioned Panama. How long did you play in that winter league?

I played for the Marlboro Smokers in Panama in 1958. I remember playing against Héctor López. We called Alonso Brathwaite, a teammate of mine, the Panamanian Jackie Robinson. I do not know how he got that nickname, but that is what we called him. I do not remember any real hard throwers in Panama. Humberto Robinson had a good sinker. Good control. It seemed like it rained all the time at the stadium there. It was big stadium. I stayed at one of the hotels in Panama City. I had not married yet. In Panama, there was a lot of drinking. The players would go and practice or play the game, and then go straight to the bar and be there for most of the evening. Next day, the same thing. They loved their beer. I drank too much beer while I was in Panama. One of the teams was sponsored by a brewery — Cerveza Balboa. I do not know if the players got free beer or not. I know when I played in St. Louis, we used to go on the road and come back, and there was case of beer waiting.

Any closing comments?

It was definitely a good experience. Good training. You played with and against good ballplayers. It was a fun time. I would recommend to any young player to play in the winter leagues and get that experience and polish your skills.

Dick Brodowski

Dick Brodowski's 1952 major league debut was a baptism of fire. Six weeks shy of his twentieth birthday, Brodowski, a Boston Red Sox pitcher, was called on to relieve in a bases loaded, no-out situation against the

Chicago White Sox at Comiskey Park. Unperturbed by a hostile Sunday afternoon crowd, Brodowski induced a double play from the first batter he faced (pitcher-to-catcher-to-first) and then retired Chico Carrasquel on a flyout. Brodowski did not allow an earned run in four standout innings of "mop-up" work, as the Red Sox were defeated 7–2.

Following Brodowski's rookie season, the pitcher's career was interrupted by a military service enlistment. Brodowski returned to the Red Sox sparingly in 1955, and that winter found himself in Puerto Rico, plying his trade for Ponce and then San Juan. Two winters later, hurling for Almendares, Brodowski, along with Bob Shaw, stood out as the top pitchers in the Cuban Winter League. The right-hander tied Shaw for most wins (14), and led the circuit in shutouts (5), while finishing third to Marianao's Shaw and Mike Fornieles in ERA.

A New Jerseyan by birth, Brodowski pitched in six major league seasons, mostly as a reliever. The divorced father of four girls resides in Massachusetts. Brodowski was scheduled for hip replacement surgery imminently following our main communication, and hoped it would not put too much of a crimp in his life of leisurely retirement.

Where were you born, and how many in your family?

I was born in Bayonne, New Jersey, July 26, 1932. Mother, father, two brothers and myself.

How did you become interested in baseball?

A friend of my mine that lived close by had a couple of gloves; I was always hounding him to play catch with me in his backyard. That is my earliest baseball memory.

What team did you root for as a youngster, and who was your favorite player?

My father was Dodger fan, and I ended up being a Dodger fan, not admiring any one player — I loved them all.

When did you start applying yourself to the game?

I played three years on my high school team, and in the summer played two years of sandlot ball. I did not do much pitching until my senior year, and I did pretty well. In the sandlot league, I did very well.

When did your professional career start?

There was a Boston scout named Bill McCarren who lived in Jersey City; he signed me for the Red Sox. That was 1950. In 1951, I was assigned to D ball in Marion, Ohio. I did well there. I started out as a third baseman. I was signed as third baseman/pitcher. The manager of the Marion team wanted me to concentrate on pitching, because we needed pitching help. I won 23 and lost 5. I nearly made the Red Sox the following spring. I was one of three pitchers vying for two spots on the staff. I pitched in an exhibition game against the Braves at Fenway Park, and did not do so hot. The team called me into the office and told me they were going to send me to A Ball. I made a case that I had almost made the big club and asked if they could send me to a higher bracket. To satisfy me, they assigned me to Louisville, which was Triple A. In my first eight starts, I was 7–1. Lou Boudreau [Red Sox manager] decided to bring me up to the Red Sox in the middle of June. I was 5–5 for the Red Sox the rest of the season.

I went onto the Army in 1953 and '54. In 1955, when I came out, I was allowed to be on the military list with the Red Sox — I did not count on the Red Sox roster. I kept asking to be sent to the minors to do some pitching. But the Red Sox did not listen, they just carried me. And I am glad they did not listen, because, at the end of my career, I needed that time for my pension. I would have given up almost a full year to my pension. And that is how I ended up playing winter ball. Since I did not do much pitching for the Red Sox, somebody on the team lined me up with somebody in Puerto Rico to pitch for Ponce.

In Ponce, you played for Mickey Owen.

Mickey Owen *was* my manager. I was trying to think who it was. Now that you mention him, he caught for the Red Sox; I am sure that is how I ended up in Puerto Rico to begin with. I pitched poorly for Ponce. I was 0–6. The team was sending me home. As it happened, on the northern part of the island, the San Juan team needed pitching. San Juan took a chance on me. I turned things around with them. I went 8–2.

North American players in Havana during the 1957-58 season. Top row, from left to right: Solly Drake, Bobby Bragan, Dick Brodowski, Bill Werle, Billy Muffett, Bob Will, Archie Wilson, Clyde McCullough, Bob Shaw, Coach Acho Varona. Bottom row: Joe Hatten, Russ Nixon, Lloyd Merritt, Bud Peterson, Billy O'Dell, Dick Gray, Spook Jacobs, Milt Smith, Rocky Nelson (courtesy D. Brodowski).

Where did you stay in Ponce?

I lived in a house that also was rented by Faye Throneberry, his wife and one child — about a year or so old. Pumpsie Green stayed there. We lived about five or six blocks from the town square. There were apartments near the square. We hung around those apartments, because that is where the pool was. I was single. That is what I did, until I was 0–6, and started packing. Next thing I heard, I was supposed to report to San Juan — and that turned out to be beautiful.

In San Juan, right across the street from the ballpark, there were these cabana-type set-ups, next to the big hotels. I lived in one of those cabanas for the remainder of the season. I walked across the street to the ballpark in my spikes. There was a hotel next to the ballpark, what was the name of it?

That must have been the Normandie Hotel.

I used to eat in that hotel, and I even stayed there before I moved into my cabana. I can still picture it. And down the street was the Hilton, I remember that.

What was the stadium like in San Juan?

The stadium was fine. Just like in Ponce. All the parks in Puerto Rico were good ballparks.

And what were the fans like?

There seemed to be more fans in San Juan. I do not remember much about the fans. No one could say my name, which was funny. They used to announce me: *el numero quince* — Dick Broduckie. [Laughs.] I still remember that. I thought that was very funny.

How did you like the food in Puerto Rico?

I never varied away from American food, except maybe when we traveled and would stop at places along the road.

Glad you brought up travel. What do you recall about that aspect of your stay?

When I was with Ponce, we would commute back and forth, wherever we played. The only time we stayed in a hotel was when we made a trip to Mayagüez, which was on the western part of the island. Otherwise, we took old Cadillacs up over the mountains from Ponce to Caguas, about two-thirds of the way, and the remaining third of the way was Santurce and San Juan. Going over the mountains, we did not have any exciting escapes of death, or anything like that. The road was just narrow. It did not make for a fun trip. When I was with San Juan, we took a big bus, which was comfortable, to play in Mayagüez, and we would stay overnight in Mayagüez.

How about teammates or opposing players?

I do not remember too many of the players. I seem to be more conscious of the players from when I played in Cuba. I had Orlando Cepeda launch a few on me when I was with Ponce. Oh, there was Roberto Clemente. I played against him, and he was awesome. The way he ran. The dirt flying up from his spikes. And he could hit the ball all over the place. He was terrific. I do not remember the pitching in Puerto Rico. It was a great experience. I loved it. I was very satisfied with my performance with San Juan, especially after that 0–6 start in Ponce. I felt a little tired when I came back, but I did not care.

You then skipped a winter before you returned to Caribbean.

I came home at the end of January, and was married on February 11. I had been traded by the Red Sox to the Washington Senators while I was in Puerto Rico. In 1956, I was whacked around early with the Senators and they demoted me their Triple A team. Washington traded me to Cleveland in 1957. I did not stick with Cleveland. They sent me to San Diego in May. I ended up 13–6 with San Diego. A man named Monchy de Arcos, a real nice man, asked me if I wanted to play in Cuba with Almendares. I met him right there in San Diego. Monchy de Arcos may have been friendly with Bobby Bragan, who managed with Cleveland and in Cuba.

Where did you stay in Cuba?

In Cuba, my wife and I stayed at a hotel that was out away from the city. A woman owned the hotel. She seemed to be a wealthy woman. The hotel was on the ocean. It was about four stories, not a lot of rooms, but it was very, very nice. Bragan stayed there. That is probably why I did, too. Although I do not remember any other ballplayers who stayed there. We used to wait on the corner of the block and somebody would pass by and pick us up and take us to the ballpark. Later, I rented a car, for convenience sake.

How was the stadium in Havana, and how were the fans?

The stadium was in good shape, the clubhouses were big and fine, from what I remember. Again, with the fans, I cannot tell you much. I shut the fans out. That was the way I operated. The fans rooted for their teams. That is all I can tell you. I had a very good year, so that would be part of not having recollections of the fans. I was pitching out of my socks—13–3. The Indians sent Mel Harder to work with the Cleveland players. Our team had Mudcat Grant, myself, Russ Nixon, and someone else. Harder showed me how to throw a slow curve, which I enjoyed using. But then after working out with Harder, and throwing a lot of pitches on the side, I went through this spell where I could not get anyone out. I think I lost three or four games in row. The loses were by scores of 4–0, games where we did not get any runs. I finished the season 1–4, because of the overthrowing on the side.

Your teammate Mudcat Grant, he made an impressive mark in the majors.

What impressed me about Grant was that he had a really good fastball. Grant was learning to throw a curve. All he had to do was bounce it in front of the plate and the batters would chase after it because they were so geared up for his fastball. Grant had a great year in San Diego—as matter of fact, I think he won 21 games. That is why Cleveland sent him down to Cuba.

Another pitcher on your Almendares' staff was Mike Cuéllar.

Mike Cuéllar, I did not have much contact with. Except when the guys used to pick on one another, he was good humored, joking and friendly about things. He was a kid. I was surprised when he blossomed in the big leagues. Off-speed stuff, with the screwball, and a mediocre fastball; he could shut down the best of them. I heard he passed away. Do you know what from? Oh, okay. Tough opponent.

Did you socialize much in Havana?

We went out a few times into the city with the Bragans. Two or three couples would be invited. Like I said, we had a car for about a month or so. There was a pool where we lived. Our kids were small and we hung around [our apartment]. Even though Bragan lived in our apartment house, I did not lean on him, so to speak. I met him occasionally away from the park. Bragan was always very kind to us—and he passed away not too long ago. I remember reading about it in our baseball newsletter. It is a baseball alumni newspaper. Among other things, it lists players' deaths. It is really odd to be reading every month or two about the deaths of all these players I played with, or remember. Gil McDougal, Cal McLish, Gus Zernial, Spook Jacobs, and good friends, George Susce and Bob Chakales, whom I played with in Washington. It is so sad to be reading about it...

Again, I'll ask about the food.

I ate as much American food as I could. I still, to this day, do not try different things at restaurants very frequently.

We talked teammates. How about the opposition? Let me toss out a couple of names, starting with Minnie Miñoso and Brooks Robinson.

Minnie was fantastic. He set the record for most decades played in the big leagues. Miñoso was a hustler, and a perfect guy to lead a team by example, to show everybody how the game is played. He used to crowd the plate. He never gave up. I remember pitching against Minnie at Fenway. I hung a pitch, and he really hit it out over the Green Monster. I later played with Minnie in Cleveland. Brooks Robinson was one of the tough guys I remember pitching to. He played second base for Cienfuegos. I would throw a flat curveball, you know, a hard curve, and Robinson used to line out to third base all the time on that pitch. It was amazing — at least once a game. I mean Robinson would hit the crap out of it — but *fweuww*, right to third for the out. I said to myself, I don't know if I should plan on getting him out this way. [Chuckles.]

Shaw was probably the best pitcher.

Right-hander Bob Shaw.

Bob Shaw. I remember one game I had a chance to beat him in a game. I was batting near the end of the game with the bases loaded. Shaw threw me a slider. I half went after it, and I bounced it on one hop back to him. He threw home, and then catcher threw to first, double play. [Willy] Miranda came up after that and popped to the infield.

Any final reflections?

Both places, Cuba and Puerto Rico, were great places to play in. Keeping a steady stream of income was great, as well.

Dan Dobbek

A September call-up in 1959, Washington Senators' rookie Dan Dobbek was one of the six North American players to suit up for the Elephants of Cienfuegos during the 1959-60 winter season, the last in which U.S. imports participated in Cuban baseball.

Dobbek and George Altman were teammates on a dominant Cienfuegos team that stomped its way through the 1960 Caribbean Series without losing a game. Dobbek hit two home runs in the Series, including a game-deciding two-run blast against Caguas' Earl Wilson on the second day of the competition. The Cuban revolution was in its infancy and the upheaval affected Dobbek in Havana on one recreational level, when he was forced to send back to the States his automobile for fear of it being damaged due to anti–American sentiment.

Dobbek followed the Senators franchise to Minnesota in 1961, his last year in the major leagues.

Living now in Oregon, the native of Michigan has been married for 42 years to Joan and is the father of two sons. One of those sons owns various rental properties which Dan spends his days maintaining.

Where were you born?

A small town in upper Michigan, spelled O-n-t-o-n-a-g-o-n. December 6, 1934.

How big was your family?

I had one sister. She passed away when she was 24.

What are your earliest baseball memories?

Playing baseball, it was not easy, because snow would not leave the ground until April, and it was muddy. We did not have Little League or American Legion. In the summers, I was batboy for the city league baseball team. I would take all the old balls and throw them against a school brick wall, trying to make myself a good fielder. I would go down to Lake Superior and get a piece of driftwood and knock rocks into Lake Superior.

How did you come to play baseball professionally?

I went to college at Western Michigan University. In the summer, I played at Battle Creek. That was where I was discovered, after my freshman year in college by a part-time scout named Dick Wiencek. He worked for the Upjohn Pill Company. Wiencek signed Jack Kralick and Jim Kaat and myself, all in the same year. We all made it to the big leagues in 1959, so that was a pretty good signing catch for him. Washington made him a full time scout after that. My first year was in Hobbs, New Mexico, in 1956. Then I spent two years in the army. Came out and went to Chattanooga. Then was called up at the end of the 1959 season with the Senators.

The Senators sent you to Cuba. What was that journey like?

I drove to Key West and took the ferry over to Havana.

Let's see, you celebrated your 25th birthday in Havana. Were you married?

I was single. I had a 1959 Impala. They did not have too many traffic lights or stop signs on the streets of Havana. [Chuckles.] It was beep-beep, and I am going through.

Where did you live?

I lived in an apartment house, right across the street almost from George Raft's gambling casino in the Hotel Capri.

Your car went over with you?

I had to send my car back to Key West a few months later. There was a little controversy, shall we say, with Fidel. There were planes flying over dropping pamphlets. At the same time, you had Batista guys running around throwing Molotov Cocktails. Fidel announced it was the North Americans bombing and strafing the city. I found a note left on my car. It was in Spanish, and I could not read it. But Dutch Dotterer, my teammate, he understood Spanish. And he told me it said I had to get my car home or they would blow it up. So I sent it back to Key West. We did not play for about a week during that time. They started the anti–American rallies. They brought in dump trucks full of people from all over, to march in protest. There was militia on every other street corner. No police. We did not do a lot of running around after that. We would sit on a veranda or something, playing pinochle. It was not the greatest time at times, but it was still a lot of fun. So much so, I still have my old cap, with the black and green "C."

Sounds like restrictions were descending all over.

We [ballplayers] were the only ones on the island that could trade our money in. We would get paid in pesos and Fidel would let us exchange. We had to go through the Hanover Bank in New York. We had allotments sent back here. We were making a thousand dollars a month. It cost us seventeen dollars to trade that amount in. Then we got three hundred dollars on top of that for expenses. It was a good paying winter league.

On what kind of dishes did you put your meal money to use?

I ate mostly American food. Ham and eggs, stuff like that.

That season, you played behind two of Cuba's most outstanding pitchers of the era. Pedro Ramos and Camilo Pascual, who were also teammates of yours with Washington.

Pedro Ramos lived very close to us. Camilo Pascual lived down there, too. Camilo was more of a quiet guy. He did not do much. But Pedro, he was the Roy Rogers of Cuba. Pedro would come to the ballpark dressed in all that cowboy stuff, wearing six-shooters and holsters. He was a huge fan of American Westerns. Pedro drove a Pontiac convertible with a Continental Kit on the back. He was the playboy. [Chuckles.] George [Altman] played the outfield and first base. George did not live with us.

What was it like to play for Tony Castaño?

Castaño was kind of strict. Never said too much. It was my first time away from the United States, so I was not going to be doing too much questioning, especially the manager.

Dan Dobbek in his Cienfuegos uniform (courtesy Charles Monfort).

The league started playing games outside of Havana that year. Your team was part of that.

We went to the city of Cienfuegos, we went down by bus, to play a league game there. But I do not remember much more, except the park there was much smaller than in Havana. It is hard for me to picture the big stadium in Havana, now, because of all the stadiums I did play in. The fans were always good. They always like a winner, I guess. I played against some of the guys from Washington — Bob Allison, he played for one of the other teams.

Who was the best player you saw in Cuba?

Well, Minnie Miñoso. [Leo] Cárdenas was good and [Tony] González. The pitchers were all pretty good. We had Pascual, Ramos and Sánchez. That was a hell of a pitching trio.

I would like to hear about the Caribbean Series. Cienfuegos capped their monumental season with a flourish in Panama City.

I remember the Caribbean Series. I remember the stadium in Panama. [Laughs.] It had canvass all around the outfield. Dark canvass hoisted beyond the walls. To prevent the fans from throwing stuff on the field. The fans kept throwing Balboas— stubby beer bottles into the outfield. One game, they had to keep calling time, to pick up the empty beer bottles. You could not see over the canvass, so no one sat in the bleachers. The ballpark was open all the way around except the bleachers. That was the first time I wore a helmet on the field on defense. There was animosity between the Panamanian fans and the Cuban team. I do not know if it had to do with something from the Caribbean Series the prior year. Our team was pretty well bombarded leaving the stadium. The people were not happy losing, or with us.

When we were in Panama, I missed a trip to the Canal. Some players went, and somehow I missed the rendezvous point. I would have liked to have seen it.

You hit a two-run home run that provided the margin of victory in game two of the competition.

The [game-deciding] home run I hit against Earl Wilson was great. You are young and full of come-what-may. I took it all in, and I was happy. We did not lose a game in the tournament.

What did you take away from that championship experience?

The plane trip back was good. Everyone was drinking Bacardí and smoking cigars. They had all kinds of people on the plane that were not ballplayers. The cabin looked like a pool room. It was a fun trip back to Havana.

Chico Fernández

Chico Fernández was one of the first players I contacted when I started my project. His wife Lynne wrote me back saying that Chico had been recently operated on and was not doing well. More than a year later, I came across a recovered Humberto Fernández at a SABR chapter meeting. Chico was the honorary invitee at the gathering. There, I arranged to interview him. I paid him a visit at his Sunrise, Florida, home.

Fernández played ten seasons in the Cuban Winter League, commencing with an eight game participation in 1951-52 as a 19-year-old with the Cienfuegos Elephants. In his decade-long career, Fernández hit over .300 twice, no easy feat in that league at any time. In a testament to his reliability and durability, Fernández three times led the league in at-bats. He also topped the league in stolen bases (14) in 1953-54 and doubles (17) in 1955-56. That latter season, Cienfuegos won the pennant and claimed the Caribbean Series championship, beating Puerto Rican representative Caguas 4–2 on the final day of the tournament. Midway through the 1958-59 campaign, Fernández was involved in a five-player trade that moved him to Habana. In a repeat occurrence the following season, the shortstop was traded by Habana to Almendares for Willy Miranda. With Almendares, Fernández started at shortstop in the last game played in Cuban Winter League history, occurring on February 8, 1961. Hitting second in the lineup, Fernández collected one hit in four trips to the plate as Almendares suffered an 8–2 defeat to Cienfuegos. The game decided the last Cuban League pennant on the season's final day.

Except for a three-pronged walking cane, necessitated by multiple operations on the same knee, the eighty-year-old Fernández appeared in fine health. His guttural voice boomed often at the chance to make several points about different players during my nearly two-hour visit. Invariably, Fernández ended up talking about his time in the major leagues, where he enjoyed an eight-year tenure with four different big league clubs. One of them, the Philadelphia Phillies, in 1957, offered an amazing bounty to the Brooklyn Dodgers to acquire the 25-year-old player. The Phillies traded four of their major leaguers and a minor league player plus $75,000 to obtain Fernández and a player to be named later from the Dodgers, the team that had first signed Chico.

You are from Cuba's capital?

I was born in La Habana, La Vibora. I can even tell you where — 20012 Avenida Lacret.

How many in your family?

There were four of us. My parents and my brother. We had other family — but we did not visit with each other much. We were very poor. My father was a mason. My mother stayed at home, but she helped out a lot.

You were able to bring your parents to the United States from Cuba.

My father died in Detroit. He lived until he was 88. He was a heavy smoker in Cuba, and we are talking filterless cigarettes. Cigarettes were a vice to him. He kept smoking here, too, against doctor's orders. My mother lasted until 2008. She was 96 when she died. I never smoked cigarettes. Cuban cigarettes were too harsh, too strong. But I took up smoking cigars, because of Sandy Amorós; he introduced me to them. I tried not to inhale the smoke of cigars. In the mid-eighties, I weaned myself off cigars. I would smoke one, but over the course of an entire day. Then I stopped. Every spring training, I would make points with the managers by bringing boxes of cigars to them from Cuba. Every manager I ever had, they all loved Cuban cigars. I was a known player in Cuba by then, and the different cigar factories—there were a lot of them — would give me boxes for free. They were always a big hit in spring camp. Of course, when I smoked cigars, they were 25 cents. Now they are five dollars apiece.

What about your current family?

I married in Detroit for the first time in 1964. My first wife is named Geraldine. I lived in Detroit for over 30 years. I have three daughters, all of them still live there. I sold life insurance for 20 years in Detroit. I married Lynne in 1994.

How did you begin playing baseball?

I started playing ball in public school. It so happened that we won our regional championship two years in a row. We won the Havana regionals, not the Cuban championship. Both years we lost to teams from the other five provinces of the island. I was studying to be an electrician in a technical school when the Marist Brothers offered me a scholarship to attend their school. After graduation, I moved into amateur baseball.

I was invited to a party, a gathering with some of my friends my first year in amateur ball. And Rodolfo Fernández showed up at this party, which was somewhat of a miracle, looking back at it. Fernández at that time lived in New York. He was coach with Alemendares, but he lived in New York. I was mentioned to him, and he invited me to a tryout with Almendares. I made a good impression with everyone at the tryout. With all the coaches, including Sungo Carrera. But Almendares had Willy Miranda at shortstop, my position. So they recommended me to Cienfuegos. I was 19. Cienfuegos also liked me, and someone alerted Andy High, who was one of the heads of scouting with Brooklyn. High signed me to a Class C ball professional contract in 1951.

What do you remember about your first year in the league?

With Cienfuegos, I hardly played in 1951, but I felt very lucky to be on the team. Billy Herman was the manager of Cienfuegos. I cannot remember my first game in the league. I became a fulltime starter at shortstop the next season at age 20.

I met Adolfo Luque in my first year with Cienfuegos. He sometimes got into with the players because they could not perform up to his standard. Luque sometimes had the same problem as Ted Williams when he managed. They could not get the players to do what they did.

You mentioned one Cuban legend. What about his equally legendary contemporary, Mike González?

Miguel Angel González. He had stepped down from managing by the time I was traded to Habana. But he still owned the team and paid everyone, every 15 days, on payday. I remember he used to tease Sandy Amorós on payday — "Are you savings your pennies, son?" — saying things like that to him. [Chuckles.]

How did you commute to Gran Stadium?

I used to take the number 14 bus to El Cerro. The bus dropped me off about six blocks from the stadium, and then I walked the rest of the way. I did that for a few years. Until 1955, when I bought my first car — a Buick. A Buick Century. Hardtop. I was crazy about Buicks. A few years later, even though I was a still a young player, I sort of mentored other players. I drove them to the games: Tony Díaz. Tony Taylor. I also bought a Buick to use here, in 1958. I bought it in Miami before Spring Training. I was with the Phillies, and we trained in Florida. Guess what? The car had air conditioning, but no heating. That came back to haunt me over the next few winters in Detroit. [Laughs.]

What was it like to play in front of the hometown fans?

At Gran Stadium, the right field bleacher fans were the ones that would get on the players the most. They would yell things at the outfielders like, "I saw you at so-and-so a place last night...."

Sundays were doubleheader days. Cienfuegos and Marianao usually played in the first game; Almendares and Habana hooked up in the nightcap. After playing the first game, I would often stay and watch the second game. Afterwards, a few of us, Amorós and [Angel] Scull, would go out to dinner. [Julio] Bécquer. Sometimes [Minnie] Miñoso. [Juan] Delís. La Primavera Restaurant was a place we liked to go. Carlos Paula was always there.

Do you remember when Cienfuegos changed managers? You had a break-out season.

Al Campanis became manager of Cienfuegos in 1953-54. He spoke Spanish. He could communicate well with all the players. Sort of like Tom Lasorda.

Boy, Lasorda had the gift of gab. He spoke Spanish and was well liked. I think we finished second in the league that year.

You scored the most runs in the 1956 Caribbean Series—ten.

In 1954-55, I hit .302 and led the league in at-bats. I am not sure where we finished [last place]. The next season [1955-56], Cienfuegos won the league and Caribbean Series, played in Panama. Oscar Rodríguez had taken over as manager from Regino Otero. Our whole infield consisted of North American players except for myself. Bob Boyd was our first baseman, and Curt Roberts played second. Milton Smith — he was a wild man — he played third. What I remember about the Caribbean Series is that the Puerto Rican team had Clemente and Cepeda. We went out to eat after one of the games. That Cepeda could eat! He could eat a whole pizza at one sitting. Clemente and I had been roommates [minor leagues with Montreal], but later on we had a bit of a falling out. I cannot remember much about the stadium in Panama or the fans ... I could have sworn it was Camilo Pascual that won the championship game, and not Pedro Ramos, as you say ... I do not remember any parade for us when we returned to Cuba. I recall a parade they had for Almendares once, when they won the championship. I attended. It passed close to where we lived. I remember seeing [Andrés] Fleitas and Fermín Guerra. Almendares was a very popular team. Monte Irvin was on that team, too.

Chico Fernández enjoyed a potent offensive campaign in 1962, slugging .410 and hitting 20 home runs as a shortstop for the Detroit Tigers.

That same season, Vinegar Bend Mizell came down to pitch in the league. He pitched for Habana and set strikeout records. A left hander. Hard-thrower. Habana did not pitch him much against us from what I remember. Habana mostly wanted him to pitch against Almendares. I tell people about a Mizell story involving myself that they cannot believe. He walked me in a game and, on the first pitch he threw to the next batter, I stole second. On the second pitch he made, I stole third base. On the third pitch, I stole home! Mizell could not hold anyone on.

Speaking of pitchers, do you remember Jim Bunning?

Bunning arrived in '56-'57. He had a great season. Marianao won the championship. Bunning pitched for them. I played with him in Detroit. Marianao also had a terrific pitcher in Bob Shaw when they won it all again [1957-58].

Another pitcher who became pretty terrific was Mike Cuéllar.

Cuéllar was with Almendares. He really became a good pitcher here. We had our doubts about Cuéllar. But he proved us wrong. We all thought another pitcher who was younger than Cuéllar, Marcelino López, was going to be the star, the 20-game winner. He threw really hard. Cuéllar developed that screwball. Rubén Gómez taught it to him.

Rubén Gómez was a character. He was some kind of auto mechanic, too. He could disassemble a car engine and put it back together like that. And he never slept. He liked the nightlife too much, and carousing. Gómez and I were roommates briefly in Philadelphia. He used to look through binoculars from our apartment, trying to spy women in the other apartments in various stages of dress. I then found him a rental home in Philadelphia, and he sent for his wife. When he did not want to go home after a game, he would ask me to stop by his place and tell his wife that he decided to stop at a local bar. And he would stay out all night.

Getting back to the winter league, the revolution culminated during the '58-'59 campaign.

When the revolution came, what I remember at the stadium was that there would be flyovers by military jets. They were conducting exercises. Tony González, our centerfielder, would become scared. [Laughs.] González came running in from center, one time, after a flyover, with all the dive-bombing noises going on; he ran right into the dugout and clubhouse. Amado Maestri [umpire] tried to stop him. [Laughs more.] But Tony was gone. There were air patrols all over the city. When those people came, they could do whatever they felt like in the city.

We [players] knew we had to leave after the '61 season. Castro had stated we could not continue to earn money playing baseball. Castro confiscated the money we had in the Cuban Players' Association fund — Miñoso, as a matter of fact, was the president of the association. It was not a great deal of money, but it was something. It did not really hit me until I had to return to the United States in 1961 via Mexico. Castro had cut off travel. We left in groups [of players]. I arrived late to spring training. And yet, after the big league season, I was planning to return to Cuba. Then I spoke to my parents and they told me not to come back. My mother told me not to return. For a mother to say that to a child.... My brother had been sent off to the fields to work under the Agrarian Reform Laws. My father told me that if he was carrying a bag of groceries on the street, he would be stopped for no reason to have the contents examined.

I finally managed to get my parents and brother out of Cuba in 1969. My brother had married, and he came over with his wife and daughter.

You played in the last professional baseball game held in Cuba. You suited up for Almendares.

What I remember about the last game played in Cuba [1960-61 season] was that Almendares and Cienfuegos finished the season tied and we played in a playoff game for the championship. [The teams were tied in the standings entering the final day of the season. Almendares and Cienfuegos were scheduled to play that day.] I had been traded to Almendares by Habana the prior season. I was traded for Willy Miranda.

Orlando Peña opened for us and Pedro Ramos pitched for Cienfuegos. I hit a double over the third base bag my first time up against Ramos. I always hit Ramos pretty well, even in the majors. I pinch hit against Ramos, once, in a Cuban All-Star Game and I hit a home run. [Zoilo] Versailles started the game, and I came off the bench. But that last day belonged to Ramos, and Cienfuegos. Ramos beat us pretty easily. And we had Amorós. [Miguel] de la Hoz, Scull. Tony Taylor. Paula.

Who was the most outstanding player you saw in Cuba?

It is difficult to say. There were many great players. Miñoso was always a favorite. He was a beloved player in Cuba. Because he hustled all the time, because when he was hit by a pitch, he would brush it off casually and go to first base. He was always on the go. Always coming at you. Amorós was a tremendous player who never got his due. Angel Scull. I can tell you who the best North American Player was— Rocky Nelson. He was the best player I saw in the minor leagues, too. There were great North American pitchers ... Mizell, Bunning, Shaw. But only for a year or two. Camilo Pascual was the best Cuban pitcher. [Conrado] Marrero I faced my first year. All he threw were sliders. He was hard to hit.

There were very few road trips made by the teams in Cuba. Do you remember any?

The year of the revolution, we played games outside of Havana. It so happened, the night before one of these first-of-a-kind travel games, I went out for some drinks with a few of the boys. We hit some "after hours" joints that were opposite *El Malecón*. When it came time to go to the airport the next morning for our trip, I was in poor shape. We reached the city we were suppose to play in, I think it was Camagüey. I was with Almendares. We played against Cienfuegos. Regino Otero was our manager. Otero was not going to play me because he saw the shape I was in. But I was a star by that time and talked him out of it. I did not make the trip to sit on the bench. I owed the people who came out to the park to try and play. The first time up in the game, I grounded out to short. As I ran to first, I thought my head would split open from the pain. On the bench, the trainer gave me a pill. After that, I came up four times and made hits all four times, including a home run. We won the game. When our team flew back to Havana after the game, I threw up all over the plane.

Mudcat Grant

James Timothy Grant's debut in the major leagues came on the third day of the American League's 1958 season. As a 22-year-old pitcher for the Cleveland Indians, Grant threw an eight-hit, 3–2 victory over the Kansas City Athletics at Cleveland Stadium. Grant had spent the prior winter sharpening his trade in Havana with the Almendares Scorpions. Grant was on the same pitching staff as league chart-topper Dick Brodowski. The circuit's stiff competition did not permit Grant to shine during the season for his second-place squad. But it did not prevent him from gaining valuable experience and enjoying immensely his time in Havana.

Almendares asked Grant back two winters later; it was the first season following the Cuban Revolution and the last in which North American players participated in Cuban professional baseball. Grant was one of two stateside pitchers that did not complete the season for cost-cutting Almendares (Tommy Lasorda, the other). However, early in the campaign, Grant turned in a brilliant 1–0 victory over Cienfuegos and Camilo Pascual.

Prior to his excursions into Cuba, the right-hander had seen winter action in Colombia in 1956-57, initiating the establishment of his two Latin American baseball residencies. Grant was voted the Colombian League's Player of the Year. (On the days he did not pitch, Grant often played the field.)

Grant did not shy away from learning Spanish while playing winter ball. Throughout the interview, Grant displayed a comfort level with many Spanish words and exhibited faultless pronunciation with surnames.

Jim "Mudcat" Grant enjoyed a distinguished major league career, racking up 145 wins in 14 seasons with multiple clubs. His best season was in 1965 as a 21-game winner with the league champion Minnesota Twins and as the first African American to win 20 games in the American League. Grant pulled in two complete game victories in the World Series against the Los Angeles Dodgers, including one on two days' rest. He also homered in that second win.

After his playing days ended, the two-time All-Star worked in the executive front offices of several major league teams. A Southern California resident, Grant sits on the boards of directors for three notable baseball organizations: The Negro League Baseball Museum, Baseball Assistance Team, and the Major League Alumni Association.

Aside from baseball, Grant's love of music is well known. Grant rendered a touching musical tribute at the Harmon Killebrew memorial at Target Field in 2011. Accompanied by the gentle guitar playing of Ric Oliva, son of Tony Oliva, Grant movingly sang Louis Armstrong's "What a Wonderful World."

Where are you from?

Born and raised in Florida. Lacoochee, Florida, in Pasco Country.

How many were there in the Grant family?

Let me put it this way: a bunch. One brother, a lot of sisters. A lot of uncles, aunts, nephews. A whole bunch.

What drew you to baseball?

As a youngster, I was the batboy for the local lumbermill team — Commer & Sons & Cypress Company, that was the name of it. They had a baseball team — the Lacoochee Nine Devils. The men made a baseball diamond near the mill. The mill made the bats. I was the batboy from the time I was five, until nine-years-old. I became interested in the game that way. The men from the mill taught me the game of baseball.

Who were your favorite players growing up?

I admired the old Negro League players. You are talking about 1944, '45, and '46, before Jackie Robinson. Satchel Paige, Josh Gibson. Oscar Charleston. Also, there was a female player that

Almendares' pitcher Mudcat Grant was acutely aware of Havana's vibrant 1950s music scene (courtesy Charles Monfort).

I admired — Toni Stone. She played with the men. She played for the [Indianapolis] Clowns, second base. She could turn the double play real well.

When did you get your first taste of playing ball on an organized level?

I started playing with the lumbermill team when I was 13 years old. The mill team used to play the prisoner's team at Raiford, a correctional facility. The lumbermill team was given a full tank of gas and lunch when we went to play the prisoner's team at Raiford. One day, there was a gentlemen from the Braves who came to see one of the games. He knew the warden of the correctional facility, and he wanted to sign me. I said I would be happy to sign. But when I started filling out the contract and came to the "Age Section" I put "16." The scout said to me, you are only 16? I said, yes. And he snatched the contract from me and tore it up. That was my first near-signing experience.

You did eventually sign a pro contract.

Two years later, I signed with the Cleveland Indians. A gentleman named Merkle, they called him "Bonehead." He played with the Giants. Merkle umpired a game when I was in high school; he was behind the plate. Well, I happen to pitch this game. I was not a pitcher, I was a third baseman/shortstop. Merkle recommended me to someone on the Indians. The Indians came looking for me later at my high school. I was visiting my uncle at New Symrna Beach. Luckily, my high school coach knew this and he came over and found me working on a roof and told me the Indians were looking for me. My coach took me over to the Indians' spring training minor league base. I stayed there and signed my first big league contract as a walk-on in 1954.

You rose pretty quickly in the ranks for a walk-on.

In those days, there were many minor league cities in which you could not play because of the segregation laws. Cleveland wanted me to go to Tifton, Georgia, but African Americans were not allowed to play in that league. So Cleveland sent me to Fargo, North Dakota. I was able to start in Class C, instead of Class D because of that. I played four years in the minor leagues. I was 21–5 at Fargo. My second year was Keokuk, Iowa — 19–3 was my record there. Then I went to Class A Reading, Pennsylvania; I was 13–12. After that, Triple A San Diego.

I would like to know about your first time playing winter ball.

My first year in the winter leagues was 1956. Cleveland had players going to South America to play. Colombia had a league. The Colombian League made inroads to me to play. I accepted the opportunity. I traveled to Barranquilla and played for the Willard Blues. It was quite an experience. I played two positions — the outfield and I pitched. I threw a no-hitter in the league that season. In Colombia, I received an opportunity to play against older, more experienced players. It was my first time in a Latin American country; it was quite interesting.

Where did you live in Barranquilla?

I cannot say exactly, but it was an apartment complex where all the ballplayers from America stayed. I cannot remember where it was, but it was quite comfortable.

What do you remember about Colombia?

Living in Colombia was wonderful. By that time, one was used to discrimination in America, depending on where one lived and where one played. In Colombia, even though you were aware of who you were, of course, it was not a serious problem like it was in the states. Everything was more relaxed. The only thing was, you had to learn a little Spanish, and I did that. There were a lot of jokes played on me by the Latin players. But it was fun.

Anything stand out about the fans?

The fans were really fans. It was more of a fanaticism. Fans reacted differently than in the states. More vocal, more active. I remember the fans would light matchbooks and set fire to handkerchiefs. That seemed to be a ritual down there. There was never any violence associated with the rituals. After my no-hitter, the fans carried me off the field. They "passed the hat" for me. They collected 2,000 or 3,000 pesos, which, because of the exchange rate came out to 200 bucks or so. That was super for one game. They held a "night" in my honor soon after, too.

You were not married at the time.

I was single. Rocky Nuñez, he was an outfielder. He played a joke on me. I met a Spanish young lady that was working at the Sears store. She was teaching me some Spanish. I was getting it, but I was not getting it. So I said to Rocky, you have to teach me some Spanish. I have a date. I am going to visit the home of this young lady I met at Sears. Rocky says, okay. Rocky gives me tips on how to act, what to say. Rocky says to me when they end a conversation and people start laughing, or become amused, say this word. [Laughs.] This word Rocky told me to say did not turn out to be a good word to say in mixed company. So I am at this young lady's house. We had dinner, and after dinner we are sitting around. The father is drinking brandy, and then somebody said something and everyone laughed. And I shout out this word that Rocky told me to say. I did it a second time, and after the third time the father threw me out of the house. It was not a good word to say. [Laughs again.]

I nearly had to walk all the way back to my apartment, which was about ten miles. Their house was located out a ways from the town. It was rather

A beaming Beny Moré (white hat) infectiously appeals to a contingent of Habana players. Seated and standing to the left of center are a more reserved Witty Quintana and Luis Boullón, respectively. At the right, next to the entertainer, an extremely tickled Hilario Valdespino exhibits a special zeal for Moré, who is widely considered the greatest musical talent produced by Cuba. This photograph was taken during the 1960-61 season, the last of Cuban Winter League baseball (courtesy Charles Monfort).

late at night and there was no public transportation at that hour. I came upon a little commercial area about halfway to my apartment, and I was able to call a cab from one of the restaurants there to take me the rest of the way back.

I told the general manager of the ball club the next day what had happened. He told Rocky that the two of us needed to make an apology to the young lady's father. After the game that day, Rocky and I went back to the home. After the father understood Rocky had played a joke on me, he burst out loud laughing. He invited us back into the home. That was my most memorable experience off the field in Colombia.

All's well that end's well, I suppose. The following winter, you traveled to Cuba to play.

I played with Almendares in Havana in 1957. Again, I received a call. I had been recommended to the commissioner of the Cuban League, and Almendares was the team interested in me. The first year in Cuba was great.

I received an opportunity to hone my skills playing against competition that was much different than in Colombia. Most of the players I played against in Colombia were Class A, Double A caliber. We are talking about major league ballplayers in Cuba.

Which players impressed you the most in Cuba?

There were some terrific players. I played against Minnie Miñoso. Miñoso was a mainstay for Marianao. I played with Carlos Paula, Angel Scull, [Daniel] Morejón. Paula played left field, Scull center, Morejón played right field. Camilo Pascual and Pedro Ramos were pitchers in that league. Tom Lasorda was there for a while. Bob Allison. I knew Mike [Cuéllar]. He was one of the best friends I had until he passed away. We attended different celebrity get-togethers. I loved the way Mike pitched. We kept in touch. He lived in Orlando.

Did you have your nickname during this period?

Oh yeah, I had my nickname then. But it had not developed into quite what it became later. It did not have that "hold" yet. Although, I remember Tony Taylor used to call me "Gato."

Where did it come from? Who gave it you?

When I was first invited to spring training the players thought I was from Mississippi. The players thought most blacks were from Mississippi. So they nicknamed me "Mississippi Mudcat." There is a catfish in the Mississippi River, it is a mudcat.

Anything else come to mind about the caliber of play in Cuba?

In Cuba, there were many more black players than in Colombia. In Cuba, I noticed the prominence of the black athlete. In baseball. In boxing. Looking back on it now, the racial issue was more noticeable in Havana [than Colombia]. There were three races in Havana. You had *negros*, you had *blancos*, and you had *mulattos*. The whites lived primarily in a section and were part of a culture that was not necessarily together with the blacks. The mulattos had more freedom to go one way or another. For example, if you went to the *Tropicana*, one of the most famous nightclubs in Cuba, they would put you in a certain section. It did not stop you from having a good time — you had a good time wherever you went in Cuba, no doubt about that. It was not a blatant thing, I will tell you. But if you went to the nightclub where Beny Moré was singing, you could sit where ever you wanted. Moré was black or mulatto, whatever you wanted to call him. Same thing with Celia Cruz.

I am impressed that you know about Beny Moré and Celia Cruz. But I guess with your musical background, I should not be.

In Cuba, I met some of the top musical performers. I met Beny Moré, Celia Cruz. I saw *Orquesta Sensación* at Tropical Park. Music was played at

Tropical Park all night long. That was where the old baseball stadium was. One band would come on and play, then another would follow. It was an incredible place. It was a celebration. The facilities were indoor. Carlos Paula was the first person to take me there. "I take you there. We have a good time," Carlos said to me. Carlos Paula could *dance.* There was always someone there you could dance with. And once they found out that you did not know the dance steps to the traditional dances, somebody would teach you. If you did not know how to Mambo, somebody would teach you. Cha-cha-cha, somebody would teach you. Salsa. Merengue. There was always someone kind enough to show you the steps.

Where did you reside in Havana?

I lived in an apartment in Vedado. It was a nice area near the beach. I was single. Solly Drake lived in the area. Drake was an outfielder with the Chicago Cubs.

What did you think about the food?

I loved the food in Havana.

Really? What was your favorite dish?

Arroz con pollo! Fried green bananas were good, too. Black beans. In fact, every time I fly home to Florida, I fly into Tampa. At the Tampa Airport, in the Delta Airlines terminal, there is a Cuban restaurant. I make sure I visit that restaurant every time. When I fly back to California, I make sure I get to the terminal with plenty of time, plenty of time, before take-off to eat at the same restaurant. I pack plenty of reading material to hold me over until the flight. After all these years, the food there brings back all these great memories of Cuba. And when I turn in my car, the attendants there, many are Cubans. I make it a point to ask them, especially the older ones. "Where are you from? Have you ever heard of Almendares?" Even though most of them were born here, through their parents, they know about Cuban baseball.

What I noticed in the Cuban League was once you played with a team, you seldom played for another. Once an *Almendarista,* always an *Almendarista.*

Almendares was the team you played for. They had a huge rivalry against the Habana club.

It was a big rivalry. The colors were blue for Almendares and red for Habana. But the league itself was a type of rivalry. Because the competition was so great. There were only four teams.

And the stadium?

The stadium was a modern structure and all of the teams played there. There was a big outfield bleachers.

Anything else you remember about the park?

Beny Moré played between games of a doubleheader. After the first game was played, we waited for about an hour, because Beny was late. Beny was always late, even at the nightclubs where he performed. The stadium was full. Everyone would be tracking his arrival. You heard a big roar when his car was spotted. The band was already set up, waiting, somewhere around home plate, a 15-piece band. People started chanting, *Beny Moré! Beny Moré!* And Beny Moré came on the stage. And the band struck a tune, and Beny said, hold it, *un momento,* and he turned completely around and shouted, *"Mi gente!"* ("My people!") The crowd went wild. It was a wonderful thing. I met great musicians all the time. Because all of them were great baseball fans. Count Basie was a great baseball fan. Ella Fitzgerald was a great baseball fan. Duke Ellington. Aretha Franklin.

You knew all of them?

Oh, yeah, I met them all, and more than that. Nat Cole. Lou Rawls. Bobby Darin. They were all great baseball fans. Remember Jerry Glanville, the football coach? He used to leave tickets [as a gag] at the box office for Elvis. Way before that, we used to leave baseball tickets for all these great performers like it was nothing. Tom Lasorda used to leave tickets for Frank Sinatra. We knew them all. We went to their concerts and they came to our games.

You skipped a winter, but then returned to Cuba in the winter of 1959.

It was different when I went back to Havana in 1959. The revolution had come. There was a time when I was not allowed out of my apartment. They canceled some games. When the season was restarted, Castro came out and threw out the first pitch. The team had a chance to meet Castro. He was an ex-pitcher, or something like that. But the person I met that I had a nice relationship with was General Cienfuegos. He was a gentlemen. It was too bad he was killed. We all felt real bad with the news.

He died under, let's say, mysterious circumstances.

Very mysterious circumstances. I respected him a lot. I saw him three or four times outside the ballpark. I saw him at an upscale restaurant. He spoke some English.

Any other remembrances of Havana?

They showed pictures in the newspapers of the assassinations of Batista loyalists. I remember distinctly this one photograph of an older, well-dressed gentleman who was shot by firing squad. I remember the sight of his hat flying straight up in the air; he was dressed in all white and had about 15 shots in his body and had not fallen. The photo was taken at a precise moment. It was graphic. Even though I remember Cuba as a wonderful place, this was one of those things that you can never forget.

I also remember José Martí. They have a statue of him in Havana on the boulevard. I remember collecting some of his works. He was a great poet.

Hopefully, in the future Cuba can get back to what it was, with a more harmonious relationship [with the United States].

What are you involved with now?

I am doing a lot of things now. I am involved in many fund-raising organizations. I co-wrote a book, *The Black Aces*. There are only 14 African American pitchers to win 20 games in the history of baseball. C.C. Sabathia became the 14th. Don Newcombe was the first, and I was the first in the American League. I do book signings, and I still do music somewhat. I make book signing appearances with Fergy Jenkins; he is one of the aces. I still do fantasy camps, even though I am an old-timer. I cannot get the ball to the plate any more, but I can instruct others on how to get it there. I am also active in community education work.

You are married?

I am married to Trudy for 35 years.

I noticed you have retained a comfortable feel for many Spanish words.

Most of the Spanish I learned, I learned in Cuba. And kept up with it later because of my friends Miñoso, Tony Oliva, Zoilo Versalles, Carlo Paula, Pascual, Ramos, Scull, Tony Taylor. I remember them fondly as teammates and friends forever.

Buddy Hicks

Buddy Hicks informed me he was an early riser (6:00 A.M. every morning), a stark contrast from his time in baseball, when "I slept in because most of our games were at night."

Hicks was a backup during his first season in Cuba, in 1948-49, and then a regular the following winter. His third winter season (after skipping one off-season) was spent in Caracas, where Hicks became part of one of the greatest teams the league has ever known. The Cervercería Caracas team posted a 41–15 record, and battled undefeated through its first 18 games (17–0–1). The team represented Venezuela in the Caribbean Series of 1952. Hicks and his teammates became forever etched in Caribbean Series history by being no-hit by Tommy Fine of Habana on the second day of the tournament. Unfortunately, Hicks did not remember the game in which he registered an 0-for-2 at the plate, with two of the three walks Fine permitted — in what is still the only no-hitter recorded in this inter-

national championship's history. Hicks only remembered Fine, who was a former teammate of his with the Cienfuegos Elefantes.

Hicks' playing career was spent in the high minors as an infielder. Hicks played in 26 games for the Detroit Tigers in 1956.

Now in his mid-eighties and residing in Utah, Hicks told me he was getting along, though suffering from heart ailments, which are controlled through medication. He and his wife Miriam have been married since 1947. Miriam, Hicks advised, had pulled out her old scrapbooks right after my initial contact. Thumbing through them again was a fond experience for the two of them, he related.

The Hicks raised two children, a boy and a girl, both of whom live in Southern California.

First off, where did the name "Buddy" come from?

My father was Clarence. My mother, when she called "Clarence," did not want both of us running, so they just called me "Buddy."

What's your background, and when did baseball become a memorable part of your life?

I went to Downey High School in California. My whole family was baseball-oriented. My dad was on a softball team; my two sisters were on softball teams. I was either playing softball or baseball. We spent probably five nights a week out watching or playing baseball.

You were signed by the Brooklyn Dodgers in 1944, and were a few years along in your minor league career when an opportunity to play winter ball arose.

I had a good year in St. Paul, Minnesota in 1948. I hit .296. I probably scored a hundred runs. They needed somebody to play shortstop on one of the teams in Havana, I think it was Marianao. And that is how I went. Cuba was really different. It made me thankful that I was born in the USA. There was no middle class people. You either had lots of money or you hardly had anything.

Where did you live?

We lived in a hotel — my wife and I — I do not remember the name of it. We had to take cabs from the hotel to the ballpark. I do not know how far it was. I did not see much of Havana at night. I pretty much stayed home with my wife.

Did you venture out to taste the local cuisine at all?

I loved their *arroz con pollo*. Oh, man, I lived on that while I was down there.

You played against Monte Irvin, to name one of the bigger stars. Do you remember anything about him?

I do not remember Monte Irvin. I remember Sam Jethroe. A real speedster. I never saw anybody go from home to third base any faster than he did. Long, long strides. Jethroe could really pick them up and lay them down.

How about Minnie Miñoso?

Miñoso had great speed. Great arm. He could do just about everything. I remember Claro Duany and Adrián Zabala. Natives that were good players, I thought, and that in later years could have played in the big leagues.

I'll throw another North American player's name out to you who participated in the league that winter: Chuck Connors.

Did he, really? I'll be darned. I do remember one thing about Chuck Conners— during spring training with the Dodgers. There were about eight hundred of us in camp in, let me see, 1947, it was. We were taking infield and batting practice. A ground ball was hit to the infield, to Bobby Morgan, and he threw to first base and Chuck was not looking. The ball hit Chuck in the mouth and split his lip. Who would know he would become "The Rifleman" later on?

You went back to Cuba the following winter, 1949.

My second winter, I was with Cienfuegos. Jack Cassini and I led the league in double plays. Silvio Garcia was on our team; he was good ballplayer. My wife was pregnant that second year with our first child. After the season, we returned to Vero Beach, and she flew home to California to have the baby. I ended up driving cross country by myself to Hollywood.

Did you feel more comfortable the second year? Did you go out a little more?

One player had a big Christmas Eve dinner, and everybody sang *"White Christmas."* I cannot remember who that player was. It was a celebration for everybody. I met Bobby Maduro [team owner]. He used to have parties for the ballplayers occasionally. He came around and introduced himself to everybody. Maduro lost everything when Castro took over. He moved to Miami.

What can you recall about Gran Stadium?

Fairly large stadium. I think it was about 350 down each line. I remember the fans more than anything else. The fans were very rabid.

Shortstop Clarence "Buddy" Hicks was a standout defensive player for Cienfuegos during the 1949-50 winter season.

Your third and last winter season was spent in Caracas, Venezuela. Why the switch?

Well [in 1951], they needed a fellow to spell Carrasquel at shortstop when he would need a rest. Ferrell Anderson, who I had played with in 1948 in St. Paul, Minnesota, took a liking to me, for some reason. Ferrell suggested my name, and he was responsible for me getting to Venezuela.

Where did you stay in Caracas?

There again, we stayed in a hotel. My wife and I.

How was the food there?

The food was excellent. We ate mostly in the hotel. They had red snapper. I loved that type of food. I was born and raised in Southern California, so I got an early start on eating fish.

And the fandom in Venezuela?

The fans were quite rabid there, also. They seemed to search the fans going into the ballpark for firearms. And still they seemed to get them through the gates. Every once in a while you would hear one fired off in the stands.

The stadium in Caracas was called Estadio Cerveza Caracas.

The [stadium] stands were mediocre. If you hit one in the gap, you could run and run. In fact, I set a record in Venezuela with three triples in one game. Then they dubbed me *"Señor Triple."* I led the league in triples, so it was apropos, I guess.

Your team, Cervecería Caracas, ran away with the pennant.

I know we had a heck of a year. We won anywhere between 16 and 18 of the first games, before anybody finally beat us. [Johnny] Hetki was the pitcher that beat us for the first time. He pitched for Magallanes. The first game we were beaten, the fans carried Hetki off the mound. The Magallanes fans set fire to the scorecards. It was like they had won the World Series.

Do you remember a native pitcher José Bracho?

José Bracho, I do remember. He had pretty good stuff.

Also on your team was Wilmer Fields, a well known slugger throughout the Caribbean leagues.

Wilmer Fields, yes sir. A good hitter. A good player.

I was hoping you could recall Tommy Fine's no-hitter against your team in Caribbean Series of 1952.

We tend to forget the bad things and remember the good. [Chuckles.] I remember Tommy Fine, the man, but not the no-hit pitcher in the Caribbean Series. During waking hours, Fine had more nervous energy than anyone. Tommy could not sit still for five minutes. Tommy always had to be doing something. He was a fidgety pitcher, too. He had a good overhand curveball, right from 12 o'clock to 6 o'clock. Average fastball. But his curveball was his out-pitch.

Any final thoughts on your baseball time in Latin America?

I really enjoyed my three years playing winter ball. As a young player, it gave me the opportunity to put the down payment on my house. The salaries, I think, were pretty much all the same. A thousand dollars a month, and expenses. It was great.

Don Lenhardt

Winter ball in 1949 irrefutably helped kick-start in splendid fashion the major league career of Don Lenhardt. The Opening Day first baseman for the St. Louis Browns in April 1950, Lenhardt stroked two hits and scored two runs in his first major league game. The 28-year-old rookie led the Browns in home runs with 22 and RBIs with 81 that season. The prior winter in the Cuban League, Lenhardt tied for the league lead in home runs with 15, with Roberto Ortiz.

Lenhardt played two seasons in Cuba, four years apart, and both with the Habana Leones. The pleasant-sounding Illinois native spoke to me with an appreciation for his winter junkets, which he felt furthered a five-year big league playing career. A career which probably would have started earlier (and therefore lasted longer) had he not lost several years of playing time in the service.

Where do you hail from?

I did not move until I was married. I married a girl from St. Louis. So now we have lived here about 60 years. But I was born and raised in Alton, Illinois. I did not have any brothers or sisters.

When were you bitten by the baseball bug?

I was brought up with baseball. My dad played sandlot ball, and I was very interested in baseball and so was my mother. My dad played catch with me constantly. I played on every team that I could, and most of those teams at that time were fast pitch softball. I played in a newspaper league in Alton called the Telegraph League. Played on Saturdays. You had to have a uniform, but most of us did not, so we played in jeans and a T-shirt.

When did the pros come calling?

Lou Magualo, who was a Yankee scout at that time, first discovered me. I signed in the Browns' office when I was discharged from the service, so I do not know if Lou received the credit.

How long was your career sidetracked because of the Second World War?

Well, I missed about five summers of playing after I went into the service. I cannot say it was bad, because you never know. It probably did not hurt me at all, because I probably matured some. I did not play ball in the service. I tried out when I was leaving, and they wanted me to stay and play, but I said no, I am going home.

Oh, who were the ballplayers that you admired growing up?

I liked all the Philadelphia Athletics. I liked Jimmie Fox and Jimmy Dykes, who later was a manager when I played for him in Baltimore. Lefty Grove. I admired every big league player. I wanted to be that big league player, but not thinking I could be. Then in Class D ball, we played the Triple A ball club and I found out that I could play in competition with them, so that made me feel better, knowing that I could play.

How did you first come to play winter ball?

I was in Double A, in San Antonio, when I went to Cuba for the first time. I was invited. Evidently, Mike González saw me play in San Antonio and he invited me to play in Havana. I wanted to go, because I knew it would help me get to the big leagues. I had a great year down there and I had a great first year in the big leagues. Obviously playing winter ball helped.

Playing for the Habana Leones, Don Lenhardt tied for the most home runs in the 1949-50 Cuban Winter League (courtesy Charles Monfort).

There was a splendid array of talent in the Cuban League. Can you speak about some of the players?

I remember Roberto Ortiz was a great player — they had a lot of good players down there. And Pedro Formental, who was on my team, was another very good player. Formental was a pretty big star down there. We had very good pitching. Al Gerheauser. Wes Bailey. Connie Marrero, who was one of the other team's pitchers and [Sandalio] Consuegra, another pitcher, they were also very good; they were major leaguers. I remember Tommy Fine, lefthander — he played with me at San Antonio — and he won a lot of games in Cuba, and you really had to pitch a lot to do that. I remember Chuck Conners very well, he went into the movies. He was a good player. [Ray] Dandridge was another good player. He played for one of the other teams.

[Amused.] I remember when I hit a home run, the players from Cuba on my team would all rush to the plate, hoping to get their picture in the paper. So when I crossed the plate, they would be there in the shots of the photographers. I enjoyed that season very, very much. They had a lot of rivalries, all four of the teams. They all wanted to win. It was very competitive.

What was your life like away from the ballpark?

My first year I lived in an apartment. My first year I was single. I did not go out at night, or at least I do not remember doing so. The second time I went down, I was married with a child. Bill Sarni and his wife went down with us. We lived out in Marianao, which was kind of like a resort area. I do recall when you were driving you had to be careful at intersections, because the first person to honk their horn was the one permitted to go through the intersection ahead of the others.

My second year, we had a great big flood from rains in Marianao. We were working out at the ballpark and when we came back to where we lived, I remember Joe Coleman took his pants off to wade through the water. His wife looked out from their apartment and said, "Joe, what are you doing with your pants off?" We all had to wade through the water to get to our apartments. And I also remember [in Marianao] there were crabs all over the place. I guess there was a migration. They were all headed to the ocean at once.

We did not go to the beach because we had the ocean right there where we were living. And every once in a while they would holler whatever word meant "shark" and everybody had to get out of the water. They also had an outdoor pool there. There was a Cuban movie producer who lived there. I cannot remember his name. He lived in a very big place. He had chauffeurs. He had guards all over the place. The movie producer had us all over for a party. I think it was Christmas. We had a good time.

Speaking of a Christmas party, what did you think of the food?

I did not like the food. I remember eating rice all the time. I saw a meat truck go by with flies buzzing the raw meat that was for sale, and I guess that turned me off. In fact, when my wife came down with me the second time, we brought a lot of food with us—canned food.

Any other recreational activities that you can tell me about, apart from driving?

I had a great time there. There were some beautiful nightclubs. We frequented those when my wife was with me. They were really beautiful. You could see Hollywood movie stars at those nightclubs.

You topped the league in home runs one winter, so you must have liked the big stadium.

I liked the stadium very much. In fact, the playing field was better than Sportsman's Park in St. Louis.

And the fans?

The fans, they were, I do not know, kind of wild, really.

You suffered an injury during your second season.

The second year, you will notice I only played sixty games. You could only play [a maximum] 60 games, if you were a big leaguer. I broke my toe that season. I cut the top of my shoe off in order to continue playing, because I did not just want to sit, inactive. I then came home after 60 games. At that time, they allowed six big leaguers per team.

I would like to hear about your manager, Mike González, and Adolfo Luque.

I liked Mike González. Adolf Luque was then a coach for González. I remember González and Luque on payday. I will never forget payday. The two of them would come in with a fat satchel. They would have all the payroll money in the satchel, and they would walk over to a table and put the satchel down on it with a pistol right on top. I think it was Luque's pistol. They would give you whatever you thought you were going to spend in Cuban money. The balance of your salary, however much you told them, they would pay you in American money. Payday was every two weeks.

Do you remember Al Campanis? I ask because he was one of the few North American managers in the history of the league.

[Al] Campanis was one of the managers [Cienfuegos]. He had a knuckleballer, Dick Littlefield. I could hit his knuckleball just as well as I could hit any other pitch. I was basically a fastball hitter. Anyway, Campanis said I was the best knuckleball hitter he had ever seen.

Who was the best player you saw?

I could not pick one; I would have to pick a bunch.

Best pitcher?

Pitcher, I would say Marrero and Consuegra.

Did you bring back any keepsakes from your time in Havana?

I have a couple of photos, I would have to look. But other than that, nothing as far as keepsakes. We were down there to earn a few extra bucks.

How is life treating you all these many years later?

Isabelle and I will be married 60 years in October. My son-in-law allowed us to add living quarters to the back of his house. We have two bedrooms, a bath. It is really wonderful for us. My daughter is here to take care of us, if we need it. Trish, my daughter, celebrated her first birthday in Havana.

We have a club here called the One Two Three Club. I am a member of it. We meet every Monday for lunch. All we discuss are the happenings in sports. You have to be associated with sports, in some way, to be a member. Even writers are allowed to be members.

Minnie Miñoso

It was most gratifying for me to speak to Minnie Miñoso from his suburban Chicago home. This long-admired Cuban baseball icon endures as one of the most genuinely likable players in baseball history.

Miñoso had recently been inducted into the Latino Baseball Hall of Fame, located in the Dominican Republic. Miñoso stated how well he was treated by his Dominican brethren and how honored he was to have a statue of himself erected at the museum there, similar to one that is stationed at U.S. Cellular Field in Chicago.

A man who loves baseball to his core, the former five-decade major league player Aman who loves baseball to his core, the former five-decade major league player seems to have grown weary over people always questioning him about his age. After my provocation, Miñoso shrugged it off and said he was 100, and then changed it to 30, with a hearty laugh.

It was clear Miñoso thought at times he has not been fully respected after leaving the game as a player. Appearance fees, in comparison with other retired players, seemed to be a sticky point. Without actually saying it, the glaring measure of disrespect he made clear emanated from Cooperstown. Again, in some gnawing comparisons to other elected players.

On that point, given the fact that Miñoso did not start his major league playing career in earnest until he was 28 (or 25, as he now states in a personal age revision that dilutes his case), it would seem to me that Miñoso should merit the same statistical consideration given to some of the great crossover players from the Negro Leagues who have made the Hall without "Hall of Fame numbers." Examining major offensive categories, Miñoso's best ten-consecutive-year stretch in the big leagues is comparable to Jackie Robinson or Larry Doby's. Additionally, Miñoso's major offensive numbers top Richie Ashburn and Enos Slaughter's over an equivalent decade-long period. Minnie Miñoso was undeniably one of the handful of best players in the American League during the entire decade of the 1950's, ranking in statistical team value (WAR) only behind Mickey Mantle and Ted Williams. (Including defense, Miñoso was second only to Mantle!) The majority of the players I interviewed for this book stated that Minnie

Miñoso was the best player they saw in the Cuban Winter League. (Note: Virdon and Schofield played during a winter that Miñoso was not permitted to participate in winter ball by his North American bosses.)

If it were up to the fans, Minnie Miñoso would be voted into the Hall of Fame by a landslide. And that should count for a whole lot.

Where on earth did the name "Minnie" come from?

I arrived my first day in Chicago as Orestes Miñoso, number nine. The next day, I was "Minnie." I do not know who or where the nickname came from — which sportswriter gave it to me. Only that I have been Minnie ever since. It has been like a legal name change. My car's license plate reads, MINOSO 9. My wife's, M MINOSO.

When then did Orestes come into this world?

I was born in Perico, Mantanzas province, November 29, 1925.

You were part of a big family?

We were three brothers and two sisters. A lot of cousins. But it was the five of us mostly.

You began your baseball career right in your hometown.

I started playing baseball in Perico on sugarmill teams with my brother, and then I went to Havana and played with semi-pro teams sponsored by tobacco manufacturers.

You played baseball professionally in the United States before you did so in Cuba.

I first played baseball in the United States with the New York Cubans in 1945. They had a good mix of black Hispanic players and black American players. I was listed as being older than I was because of U.S. travel restrictions during the War. I would not have been able to play otherwise.

That winter I returned to Cuba and was contracted by Marianao. Eloy García was the owner and he gave me a helping hand. So did Emilio de Armas, general manager. I played with Marianao my entire professional career. My first year, the league was at Tropical Park. I was named Rookie of the Year. Antonio Castaño was our third baseman. He was injured on the knee on a play in foul territory. Armando Marsans [manager] called to me, "*Oye chiquito*, take over at third base." It was about the seventh inning, in a game against Almendares. We tied the game at 1. Then I ended up winning the game with a hit against Ramón Bragaña. I won the next day's game, also against Almendares. It was a game in which there were many lead changes. I hit a high chopper to second with the bases loaded and the scored tied in the last inning. Beto Ávila was the second baseman for Almendares. I guess he did not know how much speed I had, because I beat the throw to first and we won, 8–7. After that, Castaño never played third base for us again.

As a young player in Cuba, did anyone influence or help you?

I cannot really say any particular player helped me. I was born with, what you would say, was a natural talent. I watched other players, yes, but no one really instructed me to play a certain way.

I would like to hear your thoughts on Adolfo Luque and Mike González.

I remember Adolfo Luque, managing Cienfuegos. I met Alejandro Olms there. Olms' role, at that time, was only as an "attraction." He could no longer play. He was a player who gave me a tip. "Sit down a minute," he told me. "Listen, that is not the way you tie your spikes. The laces are too long." Olms used the laces on his spikes to tie together his rings. He never left his jewelry in the clubhouse. I will never forget that.

For me, Mike González was the number one manager. He was a tremendous person, and an intelligent man. He was also owner of his team.

The Cuban Winter League spent many years at Tropical Park. But it was much more than a baseball stadium.

Tropical Park was something historic. It was a place all to itself—a town apart from the city. It was something special. All of Havana passed through there. Not only for ballgames, but because of all the activities that occurred there. There were pavilions for dancing and areas for beer drinking. It is difficult to explain how good one felt when one was at Tropical Park. It was a very sociable place.

My playing time there was short, because the following year the big stadium opened. And soon thereafter, there was a divisive split by the league's players, after which two separate leagues formed. I stayed faithful to the Cuban League, while the Federación Nacional played their games at Tropical Park. I remember the first month, hardly anyone came out to see us, preferring the other league. But after a month and a half, things started changing, and our stadium was out-drawing theirs. Some players wanted back into our league, but the league would not accept them. They were suspended. They had jumped over the wrong fence, so to speak.

That was all because of Jorge Pasquel. He was a tremendous individual. Pasquel is a man who has not been given enough due. He made baseball in Mexico. He was a man responsible for giving baseball in Cuba a boost by giving many jobs in Mexico to Cuban players. Pasquel offered me $30,000 to play in Mexico for one year with Tampico, which was managed by Armando Marsans. I told him no. My plans were to go to the United States, which is when José María Fernández brought me over to play with the New York Cubans, who were owned by Alejandro Pompez. Money was not a driving force for me. I had other intentions. It was the right decision, because not long afterward Mister Jackie broke the barrier. And I should not say just

Jackie. Mr. Branch Rickey and Jackie were the two who opened major league baseball to the world.

There was a separatist league in Cuba.

In Cuba, a black ballplayer could not play amateur baseball. There was not a law; black players were just not permitted to play with any "Club" teams. If you were not a member of the particular "Club," you could not get in to play baseball. The only exception I remember was Sungo Carreras. He was friends with the club people; he practiced with them, and, I think, even managed. Even the military teams under the amateur banner did not have blacks. Pablo García eventually became the first black player to play in the amateur league.

You were named Most Valuable Player in the league for a second time in 1956-57 and honored at the big stadium.

I remember the ceremony for me at Gran Stadium. [Master of Ceremony] Fausto Miranda was a great person. I regretted not being able to pay my respects when he died, but I was not informed until it was too late.

I saw a nice photo of you and Nat King Cole at Gran Stadium.

Nat King Cole and I were friends. He was playing at the *Tropicana* and he invited me to his show. I invited him to the ballgame. It made the news. I have a photo of Nat King Cole and me in uniform.

Tell me about the pennant-winning season of 1956-57.

Marianao won the Cuban League championship and [1957] Caribbean

Minne Miñoso at Gran Stadium in his Cuban Winter League heyday.

Series. Hal Smith was our catcher, a very good defensive player. One of the best catchers to pass through the league. Julio Bécquer played first base, a great glove man. I speak to him every once in a while. José Valdivielso, our shortstop. I think he is living in New York.

Afterwards, the team played as host for the Caribbean Series and captured Caribbean championship.

When we won the Caribbean Series. I do not remember having a parade, or receiving any rings. Marianao won, and that was it. We were not the most popular team [in the league].

Napoleón Reyes, a former major league player, was piloting Marianao.

Napoleón Reyes was a good guy. He had a sense of humor. Although he was serious when he had to be. When Reyes was bothered, he was bothered. He always gave everyone a fair shake. We were all fond of him. May he rest in peace.

Marianao repeated as league champion in 1957-58 and successfully defended your Caribbean crown. In the championship game against Puerto Rico, your all-out hustle, in the ninth inning, produced what became the winning run of the game and tournament.

In the [1958] Caribbean Series in San Juan, I scratched up my face pretty good in left field chasing a home run ball. On the decisive play with Valmy Thomas at home plate, we were tangled up and the ball trickled out and I pointed to it, "Look at the ball, there. I'm safe! I'm safe!" I remember that.

The revolution arrived the following season.

The only thing I remember about the revolution was that play was suspended for a few days. It has been many years. I was never political and never will be. I am a sportsman and I will die a sportsman. I was able to leave Cuba with my family. I have never returned, because with my constant obligations I have never had the time. I had one sister left [in Cuba], and she died last year. I have been a U.S. citizen for many years.

You headed the league's Players Association.

I was president of the Cuban Players Association for two years in Cuba, the last two years of professional baseball in Cuba. They tried to continue it here afterwards, in Miami. But I was not on board with it.

Who was the best player you saw in Cuba? Best pitcher?

I do not get caught up with who was the best player. There were a lot of good players. Camilo [Pascual] was someone who could chop you up. At that time, he had the best curveball in all of baseball.

Do you remember Tommy Lasorda?

Tommy Lasorda is a good friend of mine, but I do not remember him pitching too much.

The fans I know you remember.

What I remember about the fans was that if you played against Almendares, the *habanista* fan would be cheering you on. If you played Habana, the *almendarista* would be on your side. It was like that for years, and then Marianao started winning and Cienfuegos, too. Then Almendares and Habana became sort of like second fiddles.

Are you married?

I was widowed about thirty years ago. I have been remarried for twenty-odd years to Sharon Rice. My youngest son is 22 years old.

What is something you can look back on over your long career and say that you really cherish?

It was Orlando Cepeda who anointed me as the Jackie Robinson of black Latin ballplayers. I am grateful to him for this. Cepeda quite often makes that reference about me. I came to the United States representing Cuba, but I also saw myself as a representative of all countries of Latin America. I always respected the flag of the country in which I was playing. Next month, I will celebrate 60 years since my commencement with White Sox.

I am happy about many things that I have done in my career. I have given and will continue to give everything to baseball and its fans, especially the young fans.

Billy O'Dell

One of a select number of major league players to have never spent a day in the minor leagues, Billy O'Dell hurled for five big league teams during a 13-year career, begun in 1954 with the Baltimore Orioles.

Over the winter of 1957-58, O'Dell pitched in Cuba for Almendares and was the staff's second winningest pitcher (7–2), behind Dick Brodowski. The following summer, O'Dell earned the first of his two All-Star appearances with Baltimore, while compiling a 14-win campaign.

A trade sent O'Dell to the San Francisco Giants in November 1959. The left-hander won 19 games for the pennant-winning Giants of 1962. A winner of more than 100 games in his career, O'Dell was the starting and winning pitcher in the game that the three Alou brothers played in the outfield at the same time — a first in baseball history. The game occurred on September 15, 1963.

Though he lost his wife of nearly six decades recently, O'Dell, in his rich southern accent, told me he was still enjoying life. The father of four boys and a girl was enjoying hunting and fishing, as well.

Tell me about yourself and your family as you were growing up.

Well, I was born in Newberry, South Carolina, in 1932. In my family, there were five children and mama and papa.

At what scholastic level did you first start playing baseball?

Well, back then, it was mostly pick-up baseball, not a lot of organized baseball like you have today. Once I reached high school, I began to play high school ball, American Legion. I went on to Clemson College.

Your path to the major leagues was unique in that you never played minor league ball.

I played a lot of ball in the Greenville Textile League in my younger days. You may not be familiar with it, but real good baseball was played in the league. All these textile mills had baseball teams. Former professional players who had played in the minor leagues, played on those teams. I learned a lot from those guys. I think that experience had a lot to do with me not playing minor league baseball.

Who were your boyhood idols?

I liked them all. Ted Williams and Stan Musial, and guys like that. I always dreamed of playing against them or with them, and I did, one time.

When did you sign on the dotted line to commence that dream?

I signed with Baltimore, with a scout by the name of Red Norris. I had an opportunity to sign with any of the 16 clubs, but I chose Baltimore because they were a new franchise in the American League. They had a lot of "old" pitching. I figured if there was anywhere I had a chance to get to the major leagues in a hurry, it

Billy O'Dell was a three-year letterman in both baseball and football at Clemson University. Signing as a "bonus baby" in 1954, O'Dell went straight to the major leagues. O'Dell enjoyed his greatest success with the San Francisco Giants.

would be with Baltimore. I went straight from Clemson to Baltimore. Spent 13 years [in the majors] with Baltimore, San Francisco, Milwaukee, Atlanta and Pittsburgh.

Before you made it to the big leagues, you spent a season playing winter ball. In Cuba.

I played in Cuba, boy, that was a long time ago ... I came out of the Army in '56 ... I played for Almendares. It was my only year of winter ball. The Almendares club contacted me and Baltimore at the same time. Bobby Bragan was our manager in Cuba.

Where did they put you up?

I lived in place called Club Naútico. It was really nice. Beautiful. Of course that was about the time Castro was kicking his heels up in the mountains and things got a little edgy sometimes. But I enjoyed my stay in Cuba. I had my wife with me. We did not have any children then, so it was just me and her. I lost my wife Joan on March 18th, this year. We were married 58 years. We had a good time together.

How did you spend your time away from the ball field?

Club Naútico was right on the beach, and I like to fish and there was awful good fishing there. We would walk right down to the end of the street where we lived, with the street light there. And me and Norm Larker — he played for Habana and he was a fisherman — we would fish there every night we did not have a ball game.

You could rent a boat from there?

No boats — you had all the fish you could want right there. We caught a lot of red snapper. We caught snook when the weather was bad. That is what I did. Fish. I also enjoyed playing a good game of squash. In fact, I was accused of playing a little too much of it. I do not know if you are familiar with squash, but it is a three-walled game. I enjoyed it. Bragan might have been one of those saying I was playing a little too much. [Chuckles.]

Tell me about Bragan.

Bragan was different, I will put it that way. He did things differently. Had his own ideas. Some people had problems with him. I never had any problems with Bobby.

How did the big park play for a pitcher?

We played in the same ballpark all the time. I cannot remember a whole lot about the stadium, I have been in so many.

How did the fans treat you?

The fans were great. Some of those people came out every night.

Was the food to your liking?

The food was great. They had American-type restaurants. Some of the best beef you will ever eat. I am sure it is not like that now.

How did you get around the city?

We had a vehicle. Most everyone brought their vehicles from the states. Of course, it was only about four hours over from Key West on the boat. Ours was an Oldsmobile.

Mudcat Grant was a mound mate of yours with Almendares.

Mudcat Grant was a likable fella. He could tell a lot of stories.

Do you recall any other players?

I remember Tony Taylor. I played against him the National League for years. Brooks Robinson was there, and he was just coming up [to the big leagues].

Any final thoughts to pass along?

It was a beautiful country. I have a lot of fond memories, and I wonder about the country and people to this day. I would like to go back and see for myself one day, and I hope I will be able to do that.

I met a lot of nice people in Cuba. Most of the people I came in contact with spoke English, so there was no problem there. I wonder about those people, now, since things have happened like they have in Cuba. Like the people we rented the house from at Club Naútico. The friends we made just fishing under the street lamp. I have often wondered what happened to all of them.

Leo Posada

Two heavy wooden doors with crossed, pint-sized baseball bats mounted on the front prominently greet guests who arrive at the entrance to Leo Posada's central Miami home. In a scheduling date happenstance, Posada opened his home to me the day after Osama bin Laden had been killed. When Posada introduced me to his wife, Aida, who was in their office/den, the flat screen on the wall inside flashed reports of the global news story.

We spoke in Posada's elongated family room, looking out at his backyard patio and pool. The family room's walls were filled with photographs from Posada's days as a professional player and coach. Posada pointed out several shots of himself in uniform that were taken by his father. Posada, who played four seasons in the Cuban Winter League, told me that many of the Cuban League photos had been hard to come by because the pho-

tographers were reluctant to part with any of the shots they took, stating that they belonged to their newspapers. Posada participated in the last professional game played in Cuba. Playing for Almendares, Posada batted in the contest as a ninth-inning pinch-hitter without result. The game, which decided the pennant, was won by Cienfuegos, 8–2, on the pitching strength of Pedro Ramos.

The three-year major league player rummaged through a ream paper-size box filled with personal photos, fruitlessly looking for more from the Cuban League to show me. However, he did find some elegant shots of him and his wife contained in original San Souci and Montmartre Night Club fold-outs. I was able to take a picture of the former Kansas City Athletics player in front of a poster-size image of himself from when he was a batting instructor with the Los Angeles Dodgers.

The hearty-looking 77-year-old told me that he was one of the few athletes inducted into both the Cuban Cycling and Baseball Halls of Fame, and that New York Yankee catcher Jorge Posada was his cousin's son (grandson of Posada's uncle).

Posada's home also includes a batting practice cage, which he had built. He spends parts of his days tutoring and advising young baseball-minded athletes who come to his house to use the cage under his mentoring eye.

What part of Cuba are you from?

I am from La Vibora, Habana. I was born April 15, 1934, in el Vedado. I have one younger sister.

You were a two-sport star.

Before I started my baseball career, I was an amateur cyclist. I went to *Colegio Roque*, a private school, where I was on the cycling team. I represented Cuba in the Central American Games and then in the Pan American Games of 1950.

What made you choose baseball?

Daniel Parra — they called him "*Parrita*"— a former left-handed pitcher in Cuba, was the person who pulled me away from cycling and into professional baseball. Parra played in the U.S. minor leagues. He saw me playing with club Fortuna in 1953. Parra asked me if I wanted to play professionally. I told him, no, that I was a cyclist and I had represented Cuba in the Amateur Games, and I was still taking some courses in school. The next year, Parra again urged me to explore the professional ranks. Then some American scouts came to Cuba looking for talent. I went to a tryout held at the University of Havana's baseball field. I must have impressed, because I was signed afterwards to a minor league contract. I came over here, to Corpus Christi, Texas, to play, in a league called the Big State League. Camilo and *Patato* [Pascual], we were contemporaries. They started out in another league called the Longhorn League at Big Spring, Texas. I was then signed by Habana in 1955 and started my baseball playing the same winter in Cuba.

What do you have to say about the "eternal rivals," Habana and Almendares?

The lion and the scorpion were mortal enemies.

What about the rival managers? Adolfo Luque, for instance?

Adolfo [Luque] was a strict disciplinarian. Very knowledgeable. He was a great figure in Cuban baseball. Luque was a star pitcher that put Cuba on the map in the major leagues.

Did you know Mike González?

Of course I knew Miguel Angel González. He was the one that paid us every fifteen days.

The two most popular teams in the Cuban Winter League, the Habana Leones and Almendares Alacranes maintained a fierce rivalry (courtesy Charles Monfort).

Your play was limited as a rookie, but what do you remember about your first season?

I remember perfectly how I saw my first action. Roberto Ortiz — who had been traded by Almendares to Habana — became injured, an ankle injury, and they put Roberto on the injured list. I was then activated to the roster. I cannot tell you what I did exactly, my first hit or anything. I think I entered my first game as a pinch-runner.

In 1956, I played a bit more. Gilberto Torres was my manager. I do not have many good things to say about him. He did not treat me well nor instruct me well. It was Torres that decided the following year to leave me off the roster in favor of Hiram González, a veteran in the league. That is why I did not play in Cuba in 1957.

What did you do that off-season?

I ended up going to Nicaragua to play. I played for the GMC *Camióneros* [summer league]. Roberto Ortiz was the manager and he was the one that brought me over. There were a lot of Cubans playing in that league. Julio Moreno. Waldo González, *Bicho* Pedroso, *Guarao* Guerra were all on our team. I lived in Managua.

Unlike Cuba, there were franchises located in different cities in Nicaragua.

We played games in Managua, León and Granada. We traveled in what they called there a *microbus*, which were like buses but seated only about ten people.

How were the Nicaraguan fans?

The fans were great. At times they could get perturbed, but they were good fans. El Boer and Cinco Estrellas, which was Somoza's team, were the biggest rivals. I played later with El Boer in the early sixties.

You had a bit of a setback the next year.

I returned to the United States in 1958 to play ball and was having a good year at Rochester, Minnesota, when I broke my ankle. I returned to Cuba. May he rest in peace, Monchy de Arcos was the general manger of Almendares. I called him and told him what had happened. De Arcos came to see me at my house. I was married then. I married my wife, Aida, in 1955, and remain married to her today. De Arcos told me not to worry, and brought me an Almendares contract to sign, with a guarantee that the team would help me rehabilitate my ankle so that I could continue my baseball career. Monchy de Arcos was great to me. He put me in touch with someone I owe a great deal to, a trainer named Raudor Ruiz, who has since passed. I was able to completely recover and return to the sport thanks to him.

Did you see much action after your rehab?

I was a reserve on the [1958-59 Almendares] team. Oscar Rodríguez was our manager. He was great. Very patient. When Rodríguez had to talk to someone about something, he would bring you into his office and close the door. I remember our team well. Rocky Nelson at first. Second, Tony Taylor. At short, Willy Miranda. Baxes, Jim Baxes, third base. Catcher was Dick Brown. Centerfield, [Angel] Scull. Right field was Bob Allison and left field, [Carlos] Paula. Orlando Peña was our top pitcher. He was a hard thrower, with a three-quarters delivery. Peña had a good sinker. He did not waste pitches. Peña always went right after the hitters. Tommy Lasorda was one of the pitchers on our team. A great competitor. Always looking for a way to beat you. Art Fowler was a very good pitcher for us. Miguel Angel Cuéllar was a young pitcher, but he put in his innings.

Almendares captured the league pennant in 1958-59.

We were champions of the league and traveled to Caracas for the Caribbean Series. Sungo Carreras took over the team because of health reasons with Rodríguez. Sungo took us to the Caribbean Series. I remember it was a good trip. We won the Series. We picked up from Cienfuegos, as a reinforcement player, Camilo Pascual. There, you can see a photo of me and Camilo and Orlando Peña taken at the Caribbean Series. Camilo pitched the championship-deciding game. I traveled with the team, but was not on the roster. I could practice with the team, but once it came time for the game I had to change into civilian clothes. I remember Carlos Paula injured his hand, punching a clubhouse door, which broke glass and cut him. I do not exactly remember what caused him to do it — whether he struck out or got mad at something else, but it knocked him out of the Series.

Did the players take their wives to the Caribbean Series?

I do not remember many players taking their wives. I did not take my wife.

Where did the team stay?

We stayed at a famous hotel, one of the best hotels in Caracas, the Hotel Humboldt. It was situated high up on a mountain called *el Pico del Águila* (Eagles Nest). You had to travel up by cable car to reach it. One of the views from our hotel room was of an ice skating rink. Cholly Naranjo and Miguel de la Hoz were my roommates. I remember early one morning, we had the windows open; it was chilly, and clouds entered the room. We were that high up.

The following year came the revolution.

As far as when the revolution came, I remember a disorder descending over Gran Stadium. I was never sympathetic to the revolution. It was the beginning of a change in the discipline, in the type of behavior seen at the stadium. Arturo Bengochea, who was the league president, and González with Habana, Bobby Maduro, co-owner of Cienfuegos, Alfredo Pequeño, Marianao, and Monchy de Arcos, they were all men of great character. Bobby Maduro was a great baseball man. I know his son very well. They tried to keep things together. But you realize things sometimes too late.

As a member of Almendares, Leo Posada participated in the final game of Cuba's professional winter league (courtesy L. Posada).

Gran Stadium at that time was the best baseball facility in all of Latin America.

Our stadium did not have much to envy any major league park. Sundays were doubleheader days. Players showed up in jackets and ties to the games and their wives were dressed just as well. Marianao and Almendares shared the third base dugout, unless they played each other. Habana and Cienfuegos, first base dugout. The same pair of teams shared clubhouses that were below the stands behind their dugouts. In either of those clubhouses, without much exaggeration, you could eat off the floors. That is how well they were maintained. The players respected those surroundings totally. Almost to a military standard. From the bat boys, to the ball boy Zulueta, to the clubhouse attendants. Everyone involved catered to the players. Our clubhouse attendant would take our shoes and polish them during the game. After the game, he would take our spikes, and for the next game the spikes would be waiting for us in our lockers, cleaned and shined.

Our clubhouse chief was named Guillermo, last name escapes me. Every team had their own clubhouse chief. The clubhouses were off-limits to family and friends; it was sacred. Drinks of every type were laid out for the players, soda, juices or beer. You could take whatever you wanted and mark on the blackboard what you took. Every fifteen days, it would be deducted from your pay, plus whatever you tipped the attendants. When I reached the big leagues, I did not detect a big difference in the clubhouse atmosphere between the two leagues, except that there was more food laid out in the majors.

Who were the best players in the league?

Undoubtedly, the best pitcher was Camilo Pascual and Orestes Miñoso, the best player. I always liked Rocky Nelson. He played with Almendares, and he was a great hitter and great person.

The end came in 1960-61, and you were part of that last, historic season.

No North American players played in the last year of the league. But I can tell you there was a high percentage of Cuban players that were major leaguers or would become major leaguers that played. A very high percentage. I had already reached the major leagues with Kansas City.

After the campaign concluded, the Cuban government did not easily facilitate the return of Cuban ballplayers to the United States.

They [the Cuban government] gave the major leaguers tourists visas to travel to Mexico. We traveled in groups. When we reached Mexico, our respective [U.S.] clubs had made arrangements to cover our lodging and food expenses. The [U.S.] teams arranged for us to be picked up at our hotels and taken to the American embassy in Mexico City, where we obtained the necessary papers to board planes at the airport to re-enter the United States. That is how I left Cuba. After the '61 season in the states, I spoke to my father and mother-in-law and they told me not to try to come back. Everything was changing. I went to Venezuela to play that winter. I soon was able to bring over my father and mother and sister. I have never returned.

Any final comments?

I do not know if this is widely known, but in 1984 a group of Cuban players were invited by the Cuban government, through the Olympic Committee, to participate in a baseball "cultural exchange" in Cuba. I remember because it was the year the Soviet-bloc countries boycotted the Olympics in Los Angeles. The invited players were Camilo Pascual, Lorenzo Fernández, Cookie Rojas and myself. I was working for the Dodgers as a batting instructor, and Peter O'Malley asked me to go. I told him I would go to any country to teach baseball but Cuba. The others did not go, either.

Cuba would have been the first international country to incorporate a team into the major leagues, with Havana arriving before Montreal and Toronto.

Ed Roebuck

It was Stan Williams who facilitated my interview with Ed Roebuck, for which I am grateful. Both former pitchers have retired to the same southern California town.

Ed Roebuck was kind with his time, and related some fetching anecdotes on his off-season playing career, which was widely-based. Beginning in 1952, Roebuck pitched in three straight winter campaigns in Cuba, although the middle one was drastically shortened. (Roebuck was very enamored with his time in Cuba.) The former right-handed pitcher was able to experience the Almendares-Habana rivalry from both sides. Roebuck opened his Cuban Winter League career with the Almendares Alacranes under Bobby Bragan and closed it with the Adolfo Luque–led Habana Leones. In his final Cuban campaign, Roebuck tied with Joe Hatten for most wins (13) in the league.

Roebuck was also an important hurler for teams in the Puerto Rican and Dominican winter leagues for one-season durations. Roebuck excelled in every league in which he pitched. He finished tied for second-most wins (10) in Puerto Rico and went undefeated (11–0) with an ERA well under 2.00 in the Dominican League, in one of the all-time best campaigns recorded by a winter league pitcher. The Brooklyn Dodgers' signee also provided his services to Nicaraguan winter baseball in 1963.

A career relief pitcher, Ed Roebuck had a successful 11-year major league tenure with Brooklyn and then Los Angeles, and then the Washington Senators and Philadelphia Phillies. The valuable bullpen commodity made only one career start, but compiled a 52–31 lifetime record, with 62 saves, in 460 appearances.

You are a native of Pennsylvania. Whereabouts?

About 60 miles southwest of Pittsburgh, in the rural town called East Millsboro. It is also known as West Bend, because it is on the western bend of the Monongahela River, on its way toward Pittsburgh.

What was your family unit like as a child?

There were nine of us, six boys and three girls. I was the only boy that did not work in the coal mines. My other brothers did not want me to go into the coal mines; I was the youngest.

What sparked your interest in baseball?

With all the boys we had in the family, there were always gloves around, and we had ball games. Everyone was into baseball in that area.

Which player, or players, did you most admire?

Probably Stan Musial. I was a Pittsburgh Pirates fan, so Ralph Kiner, too. But Musial I would say; he was from the Monongahela Valley, from Donora. He was also of Polish descent, like my family.

How did you arrive at winter ball?

Our organization, Brooklyn, wanted players to go down to winter ball to get more experience. When I was contacted, I certainly wanted to do it. That was the winter of '52. Brooklyn had several players with Almendares.

A former Dodger, Bobby Bragan, was managing Almendares that season.

Bragan was certainly a baseball guy. He was a guy that made decisions; he did not fool around. Bragan was very adamant about what he was doing. I think he wanted to switch me over to an everyday player. Bobby was sort of an experimenter on changing players from where they were into maybe a better situation.

What about the players you saw in the league? Who most impressed you?

There were some real good Cuban players. Miñoso played for Marianao. Miñoso was the best player I saw and Conrado Marrero was the best from the mound. At the time, I think, Marrero was in his middle thirties; he was a very good pitcher. Marrero gave Ted Williams some trouble. Rocky Nelson was a superstar in the Cuban League; he was also a superstar in the International League. Nelson would hit somewhere around .320 every year, and he would go to Cuba and hit the same. But every time he went to the major leagues, St. Louis or the Dodgers, they had Stan Musial or Gil Hodges, so he never stayed with the big league team. Nelson was a very good hitter. Forrest Jacobs, was a very good player at that level. He was another player that had super years in the minors but when he got to the majors something happened, somebody was in front of him. Héctor Rodríguez played in the big leagues and he was a real good player in the Cuban League. I also played with Héctor Rodríguez in Montreal. Willy [Miranda] had a long tenure with the Baltimores. He was essentially the very good-field, no-hit player. Paul Smith came to the big leagues with Pittsburgh. He did well down in Cuba, and I think he stayed with Pittsburgh a few years, because I remember pitching against Paul when I was with the Dodgers.

I recall another popular player. Roberto Ortiz. Every time Ortiz showed up anywhere on the field, the people in the stands would stand up and applaud him for a couple of minutes. I was trying to figure out who this person was when I saw this happen. I did not know his history. He played with the Washington Senators. But apparently Ortiz was a real, real superstar in Cuba. You would *have* to remember Roberto Ortiz. I mean every time he showed up, the game was held up because of applause ... I was just wondering why we did not win more games with some of the players we had.

Where did you stay in Havana?

We lived in an apartment building owned by a person connected with Cuban sports, near Varadero Beach. I think he had something to do with the race track. Don Zimmer lived in the apartment above us. We did not get out to Havana that much. We hung out in the suburbs there, and there were always other players we got together with, like during the holidays. I had my family with me. Bragan was the group leader, sort of. We would visit a different restaurant every Sunday night. I always looked for American food.

My mother-in-law and father-in-law came down and joined us for, oh, a month. My father-in law, who was a veteran of the Spanish-American War, was really thrilled when we took him on a tour of Havana Harbor to see where the battleship *Maine* was sunk. My father-in-law had served in the Philippine Islands.

I must say Cuba was the best place you could probably play ball. In the sense that all of our games were at "home." And naturally, I did not have to leave my family. Everything there was great. I had some of my better times in baseball playing there. I really enjoyed playing in Havana.

The following season, you returned to the Cuban League but only pitched in two games, four total innings. What happened?

The next winter, well, I was working in Ohio at a service station, and Al Campanis called me and asked me if I wanted to go to Cuba again. And I said, uh, *yeah*. It is zero degrees here, I am freezing to death and cannot make any money. I felt like I received a call to go to heaven. I arrived in Cuba and started well. But my wife was pregnant, and she was having a hard time, and I had to come home. Very heart-breaking. Because I was very happy to have gotten away from that climate in Ohio.

Well, things worked out much better in the winter of 1954. You led the Cuban League in wins and tossed 162 innings, which is a lot for a season of 80 scheduled games.

I was just thinking about the pitch-count now. In the summer of 1954, I pitched for Montreal, which was Triple A, International League. My record was 18–15, and I had 25 complete games. I went to Cuba that winter and my record was 13 and something. I never did count up the innings, but it did sure surpass [anything by today's standards]. Oh, I did not know that I led the Cuban League in complete games, too.

Did your living quarters remain the same?

In '54, most all of the American teams had their players living in an apartment building in Havana. I do not remember the name. We stayed there.

Your manager in 1954 was Adolfo Luque.

Adolfo Luque. Boy, was he strict. He did not take anything from anybody. When Luque had his starter warming up before the game — and Mike González did the same thing — he would have another pitcher warming up alongside of him. I guess Luque figured most of the pitchers had their problems early on. I never saw that anywhere else. He did it with me; it did not give you much confidence. Mike González was a quiet, unassuming guy. He had the respect of just about everybody.

Did we talk about any of your teammates with Habana?

We had Pedro Formental on our team, and one of the American pitchers threw at Pedro and hit him. Pedro went into the clubhouse to get his pistol. I think he was going to shoot the pitcher from the other team. Luque stopped him. Every day, Pedro Formental came into the clubhouse. He would take off his pistol, lay it up into his locker, like, what is the big deal? I think Pedro was a Batista guy. Evidently, he had connections, so he could do just about anything he wanted. Sandy Amorós was a young, rookie outfielder for us.

The Habana team leaned toward the Cardinals' organization. We had four or five players from their minor leagues on our team. Kenny Boyer became a great player, and [Don] Blasingame and Bill Virdon, the three of them were just outstanding prospects.

Ed Roebuck put up stellar numbers in every winter league in which he pitched. Hurling for Habana in 1954-55, the right-hander led the league in wins with 13, and complete games, 12. With Mayagüez the following year, Roebuck won the second most games in the circuit (courtesy Charles Monfort).

I have not asked you about the fans or the stadium.

The fan participation was something else. I could not believe it, especially when Habana and Almendares played. The noise was so loud, it was all you could do to hear yourself think. It appeared to me that everybody in the stands was betting on the pitches—whether it was a foul ball, a ball or strike. Each "bookie" seemed to have their section in the stands. They bet on everything. In between, the non-bettors were even more vociferous than the bettors. The stadium was better than most of the minor league stadiums I played in. Actually, you could compare it to a big league ballpark, capacity, lights, first class structure, really.

In some respects, you made an even bigger mark from the mound while pitching in the Dominican Republic. You played for one of the two teams based in the capital, the Escogido Leones. Another former Dodger, Pete Reiser, was your manager there.

I played for Escogido in the Dominican Republic in 1959. Pete Reiser always tried to make sure everybody was happy. He had some kind of team there, I will tell you that.

Stan Williams told me a good story of how you and he wrangled some extra cash from the team owner during Escogido's playoff run.

We won everything in sight. When Stan and I convinced the Escogido owner not to spend the money to bring over Bob Bruce for the playoffs, to split it with us, instead, the owner said to us, "You boys are not only good pitchers, you are good lawyers." [Laughs.] I cannot remember his name.

Frank Howard was on your team.

Boy, would the people just stare at him. Every time you would walk down the street with Frank Howard, there would be a following right behind. All the kids would be looking at him like he was from another planet. He was six-foot-eight, 240, I guess.

Some pretty good native players were on your squad, as well.

We had all kinds of Alous there. And Juan Marichal. I was just thinking, in the playoff game in '62 — the Dodgers and Giants—I pitched against almost all the same players on the Giants that were with Escogido.

Who were the best players, in your opinion, in that league?

Probably, I would have to go with Felipe [Alou] as the best everyday player, and Stanley [Williams], the best pitcher.

As opposed to Cuba, there was "life on the road" in the Dominican.

There was travel in that league. It was interesting because we were able to see some of the island.

The stadium in the capital was a relatively new structure.

Trujillo Stadium was a well-kept stadium. It was a little bit better and had more capacity than the minor league stadiums.

And the stadium's occupants?

Very, very emphatic fans. It is really something how vociferous fans are in Latin America and how they really get into the game. When we first came out to LA from Brooklyn, you could not hear anything from the stands. I guess people were used to watching movies. And it was just the opposite down there. That is why I bring it up. LA fans, when we first got there, did not seem to be into it. It is all different now, they are great fans.

What kind of celebration did you have as league champs?

I had all of the Escogido players to my room after we won the championship. We had a big chicken dinner. Some of those native players, it was the first time they had a really enjoyable meal. What a time we had. I signed the owner's name to the tab. I just thought he would pick it up. The next day we left. When I got back home to California, there was already a call from our minor league secretary: *Send the money down or you will be ineligible to play major league baseball.*

What I find most impressive about your undefeated season in the Dominican League was that you had missed that entire major league season.

I had some arm problems later on, and it was not due to pitching; it was due to not pitching. I went to spring training in 1958 or '57. I could not throw because apparently my arm had grown accustomed to throwing year 'round, and scar tissue had formed by not pitching. I had a terrible time. As a matter of fact, I was told I would never pitch again. Every time I tried to throw, that scar tissue would stretch, and it hurt. I found it ironic, because most people who hurt their arms do it by throwing too much. I hurt my arm by *not* throwing. You see, I had my arm so stretched out from throwing all the time, my arm was really fine-tuned.

I did not mean to skip over your season in Puerto Rico. I would definitely like to hear about that experience.

I also pitched in Puerto Rico one season—1955-56. With Mayagüez. We traveled to Ponce and San Juan. Dixie Howell was our manager. We lived at the Darlington Apartments. All the American players with Mayagüez lived there. Wally Moon. [Gino] Simoli. Best player ... Victor Power, Victor Pellot. Cepeda was just a kid. I do not have that good a recall about Puerto Rico. It was a good experience. But none of the places were as good as Cuba. Cuba was outstanding.

It seemed all of the places I played in, Cuba, Dominican, Nicaragua, all had revolutions after I left. I sure hope I was not the cause.

Dick Schofield

Dick Schofield and Bill Virdon were rookie teammates with the St. Louis Cardinals in 1955. The prior winter they were teammates with the Habana Leones. Schofield had a long big league career as a utility infielder, mostly in the National League. He turned all of twenty while playing in Havana with the city's namesake team. An only child and lifelong Illinois resident, Schofield recalled numerous personal accounts of his time spent in the Cuban capital. Schofield provided a lively retelling of his winter league experience, very reflective, I am sure, of the carefree and youthful spirit that lived it.

The son of a professional baseball player, Schofield has helped perpetuate a notable baseball lineage. He is the father of major league shortstop Dick Schofield, Jr., and is the grandfather of current major league player Jason Werth (daughter Kim's son).

The 76-year-old Schofield was six weeks away from celebrating his 55th wedding anniversary with his wife Donna.

Where were your baseball roots planted?

I was born in Springfield and have lived here all my life. My dad played professional baseball for about eleven years, and he spent many, many hours with me and taught me how to play. My dad was the reason I achieved what I did in baseball.

Which baseball players did you admire?

I was always a Ted Williams fan when I was a kid.

When did you get your start in the game?

I played in high school and back in those days there were so many more minor league teams, and there were more scouts going around the countryside trying to see guys play. I was signed by the Cardinals.

It was through the Cardinals that you ended up playing your one season of winter ball.

Mike González was the owner of the Havana team, and he played with the Cardinals at one time. We had quite of few guys from the Cardinals on that team. Mike González was a real nice guy. He used to come around on payday with his little black bag and he would pay us in one hundred dollar bills. It was U.S. money. As I remember, he did not use anything but American money. I used to tell him, "Mike, keep some of this money for me until I get ready to go home. I do not know what to do with all this money." At the end of the season, I had a whole bunch of one hundred dollar bills that I brought home with me. I probably made more money playing winter ball than I did in the big leagues.

Where were you quartered?

We lived in Club Náutico. Don Blasingame and myself had one bedroom, and Ron Negray and Floyd Woolridge shared the other bedroom. We had a real nice place, right on the ocean.

Looking at the roster, it seems like quite a Cardinals' connection.

We [the team] had quite a few Americans. You could only have so many. I think we had the full amount allowed. Bill Virdon played center. We have been friends for a long time. We played together in Pittsburgh when we won [the World Series]. Bill had his little girl with him, her name was Debbie, and Boyer had his little girl, named Suzie. Blasingame and I would bring them ice cream all the time. Kenny Boyer played third. Blasingame, second, and I played shortstop. Dick Rand was the catcher.

Sandy Amorós played left field. Amorós played with the Dodgers, the *Brooklyn* Dodgers. Amorós was really a quiet guy. You would never think he was in the big leagues. Just a real nice guy. He did not speak a whole lot of English. The ballpark was the only place I saw him. I always liked him.

We had a guy named Pedro Formental who played right field. Formental was a pretty good hitter and player in his day. Formental would come to the ballpark with a gun stuck inside the front of his pants. In the clubhouse, Formental would take the gun and knock the clip of bullets out of the gun. He would put the bullets in a bag with his watch and money and billfold and rings. He would throw the gun on top of his locker. After the game, he would pop the clip of bullets back in the gun.

There was a near-serious altercation involving Formental, his gun and an opposing pitcher.

His name was Jim Melton [Cienfuegos]. Melton hit Formental two times in a row in a game. The second time Formental went down to first base and pointed at Melton with his fingers like he had a gun. After the game, we are in the clubhouse and all of sudden Formental is slapping those bullets into the gun. One clubhouse was down the hallway from the other, and Formental was going to go over and shoot Melton. About that time, a bunch of the Cuban players jumped in and stopped him.

The clubhouses were back up high under the stands. One was more behind home plate, the other was down first base. They were a ways apart, but they were down a hall from each other. Seemed like it was a straight shot to both of them down that hallway. If I remember correctly, we walked out from under the stands onto the field.

How did you get along with your Cuban teammates, and sportswriters?

Most of the native guys, naturally, did not speak English too well. We could not speak Spanish, so we did not get to know these guys as well as you would have liked. Unlike, say, Oscar Sierra, who played first base for us. He spoke Spanish and English. Oscar would tell you things. It was a lot easier to speak to him. I cannot remember any sportswriters.

Mike González was the team owner and Adolfo Luque was the manager.

Luque did not know me and Blasingame apart. If one of us screwed up, he would holler at the other one. At the end of the season, I still do not think he knew us [apart]. Luque was rather old. I was 19 and he seemed like he was 119 to me. Luque used to get on the Cuban guys really bad. Luque would holler at those guys something awful, I thought. I played for Eddie Stanky, so I know about that stuff. But I never had a problem with Luque. I always got along with him.

The youthful spirit of Dick Schofield was ever-present throughout his one season in Havana (courtesy Charles Monfort).

The biggest rivalry in the league at that time was between your team, Habana, and Almendares.

I can remember playing for Habana, we always seemed to play Almendares the second game of a doubleheader on Sundays. In between games, they would have a "riot." People running across the field with all kinds of banners. The cops would chase them with their billy clubs, shooting in the air, and you would see seven Americans back in the clubhouse — *we'll be back when you're done.* Castro was forming in the mountains in those days. At 19, I was not very politically-oriented, but I do remember people talking about Castro coming one day.

I remember one game, Bobby Bragan came out to argue with an umpire with a bottle of orange sody pop in his hand. Bragan argued all the time. The umpire was Vic Delmore. He was a National League ump, one of the few American umpires in the league. Delmore is the guy who was behind the plate, with the Cubs and Cardinals playing; we were up to bat, and there was a pass ball and Delmore handed a new ball to the catcher. The runner at first base took off and the catcher threw the ball to second and the runner was called out — but that was not even the ball that was in play. The ball in play was, hell, back by the backstop!

Who were the exceptional players in the league?

Almendares had a much older team than ours. They had Earl Rapp. Lee Walls. The guy that played third base, he was a good player, Héctor Rodríguez. Angel Scull was a pretty good player, too. I remember him playing outside of Cuba, like Amorós. I remember a pitcher named [Roger] Bowman. He threw a bunch of slop curveballs up to home plate. I was just learning how to hit, and I never saw anybody pitch like that. He always stuck in mind. [George] Munger pitched for them, as well. They had good teams in the league. Good competition. Kenny Boyer was awful good. And he got better. Boyer stood out as much as anybody to me. Of course, Virdon was a great outfielder even then. He got better all the time, too.

How about from the mound?

I guess I am kind of prejudiced. It was Bowman. I could not hit him with a handful of bats. As I say, he used to throw me a whole bunch of slop curveballs. I did silly things at home plate to get myself out, too. Oh, I will tell you who was tough: Connie Johnson. Connie could get it up there pretty quick. He had some good stuff. He was a very good pitcher.

Can you relay some more of the atmosphere at the ballpark?

The Cubans loved baseball. We had good crowds. The fans were enthusiastic. I do remember those people drinking that black coffee at the ballpark. Little tiny cups of coffee. Man, they would fire up that — what is it three-fourths sugar, one-fourth coffee? I tried that coffee once; I did not go for that. The guys in the stands wore those white shirts [guayaberas]. Everybody had one.

How did the local food appeal to you?

I almost starved to death for the first two weeks until I found a Howard Johnson's. [Exaggerated laugh.] We did not know where to go to eat at first, but after that we found our way around. I cannot remember all the places we went to — but there was a chicken place called Rancho Luna, seems like to me. I am not sure whether that is right, but the guys kind of liked that place pretty well. There was a place not too far from Club Náutico, it was just a little stand on the corner. They used to have these strawberry, I don't know, shortcake things—and some other stuff that was like a custard [flan]. I used to eat that custard like it was going out of style. I will never forget a sody pop they had down there called Caw-way [Cawy], or something like that. It was like Seven-up but really sweet. I liked it.

Describe your time away from the ballpark.

On our off-days, we played golf. Ed Roebuck and myself played all the time. I had my car there. Blasingame took his car. Blasingame drove an Oldsmobile 88. We took them over on a boat from Miami. I had a Buick Road-master. The biggest one you could find. The parking lot was right by the sea, and every day — every day — the same guys would wash your car for a buck. Playing golf, the same guys would carry your clubs all day long. And we just kept playing. If I gave the guy ten dollars after we finished, it seemed like to me, he thought he was holding a thousand dollar bill in his hand. We used to feed them after nine holes. We would buy those guys beer and sandwiches. I think they had more fun with us than we had playing golf. We had a lady that washed our clothes and a lady that ironed them. We had too much help.

We would drive those big old cars around downtown. We would do something wrong. Cops would pull us over. They would look at our driver's license. The cops could not read it. They would say, okay leave, probably hoping we would go away. After a while, they probably had to know we were ballplayers. I do not know what we did, but it seemed like the cops stopped us a lot. We took turns driving. We did not need all those cars, but we had them. Also on off-days we used to play squash. Out where we lived they had a court, they used to light it up at night. We had some serious games. We went to Jai-alai. We spent a lot of time playing golf. There were a couple of golf courses. Never went fishing.

We went to the *Tropicana*. I remember I met a girl. She was not Cuban. She was Spanish. I asked her if she wanted to go to a movie. She said I have to bring my mom, my sisters. I am thinking, I do not understand this, so I passed on that one.

We used to go to the rum factories in downtown Havana and sample the frozen daiquiris, and we would buy Cuban cigars and go down to the beach and turn green smoking those things. I definitely could not smoke those cigars. We would buy some Cuban beer and sit out there and drink with Boyer and Virdon and Blasingame. They had a place where you could buy alligator shoes and purses for women. I remember buying my mom linen tablecloths and lace tablecloths.

At the airport, players and well-wishers gather around the 1952 Caribbean Series championship trophy won by the Habana Leones. Standing to the right, with hat in hand, is a presumably unarmed Pedro Formental. The bareheaded man next to Formental is Sandy Amoros.

You would walk down the street in downtown Havana and somebody might reach out from some place and pull you into a bar or something like that. It was different. I never had any trouble. Seemed like a laugh a minute to me. I am just trying to think of some more places we went to.... Well, I am sure we went some places we should *not* have, how is that?

My mom and dad and another couple came down. They stayed at the Commodore Hotel, was that it? It was a real nice place, right on the water. It was just for about a week. They saw a couple of games. They had a good time. My dad came back to Havana to drive home with me [from Miami], and we went out to eat pork chops. By that time, we knew the places to eat. My dad is picking through his food. We are telling him how good it is. We were chowing down, and he could not get that pork chop down too good. [Amused.]

That was really great. Do you have any final memories to share?

I enjoyed Cuba. The weather was fantastic. I had a good time. I was treated well, and it was good for me. I have good memories of Havana. It was such a nice place.

It is a shame what happened. And so many good Cuban players never received a chance to play in the big leagues.

Hal Smith

Hal Smith has settled into retirement not far from the small Arkansas town in which he was born. We spoke five weeks before his 80th birthday, and Smith and his southern twanged-voice came across most amiably throughout.

Smith was the starting catcher for several years during the late 1950s for his boyhood-favorite team, the St. Louis Cardinals. As a Redbird rookie in the winter of 1956, Smith was the starting catcher for the Marianao Tigres of the Cuban Winter League. Smith caught a pitching staff led by Mike Fornieles and Jim Bunning. It had been two decades since Marianao had last won a league championship. The year Smith joined the team, the Tigers were champions of the league and the Caribbean Series. (Smith tied with teammate Minnie Miñoso for most RBIs, 7, in the Series and caught every inning for his squad in the tournament.) For Smith, a seven-year major league participant, it was his only season playing outside of the U.S.

What was your home life like during your youth?

I grew up in this little town and there were not really a lot of things to do but play baseball. That was one of the things we did. It was Barling, Arkansas. I had three brothers and three sisters. Up until a year ago, I used to play golf quite a bit. One of my brothers passed away. We used to play golf together. As a family, we still get together on certain occasions.

Who were your favorite ballplayers?

The players I admired growing up were Stan Musial, Enos Slaughter, Harry Walker. All the guys that were on the St Louis Cardinals at that time. They were my heroes.

The Cardinals were the team that originally signed you.

They did not have high school baseball back then, or a team at our college, so I played for the American Legion team here in Fort Smith, Arkansas. There were several [pro] teams interested in me, but my favorite team was the St. Louis Cardinals. When they asked me if I would be interested, naturally I said, yes.

Our general manager in St. Louis at that time was Frank Lane. He was responsible for getting me the job in Cuba. Lane was a very intelligent person as far as baseball. He was a good judge of talent, and he made a lot of trades because of that. Lane knew what he wanted. But he did make a few moves that I did not go along with. Number one was Bill Virdon. He traded Bill Virdon to the Pirates for Bobby Del Greco. It turned out real good for the Pirates. Lane wanted to trade Stan Musial, but the fans did not go along with that. Oh, yeah, Lane wanted to trade Stan. Lane traded Red Schoendienst, who was a great favorite in St. Louis, and they [fans] did not like that.

Tell me about Cuba.

In Cuba, we lived in a residential complex, I cannot remember where exactly, but that was where the American players stayed. The complex had a sentry-gate, and we had to go through that. I am sure there were regular Cubans that lived there, too. There was a couple that lived next door to us, an American couple, I cannot remember now who exactly. We spent the holidays with them. We had a Christmas tree, and a turkey for Thanksgiving. I remember a Cuban pharmacist that I became acquainted with. He was a good fan.

Were you involved in many activities away from the ball yard?

We enjoyed going downtown and seeing the sights. I loved the food. I fell in love with black beans and rice. The food was really good. Another thing I remember, when we used to go to the ballpark, we would drive down the street and there would be these machine gun nests along the way. They were manned with military personnel. This is when Castro was rumored to be coming in, you know. And then when we would get to the ballpark, and they had people with machine guns on the roof of the stadium, and then sometimes out in back of the outfield walls you could see more of them.

The stadium. What do you remember about it? And the fans?

It was a real nice stadium. I enjoyed playing there. The fans were real active. They were quite involved in the game. And I could not swear to this, but I know there was a lot of betting going on during the games. [On off days] We would have practice sometimes, but because there was only one park and four teams, we did not have too much of a chance to do so. Every once in while we would get in some extra hitting.

Havana was known for its after dark excitement.

We were not the nightclub folks, but we did go out to different places to eat. We even went to drive-in movies. We had our own car. We took a ferry from Key West to Havana. My wife and two daughters, we were all together. My daughters still remember it quite well. My wife, Carolyn, and I have now been married 61 years.

Your team, Marianao, broke the years-long domination of Almendares and Habana over the league, by winning the pennant. Can you talk about that team, starting with your manager?

Napoleón Reyes was a good guy to play for. He played for the Giants, you know, here in the states. Reyes was a tough guy, making us work at it. If you did not do what he thought you should have done, he would let you know about it. I liked him. Reyes was a very good manager.

Mike Fornieles was a very good pitcher. Had great control. He was not really very overpowering or anything like that. Mike knew how to pitch. He changed speeds well. Jim Bunning *was* overpowering. He was a tall right-hander, threw sidearm. Bunning was really tough on right-handed hitters. Back then I really did not think about it in those terms, that he would become a Hall of Fame pitcher. I just knew whenever he pitched we had a good chance to win. Julio Bécquer was a good player, we came to be really good buddies. I liked Julio. I remember him quite well. He was just a good player. We had a player who was with the Detroit Tigers, Al Federoff. He broke his ankle, I believe. Then Witty Quintana took over at second base. Hal Bevan, our third baseman, was a clutch hitter. Whenever you needed a base hit, seems like he always came up with it. Bevan was a steady player. I do not know if he ever made it to the big leagues. Minnie Miñoso was a great guy, I am telling you. He played hard every day, every game. Miñoso wanted to win. Miñoso was the best player in Cuba. Not only a great player, but a great person. He was a great help to us. Solly Drake was an excellent player. I was surprised he did not play very long in the big leagues. He had good speed; he was a great centerfielder.

What about the opposition players?

I hated to see Ray Noble [Cienfuegos] come to bat when there were runners in scoring position. I played against him in St. Louis when he was with

the Giants. Noble was a good catcher. Russ Nixon [Almendares] was another good catcher down there that I later played against in the states. I think Russ became a manager. Camilo Pascual was definitely a major leaguer. Best curveball I have ever seen, and I have caught a few good ones, like Sam Jones and Ernie Broglio. Pascual was the best pitcher I saw in Cuba.

What do you remember about the 1957 Caribbean Series?

Marianao won the league championship for the first time in, I don't know, thirty years. I really cannot remember the opening ceremonies of the Caribbean Series. I am sure it was similar to what we do here, introduc-

Hal Smith, Marianao catcher, 1956-57 (courtesy Charles Monfort).

ing the players. We played it in Havana. I became lucky with my hitting, tying Miñoso for most runs batted-in in the Series. I do not remember a parade, I only remember the on-field celebration, players jumping on each other. It was quite a thrill.

Did you bring any souvenirs back with you?

I think back and wonder how stupid I was not to have brought anything back with me. I do not have one memento or souvenir from that time. I sure do not. I have a few photographs that were given to me by the people that would take them. I have one egging a guy on at home plate. It is hard to see the uniform. At least it is something.

Any last recollections?

Perhaps the site we enjoyed most was seeing the ship that would sail us back to the United States. We had been in Cuba since early October. We were ready to come home by that time.

Bill Virdon

Before he joined the Cuban Winter League in 1954, Bill Virdon had not been a stranger to Havana. Virdon had traveled there on road trips in the summer of 1954 with his International League team, the Rochester Red Wings. A respectful man, Virdon was apologetic over not being able to remember more from his single season with the Habana Leones.

I first contacted Virdon during spring training, and he told me the interview would have to wait until he returned home from training camp. He was true to his word.

The 1955 National League Rookie of the Year enjoyed a 12-year major league career, most notably with the Pittsburgh Pirates. Virdon later skippered three different teams over 13 major league campaigns.

Where were you born?

In Hazel Park, which was a suburb of Detroit. I lived a short time there and then moved to Rochester. It was my sister, myself, mother and dad. My folks were originally from Missouri, over in southeast. They moved back to Southport, Missouri, from Detroit, when I was about 12 years old.

Where did your baseball calling come from?

I liked to play. I always played when I had the chance. I played softball.

Who were your idols?

Hank Greenberg was the main one. Hal Newhouser.

How were you "discovered"?

I was signed out of a Branson, Missouri, tryout camp by Hank Green-wade, who was a scout for the Yankees. I was 19. I spent five years in the minors. My first year in the International League was in 1954, and we played in Havana. I had a good year, in the Cardinals' organization. I had been traded out of the Yankees' organization in the Enos Slaughter deal. I led the International League in hitting that summer. The Cardinals recommended that I go and play for the Havana ball club that winter.

In Cuba, you were on a team with several other highly touted Cardinal prospects. It was Mike González, a former Cardinal manager and coach, that influenced, shall we say, that exchange. Adolfo Luque was your skipper.

I am sure I met Mike González, though I do not remember him. I remember Adolfo. He knew baseball. I had a good year for him. So it was not a matter of him over-managing. He just let me play. If he felt like a player needed instruction, he would give it. In Havana, I learned that baseball was not easy. There were a lot of good players there.

What did you do for relaxation?

The player I most associated with was Ken Boyer. He and I were kind of buddies. Our wives got along — Shirley and I have been married since 1951. Ken and I both broke in with the Cardinals the next season. We lived at Club

Bill Virdon shows off some of his keepsakes at home in 2011. The slick-fielding centerfielder was named National League Rookie of the Year, following his winter playing for Habana in Cuba.

Náutico, on the beach. Ken Boyer and his wife also lived there. One day we were actually locked in the Club. That was when Castro was in the hills. I am not sure if there was a warning, or someone thought there was going to be a problem, but they would not let us out and we did not play for a day.

Among the rooting public, Habana was one of the favored teams, along with Almendares. Did you get a sense of that from the fans in the stands?

We played generally every other day. Sundays were doubleheader days. All four teams played. I do not remember being overly intimidated by the fans [of Almendares]. I do not remember any harassment. The people certainly seemed to enjoy baseball.

Anything about the stadium that you remember?

The stadium was big, you had to hit the ball to get it out of the ballpark. To the best of my memory, it was in good shape.

I have spoken to a couple of your Habana teammates, Ed Roebuck and Dick Schofield. Are there any other teammates that you remember?

Ed Roebuck was a wonderful pitcher, a control pitcher, always seemed to keep you in the game, not over-powering. Ed always knew what he was doing. Dick Rand [catcher] was in the Cardinals' organization. Don was very steady; you always knew what you were getting from Blasingame. Dick [Schofield] was there. He did a good job. I played more with Dick later with the Cardinals. Sandy [Amorós] was one of those guys who could run and get on base. Pedro Formental was the Babe Ruth of Cuba. There was one experience, I am not sure if I should pass it along. You could use your judgment about it. Formental got into it with one of the pitchers on one of the other clubs. Anyway, the following inning, Formental went into his locker in the clubhouse and grabbed his gun. They stopped him, and nothing ever happened.

On the other side, for Almendares, there was Joe Hatten, who tied with Roebuck for most wins in the league. Their manager was Bobby Bragan.

I remember the name, Joe Hatten. No doubt gave us a lot of trouble. I was a left-handed hitter. I do not remember Bobby Bragan that much; of course, I played for him later in Pittsburgh. A very sharp individual.

Where did you eat in Havana?

There were good restaurants, good places to eat. Never had a problem with the food.

Did you and your wife have a chance to partake in any of the nightlife?

We did not go to the clubs too much. Most of the time we were playing at night. Our car went with us. We put it on a boat in Miami, and we drove it through Havana. Downtown was crowded but we were used to that.

It sounds like it was a pleasant experience for you.

It was a very good experience for me. I needed that exposure. I needed that experience. It turned out real well for me. It helped me win National League Rookie of the Year.

What are you doing now?

I still go to spring training every year. It has generally been with the Pirates. I have been to 62 spring trainings. Started in 1950. I go down to Florida in January and come back in April.

When I am home, I cut the grass, play a little golf ... and honey-do-this and honey-do-that.

Tony Zardón

I found José Antonio Zardón to be an engaging and energetic fellow, someone totally belying his age. I visited him at his home in Plantation, Florida. He cut a stout, healthy figure at six feet in height, with a full, neatly combed patch of dark hair and graying temples. He wore a blue-green guayabera and dark slacks. The Cuban native told me that he was born in 1922, not 1923, as official records indicate. (Zardón was born on Cuba's Independence Day anniversary — the equivalent of being a U.S. Fourth of July baby.)

Tony was going through mail when I arrived, and he showed me some requests for autographs that he said he receives on a regular basis. One return address envelope was from Michigan. Tony also took the time to show me a photograph of him and Minnie Miñoso, who had visited Tony's home a few weeks earlier. Tony's recall was sharp, with one exception. He could not remember the 1951 Caribbean Series that he played in Caracas in 1951. (Certainly pardonable due to the six decades that had passed in the meantime.)

The amiable Zardón played five seasons in the Cuban Winter League, and was one of the few players to play for all four of the league's teams. His greatest baseball achievements came with the Havana Cubans of the Florida International League. He was the franchise record holder for at-bats and stolen bases and second all-time in hits, runs, and games. Zardón was a one-year major leaguer with the Washington Senators in 1945.

I showed Tony an old picture of Gran Stadium that I had with me and he asked me if the stadium was still there. I told him, yes, that it had been expanded to accommodate more people and that it had been renamed. "Sad memories of glorious times," he said with traceable melancholy.

I left Tony in good spirits, as a married man of 39 years to second wife Marlene.

You were born on Cuban Independence Day.

Of course I was not around then, but I think it is a glorious thing to have been born on May 20. I would have been very bothered if I had been born on July 26.

What part of Havana are you from?

I am from Jesús de Monte, Habana. I have one sister. She is older than I am.

How did you come by your nickname?

I received my nickname — "*Guineo*" ("Guinea Hen") — when I was a rookie. One day during practice drills, Fermín Guerra, who later became a good friend of mine, picked me out to run the bases. The catchers would try to throw out base runners, outfielders as well. I was a fast runner, I would commonly win the run-around-the-bases drills. There were sportswriters in attendance this day. Fermín Guerra urged me on and called out to the sports-

Cuban baseball's greatest 20th century figures, Adolfo Luque, left, and Miguel Angel González, right. In the center is sportswriter René Cañizares. The former Major League players endured in the Cuban Winter League as successful managers. Among the teams Luque managed was Almendares, with whom he became most associated. González was a long-time player, manager and team owner of Habana, until the Cuban Revolution ended professional sports on the island (The Sporting News Archive).

writers— there was Pedro Galiana, [Jess] Losada ... I cannot remember who exactly. Sorry, I am going to turn 90 next May. Anyway, one of the writers pinned the nickname on me by saying, "There is a ballplayer named Tony Zardón on the field, we do not know who he is, but he runs as fast as a guinea hen." My father also told me that he heard it reported on the radio. *This player does not fly around the bases, he is like a guinea hen running them!* After that "*Guineo*" stuck.

When did you sign your first professional contract?

I was signed by Marianao in 1944, my first year in the Cuban Winter League. I had played amateur ball, so that helped me get recognized. I will never forget my first contract was for $200 for the four-month season. A few months later, the Washington Senators signed me for $6,000. I bought a model year Buick for $800. It had leather seats. It was a real head-turner. I cannot remember my first game with Marianao, or first hit. My first manager with Marianao was Lázaro Salazar. Tremendous player. Would have played in the majors. But Salazar left the team because, I think, he had a commitment in Mexico. Armando Marsans then became our manager. We played at Tropical Park. Beautiful stadium. Nobody could reach those fences.

I would like to hear about those early playing experiences.

In my second year, I was traded to Cienfuegos for Alejandro Olms, a famous player in Cuba, a star. Which turns out to be a rather tragic anecdote. Because Olms, who was only 40, died early in the campaign. The sportswriters tagged me as "Tony Zardón — the player who was traded for a dead man." It was meant to be humorous.

You were one of the few players to play with Almendares, Habana, Marianao and Cienfuegos during his career.

I played with all four teams in the league. One season, I asked Miguel Angel González [Habana manager], for a raise to $400. He calmly pulled out a sheet of paper from his drawer and read it to me: "Tony Zardón. *El Guineo*. Games played. Times fined, times unable to play due to sickness, times late." Well the games played were not that many; I was not a full time starter. And the other numbers were a lot more than I remembered. Miguel Angel told me that he would not give me a raise and to try Almendares, if I wanted. I humbly accepted the same $300 salary I had. Besides, my father was an *habanista*.

Your Habana team captured the flag.

Yes, the 1950-51 season, Habana won the pennant. [Steve] Bilko was our first baseman. Bert Haas, third baseman. Good player. Hoyt Wilhelm was on our team. [Gilberto] Valdivia was the one who caught Wilhelm. No one envied Valdivia, having to catch that knuckleball. Chiquitín Cabrera accompanied us to the Caribbean Series, which I am sorry to say, I do not remember. But I remember later on teasing Cabrera about how Tommy Lasorda body-slammed him when Cabrera had picked a fight during the season. Cabrera had been hit by one of Lasorda's pitches, and he took exception to that. Lasorda could defend himself, I think he knew karate or some martial arts. I remember the game. It was part of a doubleheader. Lasorda was pitching for Almendares. Both teams then got into it. I would needle Cabrera, ask him if his back still hurt; he would tell me to go to hell. [Chuckles.] I was hit plenty of times. I took it.

Using a quote from The Old Man and the Sea, ***"Who was the greatest manager—Luque or González?"***

I played for Adolfo Luque with the Havana Cubans [Florida International League] and saw him manage in Cuba. He was a smart man, a tough man. Luque went to bat for you when it came to salary discussions with the club. He would say flat out whether a player was worth what he was asking for. One time, on the field, Luque ordered me to steal second, and I was thrown out. When I came back to the dugout, Luque asked me who had given me the nickname "Guinea Hen?" He told me I looked more like a duck running to second than a guinea hen. Luque could be abrupt that way. Luque would get mad at sportswriters when he thought they had totally misread what he was trying to do with his moves. I passed Luque's office on more than one occasion and caught him crumpling up the newspaper he had been reading, disgusted with the criticism inside.

If one play ended up costing us a game, Luque would, afterwards, hold clubhouse meetings. He kept everyone from changing out of their uniforms and gathered them together, and would then instructively replay what had gone wrong. The whole team had to be present, whether or

Tony Zardón as a player in the Venezuelan Winter League.

not you were involved in the decisive blunder. The players referred to these meetings as "shower meetings," because we would all be standing around drenched in sweat — like we had taken a shower with our clothes on — listening to Luque make his point before releasing us. Miguel Angel and Luque were both of the ilks to keep the clubhouse door closed after a loss, not allowing the reporters inside.

Miguel Angel was a passive manager, compared to Luque. He and Luque were both baseball smart. But Miguel Angel was a better-educated man than Luque, and that helped him in general with the sportswriters, more than Luque.

You can say you witnessed and competed against Hall of Famer Martín Dihigo.

I saw and played against Martín Dihigo. He was toward the end of his career. I hit against him. As a pitcher, Dihigo was comparable to Adolfo Luque. In other areas, however, I believe there were two other players, both of whom I also played with and against, who were better. Better in all the aspects of what makes a great player — hitting, running, fielding, etc. ... Silvio García, Cienfuegos shortstop, and Minnie Miñoso, Marianao outfielder. Silvio García would have been a star in the major leagues. As far as best Cuban hitter of all time, in my opinion, it was Tony Oliva.

What was it like when the revolution came?

I was never politically inclined — my father was, but I was not. I was so out of it that once, soon after the revolution, an acquaintance of mine brought me a souvenir envelope with the emblem of the July 26-movement on it, which I accepted. My father, may he rest in peace, when he visited me, asked me where I had gotten that? My father turned to me and said this person, Castro — he is worse than Batista. My father knew the younger Fidel. My father knew him from Fidel's university days. My father was a customs agent most of his life and had the wisdom of his age. He was very interested in politics. Once, my father even had a run-in with Batista's government and was jailed for a time.

It was not until a certain incident occurred that the revolution became personal. I kept an apartment in Cuba after the revolution with Hiram González, a ballplayer friend of mine who died in Cuba. Some of Castro's agents broke into the apartment and took all of my trophies. I had numerous gold gloves, gold spikes from base-stealing awards. They were all stolen by these whatever-you-want-to-call-these people. They knew my father was not sympathetic to them, either, and they did not treat him well. And this bothered me a lot. My father was later able to leave the island and lived a long life. He died in New York.

As a result of these affronts and still thinking myself young enough, I impulsively joined the Special Forces designated to invade Cuba at the Bay of Pigs. I was training in Guatemala, and about ten days prior to the invasion I was injured in a parachute accident. During a practice jump, my chute did not open properly, and what saved my life was that my fall was broken by the thick branches of a seba tree. It took me two and a half years to fully recover. It was a covert operation, as you know, we did not use names. We were identified by numbers. But our photos were leaked and I was recognized by Castro, who decreed that there were certain "mercenaries" who were not punished for their acts in the invasion and that if they ever stepped foot on Cuban soil, they would be incarcerated. I was thus branded and can never go back to Cuba.

You were a much better player in the U.S. minor leagues than in the Cuban League.

Looking back on my career, I really did not apply myself to baseball as much as I should have. I was engaged in *la charada* (charade). My father once told me, half the players out there wish they had your aptitude, your arm, your hands, your speed. You do not take advantage of it. You stay out too late. Where do you go? What do you do? There were just too many temptations for a young player. Like "Ladies Day" at Gran Stadium. All women entered the park for free. Married players referred to it as "Divorce Day." [Laughs.] After the game on these days, the women could comingle with the players in a designated area outside the stadium, for autographs. Women were very imaginative on what they requested to have signed. One time a female admirer planted a kiss on the mouth of Tata Solís, Almendares pitcher. His wife, God rests her soul, saw it and she took off her shoe and tried to hit the woman with it, calling her *puta*. It was a noted incident. Security had to come to break things up.

The life of a professional athlete.... You also played several seasons in the Venezuela Winter League.

I played in Venezuela for four years with Cervercería Caracas. I beat out Chico Carrasquel for the batting title one year by two points. My locker was next to Alejandro Carrasquel. I saw the size of his feet once and remarked, "*Que clase de patones!*" That is how Carrasquel obtained his nickname, "*Paton.*"

So you're the one that gave Alex "Big-feet" Carrasquel his nickname. How about that. You must have faced José "Carrao" Bracho in Venezuela.

Carrao Bracho was a very good pitcher, but I believe Daniel Canónico was better. Also Luis Zuloaga. He was nicknamed "Mono."

What was it like playing in Cerveza Caracas Stadium?

What I remember about Caracas stadium was that it was easy to lose a ball at night, because of the low clouds.

I imagine, at your age, you can look back at a lot of things with fondness.

I thank God for my long life. But I never drank a lot, nor smoked. Nor took drugs. We had a player, Gaspar del Toro, amateur player. He offered me marijuana to try once. I told him no. He insisted I just try it, but I did not give in.

THE DOMINICAN WINTER LEAGUE

Fred Kipp

Born in Piqua, Kansas, Fred Kipp was the youngest of three children. Nearing his 80th birthday at the time of our conference, Kipp spoke to me from his place of business. A father of six and a career construction company owner after his playing days, Kipp continues to dabble in the hard-hat field, while separately engaged in the distribution of a nutritional health drink. Widowed from his first wife for many years, Kipp had just celebrated his 20th wedding anniversary to second spouse Lorraine.

Kipp was owned by the Brooklyn Dodgers when he first traveled south to play winter ball in Venezuela. A far-traveled man, thanks to baseball, Kipp also spent three winters in the Dominican Republic, where he was part of two championship-winning teams. A left-handed pitcher who had a curt major league career, Kipp hurled the 1957-58 national championship-delivering game for the Escogido Leones, besting Estrellas Orientales and Vic Rehm, 2–1.

Tell me about yourself.

I come from a small town of about 150 people. It was a German-Catholic community and we played a lot of baseball. I did not follow [big league] baseball that much, I just played it. Mainly we just played every day. There was not much else to do.

Who was the first to spot your baseball talent?

I played semi-pro ball and had a couple of chances to sign professionally but did not. I went to Kansas State on a basketball scholarship and then transferred to Emporia State University and graduated from there. Bert Wells, who covered the Midwest, had a bird-dog who was a basketball coach and coached the baseball team at Washburn University — Marion McDonald, I believe his name was. He told Wells about me. Wells was a full time scout for Brooklyn. He signed a bunch of kids across the Midwest.

How and when did you get your first taste of winter ball?

In 1955, I went to Venezuela. I had just gotten out of the army in July. I joined Mobile. We made the playoffs on the last day of the season. We won it, and went over and beat the Texas League Shreveport team in four straight games. Brooklyn hooked me up to go down to Venezuela. I stayed a month and a half, probably. I did not pitch real well. Earl Battey, was on our team, Cal McLish, also. I remember José Bracho was respected down there as real good pitcher. It was good stadium. They also had one in Valencia that was new.

Were you married?

I was single. I did not get married until my last year in baseball, 1961. It was my first time in a foreign country, I did not know quite how to eat. We all lived in a small hotel. The club paid our expenses. The base pay for winter ball was $1,000 a month. I remember the bread rolls, they were hard rolls. I grew kind of tired of those. I do not remember doing too much. We ran around with [U.S.] embassy people. I am not sure exactly if the team asked me to leave, but I do not think I would have left on my own. I do remember I came home with a suntan in the middle of winter. [Laughs.]

You moved over to the Dominican League after that and enjoyed a multiple-season stint, playing for Escogido. That time must have been more memorable.

In '56, I went to Japan after the season with Dodgers, after they were in the World Series. So I did not play winter ball. I played the next three years in the Dominican. Escogido had some good teams. We won pretty regularly. I remember Stan Williams, he played with us. I think he had just gotten married. Joe Pignatano. Ron Negray and Ken Aspromonte. Ed Roebuck. Ozzie Virgil was on our team. Frank Howard played with us one year. Howard grabbed an umpire once and he got suspended for a while. Damned near got sent home. [Chortles.] Howard was six-seven, 240, with a 34-inch waist. Howard was super strong. Stretch McCovey was there one year. He may have been 20 years old. He became a really great hitter.

I roomed with Rudy Hernández for two years. Whenever we needed something, Rudy was a great help. If we needed the power turned on, or telephone, Rudy would take an autographed baseball with him and get it done. Rudy knew how to talk to people, to get whatever we needed. Rudy lives in Puerto Rico. I talked to him about two or three years ago. He became a scout. Rudy's mother was Puerto Rican and his father Dominican, or vice a versa. Rudy always had the best looking women on that island. He was about six-three, good-looking guy. He did a lot of his growing up in New York. Rudy was a sharp guy. He knew his way around.

The second year, we stayed at a hotel. It was a nice one. I learned to eat pretty well in the Dominican. There was a store, and we would buy things and we would cook for ourselves. We ate pizza right out on the ocean a lot. There were a couple of other restaurants. We did not do too badly. It was a little different when we went in-country. Like Santiago. I think they built a

Some players socializing with unidentified hosts in the Dominican. At far left is Rudy Hernández. Joe Pignatano converses in the middle of the group. Ron Negray is third from right and Fred Kipp is at far right (courtesy F. Kipp).

new stadium there. As I remember, we took automobiles, mainly cabs. Cabs used to run up and down the boulevard and they would take you wherever you wanted to go. The roads were not that great.

The stadium in the capital was opened in 1955.

The big stadium [in Ciudad Trujillo], it was a good stadium. It had a jail, which was a bit unusual, you know. It was under the stands somewhere. I never saw it, but I remember some of the guys talking about it. They use to serve drinks at the stadium. They had a guy in the stands carrying a tray around with anisette and scotch whiskey on it. Hard stuff. Bottles of it. If you wanted a drink, they would pour you a shot. They did not have beer sales. The fans were pretty avid. Baseball has always been their sport.

Escogido won the island championship two out of the three seasons you played for them. The year you did not win, Escogido were victims of a big upset by the Licey Tigers.

Licey had a native catcher, small guy, who just played over his head, and Licey won the championship the second year I was there. They definitely were not supposed to win. We had the talent: the Alou boys. Pignatano and Bill White. Juan Marichal.

Those are some talented names. Let's start with Marichal.

Marichal started as teenager and he did not know his way around the mound. The next year, Marichal played D-ball, and he came back and was damned near a polished pitcher. You know how good he became. He was a talent, man. Marichal could throw the ball where he wanted. That was the kind of pitcher he was. Felipe was the best of the bunch. The younger one [Jesús], he was a pitcher, first. Matty, he had a hell of a year. A little guy, but Matty could run. A hell of a fielder. And he had a good arm. Felipe was probably the more personable of them all. Felipe became a manager. He was real diplomatic. Friendly. He spoke the language [English].

What else do you remember about your winter ball participation?

I enjoyed my time in the Dominican. I had the opportunity to meet quite a few people. To attend some parties. The Caribbean people are the greatest entertainers in the world. They always have something going on. They really know how to throw a party. They really know how to entertain people. They are just really gracious people. We had a celebration over at the owner's house when we won one year. I cannot put a name on him. He was a big money guy.

We played on winning teams. And that made it more fun, too.

Norm Sherry

Norm Sherry and his younger brother, Larry, played winter ball. They both played for the Cabimas Oilers in Venezuela's Occidental League in 1958-59. The following winter, Norm, a catcher, traveled to the Dominican Republic to handle the pitching staff of the Escogido Leones. Norm also took over managing the team from Pete Reiser during the season and guided the club to an island championship. The former backstop jovially disclosed several humorous occurrences he witnessed while in Ciudad Trujillo.

Norm Sherry and Larry Sherry, who passed away in 2006, both became major league performers as well. Norm was a five-year major league reserve and also managed parts of two seasons with the California Angels in the mid-seventies.

Married for twenty-five years to second wife Linda, Norm and his spouse have multiple children and grandchildren from a blended family unit.

Your place of birth?

I was born in New York City, but I was raised in Los Angeles. My mother had four boys. My older brother, Stan, myself, a brother, George, and brother, Larry.

What was growing up like in Southern California?

We lived about three houses from the high school, Fairfax High School in Los Angeles. We were constantly jumping the fences and playing on the grounds. Those guys would leave baseballs and bats behind. So we had all the stuff to play with all the time. And we were not but three or four blocks from Gilmore Field, where the Hollywood Stars of the Pacific Coast League used to play. We would go to Gilmore Field and hang around, waiting for foul balls to come over. I just wanted to be a baseball player after watching all these Hollywood players all the time. I remember telling my second grade teacher when she asked all the kids what they wanted to be when they grew up, I said a baseball player.

And which player did you most want to grow up emulating?

I did not know that much about major league ballplayers, except Babe Ruth and Lou Gehrig and Joe DiMaggio. I knew all the guys that played on the Hollywood Stars. Frank Kelleher, Tony Lupien.

The Dodgers were still happy in Brooklyn when you signed with them.

In 1949, Fairfax High School won the city championship. I graduated in January 1950, after half a term. Scouts started coming around. Then a friend of mine told me the Dodgers were having a tryout at Gilmore Field, to come down with him. I was going to go to USC; I had a full baseball scholarship. But after the tryout, I was talked into playing baseball professionally. I guess I did the right thing, I do not know. I ended up signing with the Dodgers.

I started in Santa Barbara, Class C, in 1950, then in 1951 I played at Fort Worth and finished at Class B, Newport News. The Dodgers sent me to Newport News just before June 1. The reason they did that was to avoid having to pay me more money. I was not making much anyway. The next year, I went into the army. I was in the service in '52 and '53. I was discharged from the army in February of '54, and went back to Fort Worth. The Dodgers sent a catcher from the major leagues there, and so I went back to Newport News and played the whole year there.

When did you start your winter ball excursion?

My first year playing winter ball was 1958. I went down to Maracaibo, Venezuela. The Dodgers had an affiliation with a team there—Cabimas, it was called. A lot of players from the Dodgers organization played there, including my brother Larry. He had been there the year before and he went back in '58. Rapiños was in that league. Luis Aparicio. That was his team. Toward the end of the season, that Rapiños team was in the playoffs, and I went and played with them.

Venezuela had two winter leagues at that time. In Caracas, there was the Central League. You latched on in what was called the Western League. The champions of both leagues played one another to see who would represent Venezuela in the Caribbean Series. You must have gone over to play in Caracas during the playoffs.

We did travel to Caracas to play. Less Moss was our manager. I tried to break up a double play and their guy kneed me in my side. I hurt my ribs real bad and could not play anymore in those playoffs.

How did you find Venezuela?

It was tough playing in Venezuela for me, because I was not used to the humidity. We would play morning games at 10:00 A.M., and the flag just would not move, it just hung there full of moisture from the humidity. Miller Harris was a Dodgers' pitcher. He would pitch a game in an hour and twenty minutes. We all loved him on those days. No one had the strength to swing a bat. I hit a grand slam in Venezuela once and was given a hundred dollar prize.

Food is food to me. I like Mexican food, Spanish food. We stayed at a hotel, owned by these European guys. They served meals, more or less, like what you find in any American restaurant. No favorite dishes that I recall — on yeah, rum and coke. [Jokingly.]

Escogido owner Máximo Hernández Ortega (in white suit) marches with his road team during the inaugural ceremonies at Estadio Oriental in San Pedro de Macoris on October 25, 1959. Manager Pete Reiser is at far right. Behind the boy behind Reiser is Alonso Perry. The two tallest and most visible players are Frank Howard and San Williams (front). Norm Sherry may be the player obscured by the woman (photograph by Mark Rucker/Transcendental Graphics, Getty Images).

Did you celebrate the holidays?

We celebrated Christmas and Thanksgiving. The native people down there did not. I think their holiday came in January — All Kings Day [Three Kings Day], or something like that.

The following winter, you made the transition to the Dominican Republic, and you played on a pennant-winner.

In 1959-60, I played in the Dominican Republic for Pete Reiser, who also managed me in Venezuela. I played for the Red team [Escogido]. The Alou brothers were on the team. And Juan Marichal, who no one had heard of yet. We had a pretty good team. Frank Howard was on that team. Ed Roebuck was one of the pitchers. We won the championship. Pete Reiser went home before the end of the season, and he told me to take over. I took over the club. [Chuckles.] Nope, I did not get paid extra for managing. It was not bad. I just filled out the lineup card and told the players to go play. We had good pitching and good hitting. We had a kid named Daniel Rivas. A lefty. I thought he could have been better than Marichal. Another kid at third base named Ricardo Joseph. He was a good player.

There was an on-field incident that season involving big Frank Howard and an umpire. Can you tell me about it?

We were behind in a game against the team [Licey] that had [Johnny] Blanchard and Norm Larker on it. Joe Shultz was the manager of that team. We had the bases loaded, and Matty Alou hits a ball down the left line that hits right on the chalk line. We were behind by four runs or so. This was going to drive in three runs. The native umpire on the line calls the ball "fair." All the players on the other team charge him, they had him cornered. The umpire comes out of the half-circle of players and says, "No, foul ball!" This umpire runs to the mound and starts an argument with Emmett Ashford, who was behind the plate. At first base is an umpire named Sneathen. He was about five-nine, about 250, a real stocky-built guy. Well, the umpires finally want to get the game going again. Frank Howard had been the runner at first base; he was in the dugout, thinking he had scored. Sneathen starts yelling at Frank Howard, *Come on out here and get on the base so we can get this game going.* Frank looks at him, pounds his chest, and says, *You want some of me?!* And out he goes. God Almighty, Frank is six-foot-eight, and he charges this umpire and picks him up, I am not kidding, to eye level and shakes him. The back of the umpire's uniform shirt ripped right down the middle. The umpire threw Frank right out of the game. Frank comes back to the dugout and back up the runway to the door of our clubhouse — and the door is locked. We heard a tremendous crash. Have you ever seen cartoons where a guy walks through a door? That is what Frank did. He pounded himself right through that clubhouse door. [Laughs heartily.] It was funny, I will tell you.

That is quite a mental picture you have left me with. What about the ball-parks in the Dominican?

The stadiums were like minor league parks. They were good. Showers and lockers. It was all right. We played in Ciudad Trujillo. They gave us a driver, his name was Cito Frio. Funny I should remember his name. [Stan] Williams and I, and I forget who else, we would travel to the ballgames with him. If we had to stay out of town, to play three games, he would be back to take us home when the series was over.

You mentioned Stan Williams. He was a big part of your team's success.

I remember Stan very well. We played down there together, and he was my roommate with the Dodgers in 1960. Stan was also my roommate toward the end of the season in the Dominican. One night, I heard this banging, I wake up, what is going on? Stan had a slipper in his hand, and the wall is full of blood splotches. Stan is killing mosquitoes. I look at his face; he is being eaten alive by these mosquitoes. Stan is trying to kill them all, and I never had one bite me. [Laughs.]

Stan was kind of mean from the mound. In those days, you would get knocked down. Hitters never liked it. There was a native player, I cannot think of his name, a real good hitter, left-handed hitter — he played with Kansas City [Manny Jiménez]. Anyhow, Stan and I came down out of the elevator at the hotel we were staying at and the native player was there waiting to go up in the elevator. Well, there was a history between Stan and the native player. And that native player looked at Stan and said, "Stan, one day, I *keeel* you." And Stan says, "No, no, — now is the time. Let's go, right now!" And the native guy dropped his fist and got on the elevator and did not say another word. Stan would have torn that guy apart. [More laughs.]

You caught Ed Roebuck that season. He did not lose a game. You must have been calling all the right pitches.

Ed Roebuck would just go out there and throw his game and win. He was a real good pitcher. I would go out to the mound and tell him, Eddie, you are throwing too hard, and he would laugh, because you never tell a pitcher that. Roebuck threw sinkers. You had to get the right speed on the ball or the ball would not sink.

The foreign players for Escogido were put up in a hotel. Is that right?

We lived at the hotel — Palms Hotel? — it was across the street from the fairgrounds there. Trujillo used to take his horses and go riding there a lot. The army guys would come out and block the road leading to the park. It was where Pete Reiser lived, and that is where he wanted us. I do not remember guys from other teams staying there.

Did you find the food much different in the Dominican than Venezuela?

Oh, first time I ever had, what is it called, the stuff with chicken and mussels and rice and ham and shrimp...? [*Paella*] That was really good. The food in the Dominican was good.

Besides Roebuck and Williams, any other standouts from the hill that you can remember?

I thought Daniel Rivas was one of the best pitchers. Chichí Olivo, he came up with the Pirates. His brother, Guayubin, was the left-hander.

How about non-pitchers?

Blanchard was really good, I remember. Norm Larker, who played with Blanchard.

Dick Stuart had some good seasons mashing the ball in Santo Domingo.

Dick Stuart was down there. He could hit the ball, but God Almighty.... There was a play, the bases were loaded. It would have been the last out of the game. They threw the ball to Stuart at first base. It was a little high. He jumped up and came down on the bag. He acted like he caught the ball. Stuart came over to the mound, opened the glove and no ball. Guys are running around the bases. *What is wrong with him?* Stuart thought he had caught the ball.

Jesús Alou, he was only sixteen, or so. He did not play much. He was going to be a pitcher. I remember one game, we were getting beat bad and they put Jesús in to pitch. He was scared to death. I went to the mound to talk to him. Jesús tried to spit. The spit would not come out, his mouth was like a cotton ball, so dry; he was so nervous. Jesús turned out to be a pretty good ball player.

Norm Sherry came up with the Los Angeles Dodgers as a catcher in 1959 and later managed in the American League.

What was it like to be crowned the champions of the league?

We had a party for ourselves when we won the championship. After the last game, we came across the bridge, over the river there. I do not know how many people were out on the road, banging on our car windows. The people were all excited, but the team did not do anything for us, that I recall. I do not know that we received any extra money. Maximillian was the owner of the team. I do not remember his last name. A big tall guy, like Daddy Warbucks. Always wore a white suit.

Any other enduring memories of Dominican baseball?

There was some good competition down there. The other teams had good players. It was a good brand of baseball.

Bill White

Bill White has had a long, distinguished and groundbreaking baseball life. The Ohio-reared White played 13 years in the major leagues, interrupted by a nearly two-year service hitch in the U.S. Army.

That military commitment ended prematurely White's second winter season in Puerto Rico, in November of 1956. The previous winter, his first in San Juan, playing for the Santurce Crabbers, the 22-year-old New York Giants' conscript finished at or near the top of several important offensive categories. White led the Puerto Rican circuit in runs with 54; he finished third in home runs and RBIs with 13 and 48, respectively.

White reached the major leagues as a first baseman with the New York Giants the following spring season of 1956. Two winters later, on orders from the Giants, White reported to the Escogido Leones in the Dominican Republic. White played first base for a very strong Lions team that was upset in the championship finals by the Licey Tigres.

With Orlando Cepeda and Willie McCovey coming up through the Giants' pipeline, White was traded to the St. Louis Cardinals in 1959. In St. Louis, White became a two-time All-Star and seven-time Gold Glove winner. He also earned a world championship ring.

In the early '70s, after his retirement, the former big leaguer remained in baseball as a radio and television broadcaster for the New York Yankees, becoming the first African American to broadcast games for a major sports franchise. With Frank Messer and Phil Rizzuto, White formed part of one of the most popular and best known broadcast teams for 15 years.

In 1989, White again broke through racial barriers when he was appointed president of the National League, the first African American, in any sport, to hold as high an executive post.

When I first contacted Bill White in 2011, he was engaged in touring

and promoting his recently published autobiography, titled Uppity: My Untold Story About the Games People Play.
The divorced father of five has retired to Western Pennsylvania.

Let's start at the beginning—where were you born?
In 1934. Born in Florida and raised in Warren, Ohio.

Any brothers or sisters?
I was an only child.

When were you bitten by the baseball bug?
I did not really start playing until I was about 14. We had a team in Warren that kept us out of trouble by playing baseball; it was American Legion baseball. Back then, there was a white American Legion team and a black American Legion team.

Who were your athletic role models?
I admired football players. Bill Willis. Marion Motley. Len Ford. Guys like that who played on the Cleveland Browns.

When did you commit to play baseball professionally?
I signed my first contract with the New York Giants. I worked out for them in Pittsburgh and signed in 1953. I went on to the minor leagues. I played in Danville [Carolina League], in 1953; in Sioux City [Western League], in 1954; Dallas [Texas League], in 1955. Spent a few weeks in Minneapolis [American Association], in 1956, and then was called up to the Giants in '56.

The winter before your call up, you spent playing in Puerto Rico.
Yes, my first winter season was 1955-56, with Santurce. The Giants sent most of their players to Santurce. I met the owner of Santurce, [Pedrín] Zorrilla. My recollections of him.... A good man. Open man. Treated you very well. He was an extrovert. An excellent owner. Herman Franks was the manager.

There were quite a few ballparks in Puerto Rico. The biggest one was in San Juan, where Santurce played their home games. What did you think of it?
Back then you did not rate stadiums, you just enjoyed playing in them. It was a minor league-type stadium. I do not remember the stadium itself.

And the fans?
The fans were very good fans; they were fanatics.

Santurce butted heads with the San Juan team, which shared the ballpark with Santurce. It made for a fierce rivalry.
The rivalry ... one team wore red [uniform trim] and the other team wore blue [uniform trim]. Santurce wore the blue uniforms.

Where did you reside?

I lived at *Calle Cuevillas* in Santurce. I was with Bob Thurman, Valmy Thomas, Bill Greason. We all stayed on the top floor of an apartment on *Calle Cuevillas.*

What was it like for an African American ballplayer in Puerto Rico?

There was no distinction, I don't think, in Puerto Rico between black ballplayers and whites. It was certainly different than my first year in baseball in the United States.

Did you like the food in Puerto Rico?

Oh, *si* — I acquired a taste for *morcillas* [blood sausage], *arroz con pollo con habichuelas* [chicken and rice with kidney beans], *peurco* [hog], *lechón* [suckling pig].

What would you do for entertainment?

We would have Puerto Rican families over to our place, and we would have a good time. We had such a party one night — New Year's Eve. We had a party for some American sailors that had come into port. I saw one of them — he was one of the kids with whom I had gone to high school, and that is how they came to be invited. We made a lot of noise, up there on the top floor. Somebody called *la policia.* They came in, and then they joined the party. [Laughs.] I was single. But we all had chaperones that night. The mothers and fathers of the families we invited.

You returned to Santurce in 1956, but only briefly.

I played just part of the following winter in Puerto Rico. That was the year I had to go into the army. I played maybe a month or so, I am not sure.

In the year-plus that you spent in Puerto Rico, who were the players that caught you eye?

We had some pretty good young Puerto Rican players. José Pagan. I sure recall Clemente. Certainly. You could tell back then he was [going to be great]. He could run, hit and throw it. Vic Power played with Caguas — outstanding first baseman. Valmy Thomas. Don Zimmer played second for us. We had great Negro League players, Bus Clarkson, *Ese Hombre*, Willie Brown, *El*

Opposite: The 1958-59 Escogido Leones won the Dominican League pennant by eight games over the Licey Tigres. But in the island championship series, Licey pulled off a huge upset, defeating the Leones in a best-of-nine series for the island championship. The ninth and deciding game was hurled by Licey's Pete Burnside. Juan Marichal is standing third from left, adjusting cap; Bill White is standing (unobscured) at far right. Moving left from White are Andre Rodgers, Ken Aspromonte, Fred Kipp, Bill Wilson, Gordon Jones, Felipe Alou (center) (courtesy F. Kipp).

Múcaro, Bob Thurman. Rubén Gómez pitched for us. Allie Clark. Ozzie Virgil was on our team. I remember Pantalones Santiago as a curve ball pitcher.

Travel sometimes required trips from one side of the island to the other. What was that like?

We traveled by bus. A trip was a trip to me. You take a book. You read. You go. Since it was all new, you saw it as a new adventure.

Your baseball career was put on hold by your service duty. You then picked up your winter league career in the Dominican Republic.

I spent 22 months in the army. I was discharged, and was able to play in some games for the Giants late in the 1958 season. Then I was sent to the Dominican Republic that winter. I played for Escogido. I lived about two or three blocks from the Jaragua Hotel. By then I was married and had a child. My eldest daughter Edna was with us. She learned to speak Spanish before she learned to speak English. That was the year they ran Batista out of Cuba. We would see a lot of Cubans around the hotel.

We had Willie McCovey on our team. Juan Marichal. Both Alou brothers. All three Alous played on that team, I think. [Manny] Mota. Ozzie Virgil was on that team.

Did you like cuisine in the Dominican as much as in Puerto Rico?

I liked the plantains. I tried to eat most kinds of Spanish foods. I enjoyed the food and the people. I made some good acquaintances in the Dominican.

Sounds like you spent a few agreeable winters playing baseball in the Tropics.

My experiences in Latin America were positive. I learned how to speak Spanish, enough to get around. The people I met were extremely nice to me. I enjoyed the experience.

How are you occupying your time presently?

I am fishing and traveling, now.

Family?

My five children are all college graduates, with individual degrees.

Stan Williams

As a starter and reliever, Stan Williams won 109 games in a 14-year major league career. Williams was also one of the best pitchers in the Dominican Republic during the late–1950s. Williams anchored a pitching staff that helped lead the Escogido Leones to three island championships, while topping the circuit in wins (11) in his final season (1959-60). In February, 1957, in the first of the three title finales, Williams won two games, including the championship-clincher (3–1), against the Licey Tigres. Topping that, the right-hander won three games in the 1959-1960 championship series. The third victory (9–4) came in the sixth and deciding game against Estrellas Orientales. Williams hit a home run in the game as well.

Stan was a great interview, generous with his time; he won me over with a broad knowledge of Spanish, commendably stating that he had made it a point to learn much about the language and culture that surrounded him at that time. He had very good recall. (As Stan put it, "I can remember 50 years ago, but I cannot remember what I did yesterday or why I went into the kitchen just now.") With a pitcher's memory, though, Williams remembered Dick Stuart during his worst campaign in the Dominican Republic, not Stuart's leading home run-hitting year there. Williams was able to touch on a unique aspect of Dominican baseball (one that also touched him), in which all the teams had young pageant queens as goodwill representatives. The former all-star even provided a variation to the urban legend on the origin of the Merengue.

The baritone-voiced Williams provided several interesting character snapshots throughout our conference, including an unexpected glimpse into the debauched Havana nightlife of 1959, popularly depicted in The Godfather II.

You are an East Coast transplant?

Born in Enfield, New Hampshire, moved to Denver, Colorado, at age one and a half. Went to East High School in Denver.

Picturesque country.

Enjoyed the beautiful country. A lot of hunting and fishing. Played a little baseball on the side.

How many in the Williams brood?

We were five children. Three brothers, one sister, and myself. I lived across the street from a baseball field, and I enjoyed baseball, basketball, football. We put the ball down when one season was over and picked up the other ball and played that. None of my brothers were interested in sports.

Which player did you most look up to on the baseball diamond?

When I grew up, we did not have television. It actually came out a little later. I would read the newspaper and listened to the radio. I admired Stan Musial. Probably because of his name, plus his talent. I kind of would hero-worship most of the major leaguers. I would play with a tennis ball against the stairs and pitch to these different guys, and so on and so forth, just like any other kid in those days.

How was it integrating into winter ball? Did you have any practice time with you assigned team?

I think we had about a week of training prior to the games starting. Most of us were coming out of our seasons [in the U.S.], so we were in pretty good shape. I played with Escogido, three years, in the Dominican Republic. The first year we lived in a hotel. Hotel Presidente. We all had our own rooms, but I settled there with two Giant players—a catcher named Bobby Schmidt and a pitcher, Pete Burnside. They called Pete "*Bicicleta.*" Burnside rode his bicycle everywhere. Upon seeing this, the fans put that moniker on him. We made a point of living downtown, amongst the people, so we could learn about the people and the language. We learned to say, "*Como se dice esto?*" Which means, "How do you say this?" The people would tell us how to say different things. They were very happy to help us. We learned Spanish that way. Every word I learned, I learned how to write, so I could remember it better. I can still speak Spanish 55 years later.

It had to be your first time eating Caribbean food on a regular basis?

The food was very good. My favorite dish was *arroz con pollo*. It was a delicious dish. They had an Italian place there called Mario's. Very good food.

Three full seasons with Escogido. What are some of your collective memories of the Dominican Republic?

Those were the days of Trujillo. The capital was named Ciudad Trujillo, now it is Santo Domingo. They were brothers, one was a Generalissimo and the other was president. They ruled with an iron hand. They were also Escogido owners, or rooted for Escogido. I guess that was the rich man's team. One of the managers on one of the other teams wanted to leave town and they would not let him leave. He could not get his visa to leave. The Trujillos had to allow you to leave the country. If they did not want you to leave, you could not leave.

How was your down time spent?

We did not play more than four games a week. We had a lot of time off. We played Saturday and Sundays and one or two games during the week. We

Opposite: The 1957-58 Escogido Leones won its third consecutive Winter League championship. Some of the players: Standing second from left, Juan Marichal; sixth from left, Alonso Perry; eighth through fifteenth players, Stan Williams, Rudy Hernández, Bill Wilson, Fred Kipp, Willie McCovey, Felipe Alou, Wayne Terwilliger, Joe Pignatano. Seated on bench far left, Bob Gibson. Manager Salty Parker sits behind kneeling bat boy. Matty Alou, with glove, sits next to team physician (dark suit). Ozzie Virgil is seated second from far right (courtesy F. Kipp).

had poker games that lasted 36 hours straight. We played a lot of poker. In fact, a couple of guys still owe me money. I do not remember any of the Latin players playing with us. Of course, they had their own homes, we were in the hotel.

We did not make much money, to speak of. We needed winter income. I was coming off a great year in Class B ball. It was very unusual for a 20-year-old to play in that league. It was a tough league. The Dodgers allowed me to go down to the Dominican in 1956 for a chance to make some money. So I did. After the first year there, I guess they liked the way I performed so they invited me back a couple of times. I do not remember why I skipped a winter. Maybe I figured I needed a rest.

You played with some of the earliest—and best—Dominican major leaguers.

Felipe Alou was probably the best all-around hitter, and he had the best body I have ever seen on a human being. He had muscles where I did not think you could have muscles. He was very fast for a big, strong man. He was very stiff-bodied, though. A fine young man, too. His little brother, Matty, was a hell of a player. Matty played left field for us. He played as good a left field as you ever want to see. I played with Jesús later.

I was interested to see Sparky Anderson was a teammate of yours on Escogido.

Sparky [Anderson] was George in those days. The thing I remember most about George and [wife] Carol was that I spent my first Christmas away from home that year. We had a party at George's house. I was drinking cups full of rum, cups full of scotch, cups full of bourbon. No ice, and chug-a-lugging them. And I got sick all over his house. They put me to bed and I woke up about three hours later and they gave me a wet rag to clean it all up. I felt pretty guilty about it.

Over the period of time you played there, new ballparks were constructed for all of the teams. Was there anything about the parks that stood out?

All the parks had concrete outfield walls. John Gray was a pretty solid pitcher and he had become manager of the Green team. They were short personnel and Gray had to play right field in a game. A ball was hit over his head and he ran back to chase and he hit the concrete wall and dropped like he had been shot.

All the clubs had their own beauty queens as good will representatives. Sounds like a more appealing alternative to the irritating, over-sized mascots so prevalent in the major leagues now a days.

The queen of the ball club was a cute little gal. She was seventeen. We kind of made eye contact a few times. And her family became pissed off about it. I know when we won the championship that year, we went to a restaurant called *La Cremita* on George Washington Boulevard and she was there. She came running up to me and threw her arms around my neck and gave me a big kiss, and almost caused an international incident. If you dated a señorita down there, you had to take half the family with you. Aunts and cousins walked with you as chaperones. I never had the chance to date the girl, but she was very attractive and I liked her a lot.

You came back to help Escogido successfully defend the island championship in 1957.

Salty Parker was my manager in my second winter season. I was married prior to going down. My wife was with me. I had a no-hitter in one game for eight and two-thirds innings. In the stands, the club president leaned over to my wife and said that if he gets this no-hitter, I will give you a check for $1,000. Frank Verde was the hitter and he hit a chopper to third, to Ozzie Virgil. It was one of those choppers that you are not sure whether to lay back or charge. Virgil laid back and the ball hit a rock and bounced right over his head. Cost me a thousand bucks right there. Verde said later, "If I had known that, I would have struck out." I said, "Well, if you would have struck out, I would have given you a couple of hundred." [Laughs.] It was tongue-and-cheek stuff. When I threw a no-hitter later, the team gave me a bonus of one hundred dollars. I said, what is this? It used to be $1,000. They said, well, there have been no-hitters thrown before. If you throw two in a row, we will give you a bigger bonus. I told them, no, I am disappointed with this $100. I am just not going to throw another one.

Ozzie was a blue-collar type of player. I remember one time we had the hit-and-run on. The pitcher threw an eye-high fastball to Virgil on the outside corner. Ozzie tomahawked it. He waited until the ball got there and just swung sideways and hit a line drive into right field. I have never seen that before or since.

The club president of Escogido— Martínez [Francisco Martínez Alba] was his name. He was a very nice man. Soft spoken. High class guy. After they had the revolution down there, I saw him a couple of years later in Florida, and he looked like a bum, walking the streets of Miami, in tattered clothes and what have you. He had to get out of there with his life. Could not take anything with him.

Another thing I remember about '57 was my wife's older sister, who was 25 years old, died of cancer. The only time my wife and I went to the race track — the *hipódromo*, in Spanish — my name was paged over the loud speaker. I could not figure out how anybody knew I was there. I answered the telephone. They told me my wife's sister had died of cancer. In those days, they only had one or two flights a week. The family was going to bury her the following day or the day after, and there was no way to get my wife out of the country to go to her sister's funeral. My wife cried for a week.

Dick Stuart was coming off a record setting home run year in the Western League. He played for Águilas Cibaeñas.

Dick Stuart. "Dr. Strangeglove." He hit about .130 and fielded about the same. He had a horrible year down there. [At the stadium] I remember the stands went past the dugout, down to about first base and then cut sharply in because of the bullpen area, and then cut back to the right field corner. Like an L-shape. There was a lot of room behind the first base area. We had a game, about 14 innings long. A man was on third base with one out. Somebody hit a foul pop up behind first. Stuart ran over inside that area and caught the ball. Turned and looked and there was nothing but a grandstand wall in front of him. The man on third walked home with the winning run. Another time, somebody hit a swinging bunt, the pitcher fielded and threw to Stuart. Stuart reached up like the ball hit the top of his glove. Stuart comes trotting in, like he is coming off the field. Reaches in his glove to drop the ball, and he did not have it. The ball was down the right field line, and people are running like crazy around the bases.

As you mentioned, you took a winter off, but ironically, during the following spring training, you were able to visit another well-known Latin American baseball hub.

I was with the Dodgers in spring training in 1959, and we had ten days straight of torrential rains and nobody could play baseball. The Cincinnati Reds and the Dodgers went to Cuba, so they could get some playing time in. Castro threw out the first ball in one of the exhibition games, and all the guys with sub-machines guns were all around the ballpark. There were not any problems. They were happy to have us there.

I saw Superman, by the way. The Cuban Superman. He had a *schwartz* about 16 inches long with a girth of about eight inches, I think. He used to put on a show with different girls. You would pay five bucks apiece to go in and watch his show. They would bring out like ten girls and you would get to pick two of them to put on a show. We would pick the littlest girls we could find. Superman never achieved a good hard-on. I think he had elephantitis of the penis.

Another Havana story was Walter O'Malley playing the crap table. O'Malley was on a hot streak and won an awful lot of money. I do not remember how much. He left the table and threw the dealers twenty bucks. They were all upset O'Malley did not leave more.

After the major league season, you put in your final winter league campaign. Another most successful one.

I returned to the Dominican that winter. One of the most popular players in the league was Alonso Perry. A big, black left-handed hitter. Another was Guayubin Olivo. Guayubin was the older brother, a left-hand pitcher. Chichí was a big right-hander. In fact, I hit a home run over the centerfield fence off Chichí Olivo. Guayubin, he must have been about forty at the time, but he was still able to throw fast balls past Frank Howard. And that was pretty hard to do with Frank Howard. I remember them listing Guayubin as being 40 when he made it to the majors. But he was 40 when I played with him, four or five years earlier. He somehow became a lot younger with Pittsburgh.

Hondo struggled for a while. Howard struck out three times in a game on about nine pitches. Guayubin Olivo was pitching in that game. So Howard was a bit, uh, unhappy with himself, let us put it that way. There was an umpire, the funny thing is I still remember his name because of the incident. Bill Sneathen. The umpire was pee'oed at somebody yelling at him from the dugout. Sneathen yelled back and Frank thought Sneathen was yelling at him. Frank looked at the umpire and said, "You talking to me? You talking to me?" The umpire kept pointing and yelling. Frank ran out of the dugout and reached out and grabbed the umpire by the shirt and twisted his shirt and slit it right down the back. The umpire was a real stocky little guy. I came out of the dugout and jumped on Frank's back, trying to keep him out of trouble, figuring he is going to get thrown out of baseball, and Frank shrugged his shoulders and I end up about ten feet away on my back. The umpire said to let him go, "I used to wrestle." Frank would have eaten him like a sandwich.

Two other franchises, were located outside the capital. The aforementioned John Gray's Green team was one of them.

Águilas was the Orange team [uniform-trim]. Estrellas were the Elefantes, Green team. Licey, the Blue team, and Escogido, Red. When we played Águilas, we stayed at the hotel Matum, in Santiago, about two blocks from the ballpark. I remember Frank Howard eating there. Frank would go in and order a dozen eggs, a package of bacon, sausage, toast and everything else with it. Two hours later, Frank would have lunch and he would have four fish dinners, seven bread puddings and six or seven large ice teas. That is the way he ate. I always said Frank received a $108,000 signing bonus, and he ate it in his first year. Carol [Howard's wife] was five-foot-two and 101 pounds.

We had a victory party that year. We threw it at one of our apartments. We invited all the players. Frank Howard left the native players in awe with his eating. He was chewing the meat, the bones, sucking the marrow off. We signed all of it to the ball club and they paid for it.

The championship series was a best-of-nine game clash. You and Ed Roebuck pitched Escogido to the championship over Estrellas Orientales.

The way they did things in those days was to try and stock up at the end for the playoffs. In '59-60, Escogido was going to bring over Bob Bruce from either Cuba or Puerto Rico. [Ed] Roebuck and I went and talked to the general manager and told him — he was always complaining he did not have any money — it is going to cost you $5,000 to bring Bruce over. What you should do is give half that money to Roebuck and I, and we will pitch every game. It was a nine game playoff. So the general manager decided to do that. It turned out the playoffs went six games. I won three games. Roebuck won two.

A young Juan Marichal was on your staff.

We had a left-handed pitcher named Daniel Rivas that was as good as Juan Marichal, but he later hurt his arm. Rivas was involved in a fight caused by Jim Coates that broke his hand. It happened in Triple A, in San Diego. Coates was knocking everybody down, drilling people. Their teams started fighting. Rivas hit somebody on the helmet and broke his hand. I guess Rivas ended up favoring the hand and he ended up hurting his arm. I do not think Rivas ever made it to the major leagues, but he was pretty fantastic. Marichal, he was young. Marichal won 20 games in every league he ever played in. He played in Class D and won 20; he pitched in Class B and won 20. They put him in Triple A and he won 20, and then in the majors. Marichal was a hell of a pitcher.

Escogido won the championship all three years I was there. We were triple champions. *Triple campeones.*

I haven't asked you about the Dominican fans.

The fans were wild fans. What I remember most about them was that they would shake hankies at you if they were displeased. They were a raucous crowd. They yelled out a lot of things. They liked to yell *maricón*, which means queer. I certainly did not go for that. We used to play games in less than two hours. Not a lot of stalling going on. By the time the centerfielder reached centerfield, the pitcher was supposed to be done warming up.

There was a player in the Dominican Republic, Rudy Hernández. Rudy was very good about helping the players with interpretations and teaching you about the club and the country. The problem was everybody thought Rudy was gay. Now whether he was or not I have no idea, nor do I care. But it became embarrassing at times when he would come to the plate, and there are 15,000 people in the stands chanting, *"Roo-dee. Roo-dee."* [Effeminately.] I felt sorry for Rudy in those cases. I think he was more of a pretty boy than a gay guy.

Did any Dominican batter give you trouble? Have your number, so to speak?

I do not remember anybody getting four hits off me in the majors, or minors. But there was a guy in the Dominican named Manny Jiménez. He got five hits against me in one game, and a home run. He later played with Kansas City. Brother was Elvio.

It seems to me like you assimilated pretty well to winter ball.

You would get a little bit on edge at times, being away from home. You would get tired sometimes of listening to Spanish and Merengue music. Although we danced Merengue all the time at parties. [Chuckling.] The Merengue was developed by a club-foot politician. The politician had a limp in his dance, and people started mimicking him and that is where the Merengue came from. *Buenas tardes.*

The Mexican League

Monte Irvin

Monte Irvin was the oldest player I interviewed, and one of the most keen. (Both Irvin and Luis Olmo were born in 1919.) It was a privilege to speak to Irvin. The former Negro and National League standout related some of his experiences playing professional ball, first in Mexico for one season and then from two winters in Cuba. Irvin provided a great Jorge Pasquel story and recalled his favorite dish from Cuba with a mouthwatering delight. Irvin also perpetuated a Fidel Castro connection to Cuban baseball.

A few months after starring in the first Caribbean Series in 1949, Irvin made his major league debut with the New York Giants, at age thirty. The outfielder played eight seasons in the major leagues, which, along with his credentials from the Negro and Latin American Leagues, earned him election into Cooperstown.

Listening to Irvin, I gained a much greater measure of respect for him, and others like him, in the way he did not permit the doctrine of inequality that was all too prevalent during his playing days, to leave any lasting degree of bitterness in his heart. I felt the same admirably benevolent sentiments from George Altman and Minnie Miñoso and Dave Roberts and Félix Mantilla. Also, Pantalones Santiago, Julio Navarro and Mudcat Grant.

Irvin, enjoying retirement, resides with his daughter and son-in-law and grandchildren in southeast Texas.

Where did it all begin for you?

When I was eight years old, my family moved from Alabama to New Jersey, and that is where I grew up.

You had quite a few brothers and sisters.

There were 13 of us originally. I have a younger brother, age 86. I had a brother, 89, just died last week. There are only two left now from 13 children.

How old were you when you started playing baseball?

I started playing baseball in grade school when I was eight. I played until I was 38. In school, I was the biggest, strongest, fastest. I started out as a pitcher. Later on, I started catching. From catching I went to shortstop, then third base. From third base to first, and then later on to the outfield.

Who were your favorite players?

We lived about 45 minutes from New York City. We used to go to see the Yankees play. I used to enjoy watching Babe Ruth and Lou Gehrig and Joe DiMaggio. My brother was a big fan of the Philadelphia Athletics. That was in the early thirties. They had Lefty Grove and Jimmie Foxx and Mickey Cochrane. Rube Walberg. I rooted for who my brother rooted for. When I became older, I realized how great some of the Negro league players were. At that time, Satchel Paige was very popular. And there was Oscar Charleston, John Henry Lloyd. Cool Papa Bell. Buck Leonard. Raymond Brown. They did not have a chance to play organized ball at that time.

When did you become a professional?

A man by the name of Abe Manley had seen me play. He and his wife, Effa, owned the Newark Eagles. In 1937, Manley came to my house to talk to me about signing with the Eagles and told me that I should be happy and proud to play with his team. I asked him about a bonus. Abe said he did not do that. Abe said that I should consider myself lucky to be living right near his team's office and the team's stadium. You can live at home and will not have any expenses. I said, well, I will not have expenses but my mother will. But Abe still would not give me a bonus. I signed with him, anyhow, for $125 a month. Which was not that much, but this was during the Depression and money was very scarce. I was happy to be able to contribute to the household. Everything I made, I brought home and gave to my mother and father. That Christmas, I received a check in the mail for fifty bucks from Effa Manley. I guess she felt a little guilty that Abe had not given me anything. I started playing right out of high school. I played with the Eagles until 1942.

That's when you headed South of the Border.

George Pasquel had a friend in New York. Pasquel contacted the friend and told him to look me over, and then to ask me if I wanted to go to Mexico to play. Pasquel's friend offered me $400 a month, plus an apartment and a maid in Mexico City. My wife and I jumped at that. We had just gotten married and we viewed the trip as a honeymoon.

We left on the first of April. I hit .397 and was named Most Valuable Player. I led the league in home runs and missed the triple crown by two runs batted-in. I played for the Veracruz Blues. They decided to move the team from Veracruz to Mexico City. We played all of our games in Mexico City. We shared the ballpark with the Mexico City Reds. We drew pretty well. It was a year George Pasquel was able to make some money. Pasquel was a very rich man. He did not worry about spending money to bring the best players there. It was an exciting time and one of the best years I spent in baseball. The fans liked me and I loved them. At one point I could have run for mayor. There were players from Cuba. Some from Panama. Mexico had good players. A lot of Cubans and Mexicans and African Americans that could play. It was a good league. It was good baseball. It was not as good as the Cuban Winter League. But it was a good league.

Please tell me about Jorge Pasquel.

Pasquel was a great person. He was handsome. I call him the George Steinbrenner of Mexico. Pasquel was young, rich, impulsive and demanding. All of that. He was the reason some of the players in organized ball received decent salaries. He brought down to Mexico Sal Maglie, Max Lanier, George Hausemann, Danny Gardella. They came and received a lot of publicity. Pasquel helped increase the attendance at the ball parks. He improved the parks, trying to make it comfortable and exciting for the fans who came. He sent Stan Musial a blank check and told him to fill in the salary he wanted. Stan turned it down. A fellow like Vern Stephens was given about 25 or 30 thousand dollars, and most of those guys were not making but ten or twelve thousand in the states. The playing conditions were not major league caliber, but they were good enough. The stadium had clubhouses and showers with hot water. Pasquel also improved that.

Roy Campanella arrived in Mexico about three weeks after I did. He played for Monterrey. There was a game we played against Monterrey. We were the home club. Last game of the season. They were leading us, 1–0, in the bottom of the ninth. Ray Dandridge, who was a Hall of Famer, singled, with two outs. I was next up to hit. George Pasquel beckons me over to where he was sitting in the front row. I said to him, "George, this is mighty unusual, I am getting ready to hit." He put his arm around me, "Please hit a home run for me. We want to win this ball game." I became a little teed off at that. I had always tried to do the best I could every time I came to the plate. Never had been ordered to get a hit, particularly not to hit a home run. I told George, "Do you see how hard [Lázaro] Salazar is throwing that ball? I cannot promise a home run. I will try and keep the rally going." "But for me, Monte, you hit a home run," he said. So I come up to batter's box, and Campanella asks me, "What did George want?" I told him, and Campanella said that George must be crazy, that I was not going to hit a home run now. The first pitch was called, strike one. The second pitch I fouled over the grandstand. Something told me, be ready now, Campy wants to strike me out on three pitches. I guessed fastball and got it. I hit a home run over the centerfield wall and we won the ball game, 2–1. When I arrived at home plate, George met me.

We shook hands and in his right hand there was five hundred bucks. Now Campy had not gone in, and he said to me, "Jesus, you have got to be the luckiest SOB. You will never do that again." I said, "Well, I did it that time." Campy is stomping up and down. I told him to calm down, that George had just given me five hundred dollars and told me to give you $250 for calling the right pitch. Campy said, "*My main man.*" That is an absolutely true story.

That's something. It's too bad Pasquel died at such a young age.

I was sorry to hear that George died in that plane accident, because he did a lot for the league, trying to improve the caliber of play,

National League opponents for many years, Monte Irvin, left, and Roy Campanella also opposed one another for one season in the Mexican League.

the ballparks. He was a great guy. George had three other brothers—there were four of them. Mario was the lawyer, he was the youngest. They wanted Mario to take care of the family fortune. I grew to know Mario.

George loved to hunt. He bought a house over there in Africa. Every year, George and whoever would go [big game] hunting. One year Mario went, and he wounded a lion. You had to finish off a wounded animal, that was the law of the jungle. I asked Mario how did he finished the lion off? Mario said that when a lion is wounded, that is when it is really dangerous, because it wants to get even. In order to make sure you do not miss, you wait until the animal charges you and goes into its leap — and then you fire. That is what I did. Mario said this big, wounded lion charged him, and he waited until it leaped at him and then shot it when it was in its leap. And then what happened? I asked. Mario said, well, I killed the lion, but after the shot I went over into the bushes and cleansed myself.

Mario and I became great friends. We were the same age. While he was alive, we stayed in contact. Mario had a condo in New York City, right near the big Catholic church there. He came to New York, and I went to visit him, along with Dandridge. We all went to the racetrack.

They hunted polar bears, too. George's son, George Pasquel, Jr., has a house in Mexico City with a room full of stuffed animals. Very impressive. The most dangerous mount is the polar bear, more fierce than a grizzly or a brown bear or whatever. It has been about five years since we were in Mexico City.

The last time I saw George was in 1947. That was in Cuba. We met at that hotel there, the best hotel in Havana, up there on the hill, I cannot think of it [Hotel Nacional]. George wanted me to come back to Mexico. Well, I said, they are taking African Americans into baseball, I think I might want to stay in the states. We parted friends.

Martín Dihigo played in Mexico with you that year and was stellar.

Martín Dihigo was a pitcher with a one-point-something ERA, who hit third in the lineup. Dihigo was a great performer. He did everything except catch. Dihigo played with Torreón and I played with Veracruz, so at the ballpark was the only time I saw him. Dihigo struck me out three times one night in Torreón. The lights were bad. I said to him, "Martín, dammit, wait till you get to Mexico City where I can see the ball. I will get you there." He said, "Yeah, Monte, you will get me there the way I got you here."

In a box at Gran Stadium, managing general partner of Almendares, Dr. July Sanguily, left, along with his wife, respond cheerfully to a photographer's presence. Directly in back of Sanguily is son July Jr., while in the middle, Walter O'Malley listens to comments from sportswriter Rubén Rodríguez (The Sporting News Archive).

Did your wife enjoy Mexico?

We enjoyed our time in Mexico. There was a lot to see. There were great theatres and restaurants, and wonderful hotels. My wife and I enjoyed going to the bullfights. On Sundays, the baseball game in Mexico City would start at ten o'clock in the morning. We would play the game, come home and change, and then go to the bullfights in the same stadium. We went sightseeing. The parks in Mexico City were beautiful. We saw the pyramids.

I suppose it was your first time sampling Mexican food?

There was a great restaurant right down the street from our apartment. We would eat there at least five or six times a week. I came to know the Mexican cuisine and liked most of it, particularly the beans and cheese and rice.

You were a bit more seasoned as a ballplayer when you headed to Cuba to play.

Cuba was a little more professional than it was in Mexico. We played in one stadium. There were four teams. Almendares. Habana. Marianao and Cienfuegos. A doctor by the name of July Sanguily [club owner] had heard about me. He offered me a good contract to go to Cuba and play for Almendares. That was in 1947. I played '47–'48 and '48–'49. In 1948-49, we won the league championship and then won the Caribbean Series. We played about four or five games a week, right there in Havana. The competition was wonderful. They had young major leaguers playing, and they had players that had starred in the majors and maybe were on the way out, so it was real good baseball. The crowds were huge. A lot of enthusiasm. You could bet on baseball there, openly. And some of the fans would bet on each pitch. High, low, ball or strike. The money was wonderful. Guys were making a thousand, twelve, thirteen hundred a month. It gave you a chance to make some money and gain some experience.

Where did you stay in Havana, and what did you do for relaxation or entertainment?

I lived in an apartment. I took my wife and two daughters with me. We shared the apartment with Sam Jethroe. He had his car with him — his family was not there — so we kind of took advantage of Sam's transportation. It was a Pontiac sedan. We went sightseeing, we went to the beach, we went fishing. We caught red snapper. We really enjoyed going fishing. We used to know a couple of guys that would take us. We never went out far enough to catch the big ones.

Some of the nightclubs that we wanted to go to were not open to us. We went to some lesser clubs. Some of the bigger ones, they would not let us in. Some hotels you could stay in, some you could not. Just about all the other places we could go. The Mob had control and they introduced that segregation policy. You know, when in Rome, do what the Romans do. We did not worry about it. There was a lot of other good places where we had a good time. The beaches had some of the whitest sand I had ever seen. There was a lot to do and see. We enjoyed it. The main thing was, we had the family with us.

Of course, I have to ask you about the food.

Some of the Cuban dishes were very good. Good restaurants. Some of the restaurants were rather Americanized. My favorite dish was *asopao de langosta*. It was like a lobster stew. It was great.

Your Almendares team won the first Caribbean Series ever played in 1949. Which teammates were most responsible for achieving the feat?

[On our team] We had [Al] Gionfriddo and Sam Jethroe. Chuck Connors. He had a pretty good season. But Chuck was having trouble hitting left-handers. I remember we played a key game and Chuck struck out four times—all against southpaws. Chuck came back to the dugout the last time and said, "Holy Smoke, the Lord must be left-handed." [Laughs.] If we had a rain delay or if we had time on our hands in the clubhouse, Chuck would always recite "*Casey at the Bat.*" I think Chuck knew he was going to be an actor. He would do some other skits, too. Chuck was good to have on the team, because he was entertaining. Chuck was married in Havana. His wife, I think, was from Montreal. Dr. Sanguily paid for the wedding on the beach. During the ceremony the players did that thing, you know, where they cross the bats and the bride and groom walk underneath. That was a big thing, attending the wedding, with a party afterwards. Sanguily was a great doctor. If you did not have any money, he still operated on you.

Who were the all-round top players that you remember?

Héctor Rodríguez was one of the best infielders I have ever seen. Héctor played third like Ray Dandridge. We had Cañizares at short. Conners at first. Fermín Guerra was the catcher and manager. He was a stud catcher.

Conrado Marrero was our star pitcher. He was a little, short stocky guy. He threw like a half-curve, you could not hit. Marrero was very stingy with runs. We had good times together. He is still alive? He did? 100? Oh, boy. When I went back to Cuba some years ago, I saw him. He was still smoking those long cigars. I asked Connie, why he did not stay in the United States? Too hard to learn English, he said, so I stayed here in Cuba. How much pension money do you get? He said, ten dollars a month. So the group I went with and I gave him some money, which he really appreciated. B.A.T. started sending x-amount of dollars to him.

Santos Amaro and Miñoso. [Claro] Duany was a great home run hitter. They were the best players. Marrero was the best pitcher.

You played in what was considered a state-of-the-art stadium at the time.

We played at the new stadium. *Estadio [del] Cerro.* They had moved from the old stadium. The new stadium held about 35,000 people. Many times it was filled when we played. We would play a four-team doubleheader on Sundays.

At that time, Fidel Castro was a student at the University of Havana. He used to work out with us. Fidel would come out and pitch batting practice for Almendares. Yes, it was Fidel. Fidel *did* work out with us. He could throw hard but he did not have any control. About six or seven years ago, when I went to Havana and got together with Marrero, we held a press conference. Marrero said, if we had known Fidel wanted to be a dictator, we would have made an umpire out of him.

What do you remember most about Cuba?

We played our best ball in the Caribbean Series. We swept everybody. Jethroe was running and I was hitting and [Wesley] Hamner was fielding. It was a great team effort. I do not think we had a team party. I think we just celebrated in the clubhouse, and then everyone went their separate ways. There was always so much to do and see there.

Evans Killeen

Evans Killeen saw the light of the major league day with the Kansas City Athletics in 1959. As a minor league player in his early twenties, Killeen viewed and lived more worldly and enlightening experiences than most people his age.

Killeen, whose name sounds like it is right out of an old Louis L'Amour dime store western, played winter ball in Panama in 1956-57 and in the summer league in Mexico in 1960. As a member of the Carta Vieja Yankees, Killeen was the winningest pitcher in Panama with a 6–3 mark. In Mexico, Killeen pitched for the Monterrey Sultans. During his time in Mexico, the hard-throwing right-hander revealed a compassionate side, not often found in a person of his age, with generosities toward exploited women.

As a high school hurler, Killeen passed along an assured "true story" on how he struck out football legend Jim Brown in all of his at-bats during an all-star exhibition game. Brown later told Killeen that he had helped Brown realize that he would never be able to get around on anybody who threw the ball hard and that baseball was not going to be his sport.

A New York Mets' fan and father of two, Killeen works at his floor covering business. He was dealing with the particularly adverse circumstances of his girlfriend's brain cancer affliction.

You are a New York boy.

I was born in Brooklyn, but lived mostly in Richmond Hills, Queens. We then moved to Elmont, New York, which is in Nassau County.

Any siblings?

I had two sisters.

How did you come to embrace the game of baseball?

I lived across from a city park in Richmond Hills and I guess I spent every day there. I had a ball in my hand since I was seven years old. In those days a lot of kids played baseball. The sport was baseball. I was a real Dodger fan. I loved Duke Snyder. I loved Pee Wee Reese. I loved most of the Dodger team. When I was a little boy, I used to cry when they lost. When I was growing up, we had three teams in New York. The Dodgers, Giants and Yankees. We were very competitive with each other, rooting for our teams. It was a great time.

When did you start getting good at the sport?

I remember having a tryout at Ebbets Field when I was a youngster — local talent from Long Island. It was quite a thrill to be in Ebbets Field, inside the ballpark of all my heroes. I will never forget later, during my first major league spring training camp, when we played the Dodgers at Vero Beach, I was walking around and looking around at all my heroes. What a thrill to be part of that.

After the War, there was a lot of movement out to the so called suburbs. At my high school, it was quite a school. We had over 4,000 kids going to this school. To play on the baseball team you really had to be good. I really did not show anybody my talent until my senior year in high school. My junior year I could not make the team. We had three pitchers that were seniors. If you know high school baseball, you played Monday and Thursday. I remember the sub-varsity coach saying, you have got to pitch this kid Killeen. Well, I turned 17, and in my senior year I never lost a game. Never gave up a run. I was the most valuable player on Long Island. I did it all overnight. It was amazing. I received a scholarship to a prep school. My parents wanted me to go to college. But I wanted to play baseball so badly. So at 18, I signed with the old Philadelphia Athletics. Connie Mack, Jr. signed me.

Where did that first signing lead you?

My first year in pro ball I played in West Virginia, in the old Appalachian League. That was quite experience, I will tell you. [Chuckles.] You had the coal miners. The women used to fist fight in the streets. My mom and dad came down to see me. I am 18 years old and making $250 a month at the time. I am living in a kind of boarding house with a river in the back that was nothing but black from the coal dust coming down from the mountains. My parents took one look and told me, *You are getting out of here.* I said, *No, no, I am not going anywhere.* It was quite an experience for an 18-year-old, first time away from home. It was kind of cool.

I played in Abilene, Texas, in the Big State League, the following year. I went from D-ball to B-ball. I had a pretty good year. I went 17–13 and led the league in strikeouts. That is when the A's wanted me to go to winter ball, to Panama.

The season in Panama started a little later than other winter leagues.

We spent a week or ten days in Miami, Florida, before we went to Panama. We had a little spring training down there. Billy Shantz was our manager. He was also the team catcher. Billy was quite a student of the game. Not much with the bat but he was a great catcher. Billy treated me great. I was impressed with most of the guys I was playing with. I did great. I was 6–3. I think I had the most games won in the league that season. I was on my way. After that winter, I received my first shot at a big league training camp.

Where did they put you up in Panama?

I lived at the Roosevelt Hotel. I think we all lived there. It was in the Panamanian section, but we spent most of our afternoons, most our time in the American zone on the other side by the Canal. There was a swimming pool there and a club. We spent a lot of time there. It was great. We ate at a place called the Key Club. They had a restaurant. It had the most fantastic steaks. It was near the Roosevelt Hotel.

What can you tell me about the stadium in Panama City and clubhouses?

It was a fair stadium. Clubhouses. Nothing was elaborate in those days, and when you are a kid you do not know what good is yet. Until you get to the big leagues— I had a cup of coffee there. That was pretty nice.

Fans in Latin America seem to rise to a different level of enthusiasm than they do here. Did you get that sense?

The fans in Panama would shoot Roman candles at us. [Amused.] It was

Evans Killeen as a Kansas City Athletics rookie (courtesy E. Killeen).

really, really different for me, a 19-year-old kid. A great experience. The fans knew the game very well. They were into the game. But they were fans that had to be controlled. The police were in force all the time, from what I remember. I guess they did not want to take any chances with anybody doing something crazy.

What about the degree of competition in Panama?

There were good players. Héctor López was a well-known player in Panama. Eli Grba was my teammate. He got to the big show. We were good buddies. Another teammate, who played with the Pittsburgh Pirates, was Tony Bartirome. He must have been five-eight, playing first base. What a phenomenal fielder Tony was. He was like a shortstop playing first base. A left-handed hitter, no power, but, wow, what a fielder.

I felt I was as good or better than anybody. I was kind of cocky. When you are a young ballplayer and you compete, you always think that you are better than the next guy. And Billy Shantz kept telling me how good I was. And I was striking out people. Héctor López was a tough guy to get out; he

The men most responsible for the Mexican League and organized baseball entering into a mutually beneficial relationship. Left to right, National Association president George M. Trautman, baseball commissioner A. B. "Happy" Chandler (seated), NA Secretary Walter Mulbry, Mexican League president Eduardo Quijano Pitman, and Anuar Canavati, owner of the Monterrey Sultanes. The Mexican League eventually joined organized baseball in 1955, after an extended disaccord following the post–World War II "player raids" of Jorge Pasquel (The Sporting News Archive).

was just a good hitter. He was not afraid up there. You could get two strikes on most of those guys and you would get them out. López was different. He hung in there. The only pitcher that really, really impressed me in the minor leagues was Juan Marichal. I faced him in the Eastern League. I actually got to the big leagues before he did.

I threw very hard. I can remember after a game once, a huge black player, one of the Panamanian players— we were out somewhere socially — he looked at me and someone said, this is Evans Killeen, the kid who pitched tonight. "Nah," this player said, "You cannot be Evans Killeen. You have to be seven feet tall and three hundred pounds to be Evans Killeen. You scared the crap out of me tonight." I look back and feel good about things like that.

Anything else you remember about Panama?

We took a plane to Davíd, which is in the middle of Panama. The people there had never seen white people before. We came off the plane and the people were right next to me, staring at me. It was like, wow, look at this, a white person. It was kind of interesting. Kind of fun. The plane ride was not fun. We flew a two-engine plane. We were over Davíd and there was a thunderstorm. I am telling you, I was scared. That plane was pitching up and down. It was nerve-racking.

How did you arrive as a player in Mexico?

In 1960, they farmed me to one of the White Sox teams. I was not starting. I knew I had a bum leg and everything, but I was not happy about it. I wanted to do something different. So I inquired, and they said, you know, if you want to, we can send you to the Mexican League. I said, why not? I played for Monterrey, and it was something different. Again, it was an experience. I had a major league contract, so I was making decent money. In Mexico, I was getting paid 8-to-1 [exchange rate]. The money was more than I had ever made before. The value of the American dollar was high in those years. I had a few bucks in my pocket.

I remember after the ball games in Monterrey, all the kids would sur-round me. I would buy them all sodas. Everybody was so poor. On Sundays, I would go to the jail and bail out the young prostitutes. They were underage, selling themselves. The parents would send them out to sell themselves. It was the only way they could make any money. It was a wakeup call for an American kid who had never seen life that bad.

And I was not afraid in those days. I went out. I was at a place, and I was dancing with some girls. Some of them may have been prostitutes, but I was not interested in that. I liked to dance and "Lindy," and they liked to dance. The place had a juke box. One of the soldiers who had too much to drink put a gun to my head. He called me a Gringo and all this kind of stuff. The girls screamed at him and told him who I was. *Béisbol player. Evans*

Killeen. The owner of the Monterrey team was [Anuar] Canavati; he was a Monterrey billionaire. And the soldier, I guess, realized he would be in a lot of trouble, and that scared him off.

If I remember right, Canavati was a gay man. A couple of the guys mentioned it. I was young, so I do not know for sure. Canavati treated me nice. I remember he used to come around, he was interested in the ballplayers. Canavati was a pretty good owner, I imagine.

Your lodgings in Mexico?

I lived in the Ambassador Hotel. I probably made the most money on the team. I was able to have cabs drive me back and forth. I dated a girl named Helia Luna, she was a recording artist in Mexico. The girls were, of course, after the ballplayers. They would sit over our dugout. They idolized us. Most of the players were Cuban, or Latin. Myself and another player were the only American white kids on the team. And I loved it. I got along with all the guys. I learned about other people's lives and cultures.

Any high-grade players you remember?

There was a fellow I played with in Monterrey, this guy Clyde Parris, small compact guy. To me, he was one of the greatest hitters I have ever seen in my life. He would have been a great major leaguer. But he never got the chance. Parris was a third baseman with the Dodgers, and Billy Cox was with the Dodgers. Parris played in Montreal for a few years. All Parris hit was line drives, and he was a tough out. He had a small strike zone. What a hitter.

We had some good players. But sometimes guys went through the motions. I mean, you are talking, 1960, there were only eight teams in each of the big leagues. How many jobs were there? How many guys could be there? The blacks, Cubans, they knew they were not going to get much of a shot, as good as they were. Some of those guys were really good. It was tough to get a job. You had Clyde Parris. Could you imagine him today? This guy was some hitter. Holy Cow! There were some natural hitters around in those days.

The Mexican League teams competed against clubs in the U.S. Southwest during the season. A unique international league association existed.

We played against the Texas League, in places like San Antonio. The travel never really bothered me. What I do remember was how tough it was to pitch in Mexico City. I remember them fanning me and washing me down with ammonia and stuff in between innings. The high altitude was tough.

Where did you play your home games?

In Mexico City, we played in a place called Social Security Stadium. The police would come in with their horses and one would go left and one would go right. Peel off in rows and station themselves in front of the stands. Mexico

City had two teams— Mexico City Reds and another team, I cannot recall the name.

I don't have to put you on the spot and ask which country you enjoyed more because you have sounded equally enthusiastic about both.

That whole time — Panama, Mexico, it was terrific. It was a great experience for me, and for the rest of my life.

There are many what-could-have-been stories in all sports, but I would like to know more about yours.

You know what happened with me? In those years, they did not count your pitches. I threw very hard and nobody would swing at the ball, and I threw a lot of pitches. You can imagine how many starts I had in my second year in baseball. Then I went to winter ball and pitched. I think they should have watched me a lot better. There were no agents. My third year I hurt my arm. I hurt my elbow. It took me a while to get back on the ball, to where I could throw really hard again. I went into the Marine Corps reserve for six months. Finally, when I came out in 1959, I started to put things together. And I was called to the major leagues. I think in my fourth game, I had a freak accident. I was backing up a play at home plate. Roger Maris threw the ball home and the guy was out. But the catcher threw his mask and I stepped right on the mask, hurt my ankle very badly. It was my right ankle. My main pitching ankle. I was never the same. In '61, I was out of baseball and was talked into playing semi-pro. But I was too good for them. A couple of scouts had seen me and the Mets, who were coming into the league in 1962, invited me to spring training. I hurt my leg again, on a play at first.

The following year, the Mets wanted me to come back. I was 26 years old. My brother-in law owned a big company in Garden City; he was a wholesale distributor. He offered me a great job. I packed it in and went to work for him. I regret it today. But the handwriting was on the wall, and there was no money in baseball in those days. No money. I lost my drive to keep at it. George Weiss was the general manager of the Mets. He was as cheap as could be. He offered me a lousy contract to come back and play. I said get the hell out of here. There was not a great feeling that they really wanted you.

Well, you made it farther than most.

I feel so good sometimes about being a ballplayer, even though it was only for about eight years. I get fan letters from people. People, you know, that if you played in the major leagues for a short time, you are like a rare stamp to them. They want your autograph. That is kind of neat, even at my age, now.

THE NICARAGUAN WINTER LEAGUE

Joe Hicks

I did not know it at the time, but I received a two-for-one interview ticket when Joe Hicks agreed to speak to me. Hicks was happy to talk to me about his winter playing days, the majority spent in Nicaragua. His wife and Nicaragua native, Antonia, also chimed in nicely, providing some interesting observations on the conduct of some fans attending games in her home country.

Hicks played five seasons in the major leagues, four in the Junior Circuit with the Chicago White Sox and Washington Senators and one with the second-year New York Metropolitans. The outfielder played ball for nine consecutive winters, seven of which were in Managua.

Clearly a friendly man with an outgoing personality, Hicks remains involved in his Northern Virginia community, years after retiring from a long-held civic government post. Hicks and his wife have three daughters: Francesca, named after his wife's mother; Debbie; and Esperanza, named after the chaperone accompanying Hicks and his wife on their first date.

Where are you from originally, and how many were in your immediate family?

I was born on a little a farm, about ten miles west of Charlottesville, Virginia. There were seven of us, five kids and my mother and father. I had two brothers and two sisters. We did not have television. The family had a radio and at night when the local stations went off the air on a clear night you could pick up stations as far west as St. Louis—that is as far west as major league baseball went in those days. I could pick up games from the Brooklyn Dodgers, Red Barber was the announcer. I could pick up Cincinnati and Pittsburgh and Philadelphia, and I just fell in love with the game. St. Louis was my favorite team. I was about nine years old when I started listening to those games. Right around when Stan "the Man" Musial came up.

How did you receive the baseball "calling?"

In the backyard when the broom sticks were out, I would saw the end off one and use it to hit pebbles. I would play pretend games between the Brooklyn Dodgers and St. Louis Cardinals. When the Cardinals came to bat, I would try to hit those pebbles a bit farther.

We did not have any Little Leagues. My brother, who was a year and a week older than me, he was good enough to play on the high school ball team when he was in fifth grade — ten years old. We only had eleven grades. We graduated after eleven years. So that is when I really became interested in the game.

It was not the norm for baseball athletes to attend college, but you did.

I was a pretty good student in school. My principal obtained for me an academic scholarship to the University of Virginia. UVA only gave football and boxing scholarships, and a couple of basketball scholarships, too. No baseball. I tried out for the baseball team. The freshmans — we were called "first years" — could not play on the varsity team, and had to play freshman ball.

My second year at UVA, we were playing our archrivals, Virginia Tech. We used to play them twice a year. Over in Blacksburg, I had hit a home run late in the game to win the game over there. They came over to Charlottesville to play us. They were ahead in the ninth inning, 6–5, and we had a runner at second with two outs and I am the next hitter up. The manager calls time out and walks out to the pitcher's mound. The catcher meets him there. I know they are talking about me. Anyway, all of a sudden, I am standing there and the home plate umpire takes off his mask and says, "Hey Joe, how would you like to play pro ball?" I said, "Mr. Ump, that is my dream!" This umpire tells me he is a birddog scout for the Chicago White Sox, and that he would contact his boss, Harry Postove, who was in Norfolk, Virginia. The ump tells me he likes the way I swing.

They both came out to my house a short time later, the ump and Harry Postove. I signed a minor league contract for the Class D league in Madisonville, Kentucky for $250 a month and a $500 signing bonus. I could not believe they wanted to give me bonus, too. I loved playing in Madisonville because we played every day. I had never done that before. I had a good season, good enough for the White Sox to bring me up to their Colorado Springs team, Class A.

I made it up to Double-A ball in 1955, which was the last step up before Chicago. On my team, Memphis in the Southern Association, was Lou Aparicio from Venezuela, who had signed with the White Sox. Louie was my roommate. I spoke a little Spanish. I took Spanish classes at UVA. I was the only one who could converse with Louie, because Louie could not speak much English.

It was the norm for baseball athletes to be conscripted for military service, as you can attest.

I missed '56 and '57 because of military service. I came out of the army, and in those days when the season was over, ballplayers had to get jobs. We did not make much in the minor leagues. I made $350 a month after Madisonville. Double A ball was $500. In the majors, it was $6,000, the minimum salary. I called up my old scout. I said, "Harry, I just came out of the army. I need a job." He said, "My friend is going to manage a baseball team in Colombia. He needs somebody to play." I said, "Oh, Columbia, South Carolina?" He said, "No, no. Colombia in South America." The manager was Frank Scalzi, he was a minor league manager in the White Sox' organization. We met in Miami on such and such a date, and flew down to Cartagena. They [league] had two teams in Cartagena and two teams in Barranquilla. And that is how I was introduced to winter baseball in the winter of 1957-58. I played for the Kola Román team. I loved it. On Christmas Day, it was 75 degrees out and we were playing baseball.

I came back to Colorado Springs in 1958. I had met Earl Torgeson in spring training in Tampa. He was a first baseman, getting up in years. I think he was 36. The White Sox wanted Torgeson to get some managing experience. They assigned him to a winter league team. And he asked me, "Hey Joe, how would you like to play some winter ball? I am going down to Nicaragua to manage a team." "Nicaragua? Where is that at?" I said. I had played in Colombia the previous winter and had enjoyed it, so I told Earl I would love to go with him.

I traveled to Managua, Nicaragua, and played for the Boer Indians. They had another team called Cinco Estrellas — the Five Stars team. It was named after the military rank of Anastasio Somoza, the top army general. Those two teams were based in Managua. They had another team in León, about an hour's drive. It was a 45 minute drive over to Granada; the Oriental team played there. Ronnie Hansen was on our team. He played in the major leagues. Jim McManus. Phil Regan. Another pitcher was Jack Kralick. Torgy was the manager. He was not a player-manager. Johnny Pesky was the manager of the Cinco Estrellas team. My second year, Torgeson had to leave the team and I became the player-manager. Jim Kaat was one of our pitchers that year.

How were the accommodations in Managua?

They put us up in a hotel in the middle of town, but it did not have a swimming pool. On one of the off days — we usually played four days a week, every Tuesday, Friday, Saturday and Sunday — we were walking and saw a hotel with a swimming pool. The hotel was the Lido Palace. They had this young girl working there behind the desk. This girl was in charge of everything. I had an eye out for her. She spoke a little English, not too much. I had taken Spanish in college. I asked her for a date after a game one day. I asked her if she wanted to go to the movies. She said, okay. I took a taxi to her house. I am waiting for her. And she comes out and we are ready to go, and her little sister comes out and is coming along. I said, what is *she* doing? Well, *she* was the chaperone. Anyway, that is how I met my future wife.

In Nicaragua, there were not any mailboxes on the street you could drop mail in. You had to mail letters through the hotel. So, I had met a couple of girls in Colorado Springs, and I was mailing letters to them. I never received a reply. I later found out that my future wife was throwing my letters in the trash can. [Laughs.] We were married on New Year's Eve, 1958. My wife's name is Antonia. She goes by Toni. She grew up in a gold mining town called Bonanza. It is a beautiful little village. You can only get there by plane. At the end of the season, I went over there and spent a few weeks. Toni's parents had sent her to Managua, to Catholic schools there. The schools were better in Managua.

Did you have the same affinity for Central American food as you did for Central American women?

We had good food at the Lido Palace Hotel. They had a good cook. My wife was in charge of the kitchen, too. She was more or less running everything for this American guy, who was the owner. My wife did not like the American players too much, because they were always drinking at the bar, they were a little rude. Except for one little player, who never went back to the bar to drink anything — that was me. I just drank Coca Cola. I had to behave myself in front of her. Though once we were married, we found an apartment.

How did you spend your free time?

Some of us went deer hunting once. I was waiting for the deer. It was warm, and I fell asleep. I heard a noise — a deer came right by, and before I could compose myself, the deer was gone. I could not even get a shot off. We spent time at the swimming pool. They had a beach at León.

Joe Hicks as a member of the Boer Indians in Managua, Nicaragua (courtesy J. Hicks).

What top-notch players can you recall playing against?

When I first arrived in Nicaragua, Marvin Throneberry had had a great year the prior season and they brought him back during my first year. Silverio Pérez was tough. He was a left-hander and we had a predominantly left-handed batting order. Duncan Campbell was a Nicaraguan player. He was a star with León. Campbell finished near the top in batting one year.

You played for Boer. They were the team in the league with the largest fan base.

Julio Martínez was Boer's owner, and he had a son named Héctor. A guy named Morales was the treasurer. The owners would bet. Fans would bet. Fans bet on everything. Córdobas was the Nicaraguan money. A guy would hit a triple. They had a standing bet: *Habre con triple, no anota.* You could bet on whether the guy would score from third base. They would bet on whether guys would strike out.

We would play in León or Granada on Sunday mornings and come back to play a night game in Managua. *Estadio* Somoza, that is what it was called. In those days, Somoza was a big name in Nicaragua. We dressed at the hotel. We came to the stadium dressed [in uniform] and ready to play.

I always ask about the stadium and fans. What can you tell me with respect to each?

The fans were rowdy. Really rowdy. One time I guess I had a bad game, and somebody cut the canvass top on my jeep in the parking lot. The fans would light fires—hold on...

... Antonia Hicks: The stadium was cement. If the fans did not like a play or a sequence of events, they would start a *fogata* (bonfire). They would burn whatever they could, papers, wrappers—even their shoes. It was their way of showing displeasure with what was going on. And after that, would come the iguanas. The fans would throw iguanas at the opposing players in the outfield. To scare them. [Laughs.] One time, an iguana landed near a player and he took off running. The fans were fans.

Jack Kubiszyn

Prior to Jack Kubiszyn becoming a two-season major league player with the Cleveland Indians in the early '60s, he spent the winter of 1959 in Nicaragua. A teammate of Jim Weaver with Cinco Estrellas, the infielder went 5-for-5 in Weaver's no-hitter against León.

Kubiszyn accumulated four sports letters in high school and was an accomplished collegiate athlete in his adopted state of Alabama, where he still holds several University of Alabama basketball records. After baseball, the Buffalo-transplant established a successful insurance agency and became a lifetime member of the prestigious Million Dollar Round Table. A father of five and devout Catholic, Kubiszyn had his life story published in 2009 in a book titled When a Star Fell on Alabama. *The book was written by Lucy Stallworth Kubiszyn, Jack's wife of more than one-half century.*

In the book's dedicated Nicaragua chapter, it was related how Kubiszyn, on the day he was leaving Managua for the United States, wanted to purchase and bring back with him a pet monkey that was for sale at the airport. After a protracted discussion filled with strident objections from his wife and being notified of a U.S. requirement to quarantine the animal for a time, Kubiszyn forwent the idea. On the same ballplayers' flight home, another U.S. recruit, Maury Lerner, brought back from Nicaragua a baby wildcat and luckily smuggled it through customs in Miami inside a travel satchel.

You are from upstate New York.

The west end of Buffalo, New York, until I went to college.

How many children did your parents raise?

Three of us, a brother and a sister. Buffalo was a real good sports town.

Baseball was not necessarily your primary sport. Did you admire athletes from other sports?

I was never really a fan [of players]. I played baseball and basketball and football and tennis in high school.

But baseball won out.

I came down to the University of Alabama on a basketball scholarship. I played basketball and baseball in college. There were about 20 or 30 scouts looking at me at one time when I played baseball. Coach Sewell signed me. Joe Sewell. He used to live here. Sewell played with the Yankees, with Babe Ruth. He is a Hall of Famer. Sewell only struck out three times in one season. I signed with the Cleveland Indians and they sent me to Nicaragua in 1959.

What can you tell me about that?

Johnny Pesky was my manager, and I always remember him preaching to "develop a base hit stroke." I had a real good year for him in Nicaragua. I went to Mobile the following year and finished second, I think, in hitting. The winter baseball really helped.

You played with Cinco Estrellas, so you were based in the capital.

We lived — I was with my wife — in an apartment about a block from the Gran Hotel in Managua. We stayed at the hotel for maybe a week, until we found the apartment.

How was the national stadium in Managua?

At the stadium they had regular fold up chairs. At that time, Somoza was the dictator. I remember seeing guns being carried on the street. At different times there would be talk about there being a revolution. At one game, the fans threw a bunch of fire crackers in the stands and the players' wives, sitting together, I guess with all the talk recently, hit the ground and all the chairs went flying. They thought it was gunshots.

Did you pick up any Spanish?

I never heard the word *mañana* until I went to Nicaragua. Everything was *mañana*, there. We were never paid on time. It was always *mañana*.

Did you get to see much of the city or surrounding areas?

Over there it was rich and poor. No middle class. That was a culture shock. The people were so poor. One of the people who owned an apartment house brought us out to the jungle, he had a picnic for us. This guy was raising deer. He had deer in a pen. That was kind of interesting. We went shopping a little. But everything revolved around baseball. It was pretty good baseball down there.

Was the food and drink to your liking?

We did not drink the water. We would boil the water. We would drink bottled beer. We had a girl named Matilde, a really sweet lady, that did our shopping for us. We would hire her for the day. The food was very adequate. Matilde cooked for us. Mostly American food. We did not eat out at all.

What players can you recall?

Don Mincher played against us. Jim Kaat pitched against us. Maury Lerner, I remember. Walter Bond played with us. There

Jack Kubisyzn reached the major leagues with the Cleveland Indians in 1961 (courtesy Lucy Stallworth Kubsizyn).

is a funny story about him in my book. It is funny now. It was not so funny when it happened.

I would like to hear it.

Walter was six-foot-seven. I hit a home run one game. Walter was up next, and the pitcher beaned him. Walter is laying out there motionless, and they call for an ambulance. The ambulance comes in from the outfield, with sirens blaring, and it stops with a hard half-spin at home plate that kicks up a big cloud of dirt that envelops everyone around. There are two guys on the back of the ambulance, on the running board, who jump off. These guys move fast, like a cartoon, opening the door and getting the stretcher out. After that ambulance entrance, the fans are loving the actions of these attendants, applauding and screaming at the ambulance guys, who become like actors on a stage. The guys put Walter in the back of the ambulance and take off fast, kicking up another big cloud of dirt. Well, Walter is so tall that his feet are sticking out of the ambulance because they could not close the door. And the ambulance guys on the running board in the back are waving to the cheers of the fans as they speed out. To everyone's horror, Walter then starts sliding out of the moving ambulance. The ambulance guys see it and push Walter back in and just keep waving like nothing happened. What turned it so comical was that the ambulance guys keep waving to the fans while Walter starts sliding out again. It turned into something out of Laurel and Hardy. The ambulance guys would wave and then they would quickly push Walter back in. Wave. Push Walter back in. It is funny now because Walter was all right. He came to the ballpark the next day. He was okay. But Walter kept wondering why he had a bump on the top of his head, along with one from the beaning. [Laughs.]

That was funny. Anything else to add?

It was an enjoyable time. The experience taught me that you did not need to play baseball for eight or nine months, you needed to play baseball all year 'round.

Phil Regan

Phil Regan was traded by the Detroit Tigers to the Los Angeles Dodgers in December 1965 for Dick Tracewski. The following season, with a record of 14–1, Regan won the first of his two Sporting News Fireman of the Year Awards for the National League champion Dodgers. Regan began his 13-year major league career as a spot starter with Detroit in 1960. That win-

ter, he gained confidence-boosting experience pitching for the Mayagüez Indians. A right-hander, Regan led the P.R.W.L. in wins with 11. Two earlier winters had found the 21-year-old honing his trade for Nicaragua's Boer Indians.

A winner of 96 big league games, Regan was a pitching coach for the Seattle Mariners in the 1980s and for Chicago Cubs during the following decade. Regan managed the Baltimore Orioles in 1995 to a third-place American League Eastern Division finish. Regan expressed an affinity for Baltimore. His first game as a starting pitcher came on the road against the Orioles. His first World Series appearance came against the Orioles, and his first and only managerial post occurred in the Charm City. (Regan also managed the Caracas Leones to the Venezuelan Winter League pennant in 1989-90.)

Regan was coaxed out of retirement by Omar Minaya a few years ago. Minaya, the general manager of the New York Mets at the time, asked Phil to be the pitching coach of the Mets' minor league team in Port St. Lucie, Florida. Regan accepted, and the baseball reintegration led to a permanent relocation. "I came down to Florida and loved it," Regan stated. "I sold my house in Michigan and bought another one here in Port St. Lucie."

Where did you grow up?

I was raised in a small town in Michigan, right outside of Grand Rapids. I lived in the country and did not play a game of baseball until I reached high school.

That is amazing. Were you able to follow the game?

I knew the whole Detroit Tiger team. Hal Newhouser was one of my big heroes growing up.

You must have made up for lost time in high school then?

I started playing American Legion ball, then I went to college at Western Michigan. After one year at Western Michigan, I signed a contract with the Detroit Tigers. I was signed by a fellow by the name of Ray Meyers. He had seen me in a tournament over at Battle Creek, Michigan. There was no draft. They had what they called a bonus system. If you received *more* than $4,000 in salary and bonus, you had to remain with the major league club for two years. This is why guys like Al Kaline never went to the minor leagues. I received a signing bonus of $2,700 and $250 a month to make a total $4,000.

I started off at Jamestown, New York, in the PONY League. That was Class D, the lowest you could go. That was 1956. I had a good year at Jamestown, I won 17 games. They moved me up to Durham, North Carolina, in the Carolina League in 1957. That was Class B. Then the Tigers gave me a chance in the spring to make the Double A team. I went there because the Tiger manager at the time was a guy named Jack Tighe. He lived in Spring Lake, Michigan, which was not too far from me. Tighe saw me over the winter and said, I am going to give you a chance to make the Double A team. I made the team, the Birmingham Barons.

So it was after a couple of years of minor league ball that you first ventured to play winter ball?

I had a friend back in Grand Rapids by the name of Bob Sullivan. He had a semi-pro team that did a lot of barnstorming. Sullivan knew Earl Torgeson real well. Earl Torgeson went down to Nicaragua to manage, and Sullivan called him and said, you ought to take Regan with you. Torgeson called me and asked me to go to Nicaragua with him.

Torgy was an intense guy. He had played in the

Phil Regan began his career with Detroit as mostly a starter. He later won two *Sporting News* Fireman of the Year awards in the National League.

major leagues, and you really respected him. You liked playing for him because of his intensity. In 1959, the White Sox had been to the World Series, and Torgeson was a member of that team. The White Sox came over to Lakeland, Florida, the following spring training, and I was pitching against Torgeson. I threw Torgeson a curve and it was called strike three. It was questionable. Torgeson asked me later if I thought it was a strike. I said, I thought maybe it was. I am not sure whether Torgeson did not take that pitch just for me, you know what I mean? He was at the end of his career and he knew I was just starting out. I just did not see him taking that pitch too many times. I always wanted to ask Torgeson if he took that pitch just for me, but never had the chance. He was that type of person.

In Nicaragua, you stayed in Managua?

I played for the Boer team. Most of the players stayed downtown in a hotel. We rented a home — my wife and I — outside of Managua. It was a two-family home. Another ballplayer, Jack Kralick, and myself, stayed out there with our wives. It was in the country, and we had a great time. My major in college was history. I have always tried to study the history of every country I have been to. Nicaragua was interesting because the other big team was the Cinco Estrellas, the Five Stars team, which was Somoza's team. Somoza was in power at that time. I would read about fighting going on in the hills. I would ask, who are these people? They told me, do not worry, they are named after a general that was a martyr. You will never hear from them again. Twenty-five years later, the Sandanistas were in power.

Frank Kostro, a good friend and roommate of mine in the Tigers' organization, went down to Nicaragua the following winter, or two winters later. I talk to him quite a bit. Frank played for Cinco Estrellas. Something happened one night at a game and he made some gesture toward Somoza's box, kind of in defiance of him. The next morning, Frank says, they came into his room and pointed a gun at him and told him, you are going home on a plane. Right now. Get out. Kostro did not want to come back. [Laughs.]

I don't blame him. What can you tell me about the stadium?
It was a very big, round Olympic stadium. A lot of cement seating. It was not great seating. Whenever we played Somoza's team, the stadium was full. We dressed at home. As I remember, the locker rooms were not great, but, you know, when your 18, 19, 20-years-old, you do not complain about it. You could walk outside our home, which was kind of on a main street and you could get a cab for 15 cents or 20 cents to take you to the ballpark. We did not have much travel. The only time we traveled was to a place called León. We played there, and we had a guy named Jim McManus on our team. McManus slid into third base, hard. There was a fight between he and the third baseman, and the fans swarmed the field. They called the game. They got us on the bus. The fans stoned the bus and knocked all of our windows out. We made it back to Managua. We never traveled there again.

Did you have a better experience with the local food?
I liked the food. We had a person that prepared our food. The lady's name was Carlota.

What about at holiday time, being away from home and all?
We had turkey for Thanksgiving. I can remember the native people would come out around Christmastime and wrap the trees with white crepe paper to make it look like snow, and they would serenade us with Christmas carols. It was a long way from Michigan, but it kind of reminded me of it, with the fake snow. It was pretty nice.

I interviewed a teammate of yours. Joe Hicks.

Joe Hicks was from Virginia. He was an outfielder with, I think, the White Sox. He married a girl from down there. You know, when we got down there the owner of the club told us, "One of you guys will probably marry a girl from Nicaragua." The single guys snickered. And Joe Hicks married a girl from there. I wish I could remember the owner's name, I cannot.

Any other players come to mind, teammates or otherwise?

I left there a little bit before the season ended. I did not play in the play-offs. Kralick won a lot of games, he stood out to me as the best pitcher. I cannot remember too many of the other guys. I loved the people. I had a great time and enjoyed it.

You also experienced winter grooming in another locale.

I played one other season of winter ball. In Puerto Rico. The person who contacted me was one of the owners of Mayagüez, Babel Pérez. Bill Adair was the manager. I had a pretty good year there. I had a lot of positive experiences in Puerto Rico. I made $800 a month, plus $300 for expenses. That was 1960. In '61, I pitched for the Tigers, and won ten games for them. And Babel Pérez called me. He said, "We would like to have you back, but we can only offer you $700 a month." He wanted to cut me a hundred dollars. [Laughs.] I told him no.

What was Puerto Rico like?

It was a great learning experience for me because I received a chance to play against Clemente and Vic Power. Orlando Cepeda. I pitched against guys like that. It made me know that I could pitch in the big leagues. Juan Pizarro was there, a great pitcher. I played with him later on in Chicago. Charley Lau was our catcher. I remember him saying — he was with Detroit — that he tried to hit home runs, because Tiger Stadium was a small ballpark. You could hit the ball out to right field. Lau was a left-hand hitter. But Lau was only a .240 hitter. Lau made the choice in Puerto Rico to quit trying to go for home runs. *I am going to hit down on the ball and I am going to hit the ball through the middle.* And that was the year he started to develop the Charley Lau theory of hitting, where you hit down on the ball and back up the middle.

Where in Mayagüez did you stay?

We lived at the Darlington Apartments, a high rise building, all of the players lived there.

Mayagüez is located on the western part of the island. That mandated some travel.

We traveled mainly by bus. When we went to Ponce, we would take a back road going over the mountains, and I can tell you that was not fun. A lot of times when we had to go to San Juan, Babel Pérez, would say, hey, I have plane ticket for you. I am going to fly you there. I still remember the name of the hotel in San Juan. A big, white hotel, it looked like a ship, the Normandie Hotel. That is where we stayed when we went to San Juan.

What was your home park like?

The Mayagüez stadium was small, nothing real fancy. It held seven or eight thousand. The thing I still remember is that you would practice in the outfield and you would see these big land crabs that came out of holes in the ground. It was interesting to me because I had never seen them before. San Juan's stadium was an older stadium. It did not have a lot of lights.

What did you do for relaxation?

Whenever we had two days off, my wife and I would go to a small town called *La Parguera*. It has this phosphorescent bay. At night, you could see the fish glowing and shimmering in the moonlight because there was so much phosphorescence in the water. It was really a unique place. It was really beautiful.

You mentioned some well-known players earlier. Juan Pizarro was one of the league's leading pitchers that season, along with Luis Arroyo.

What I remember most about Luis Arroyo was the following year, I won ten games with Detroit, and we won 101 games and finished behind the Yankees, who won 109. Arroyo was instrumental in that for the Yankees. Aside from Arroyo, Juan Pizarro was just outstanding. Pizarro threw the ball hard and he was a dominating pitcher at that time. Orlando Cepeda never came to Mayagüez to play. The fans got on him too hard. Clemente was the best player I ever pitched against.

How did you spend the holidays in Puerto Rico?

Babel Pérez invited us over to his house for Christmas. What I remember were these huge crystal bowls filled with fresh shrimp cocktails. You would go over and eat as many as you wanted. Both holidays, Thanksgiving and Christmas, we went to Babel's house. They do not celebrate these holidays there, but they kind of honored the American players. When I played in Venezuela in the sixties, I remember, they had the players to a restaurant and they served turkey and mashed potatoes. They tried to do it like in the United States.

How were the Puerto Rican fans?

The fans were good to you, if you played hard. If you did not play hard, they did not like you.

Well, I have to be going. I have to get my pitchers warmed up.

Dick Stigman

Dick Stigman's current family unit would have made up one-third of the population of the small town in which he was raised. The father of nine and current horticultural devotee took time to reminisce with me about his single season of winter play in Nicaragua in 1959-60. Stigman was one of the top pitchers in the league with nine victories for the Boer Indians. It was an experience he looked back upon fondly and one which assisted his budding major league career.

Stigman played seven years in the major leagues, four of them with his home-state team, the Minnesota Twins. (The same week I spoke to him, Dick and his wife were preparing to attend the memorial service at Target Field for Harmon Killebrew, whom Dick called a great teammate and a wonderful man.) The former left-handed pitcher split nearly evenly his 235 mound appearances in the major leagues as a starter and reliever.

What part of the country are you from?

I am from a small town in north central Minnesota called Nimrod. It was a town of about 70 people. I had two brothers and a sister. My older brother was a year older than me, my sister a year younger, and another brother was three years younger. My father managed the Nimrod baseball team. In those days, every little town had a ball team and that was the way we spent our Sundays. On weekdays, we practiced. It just came naturally to me.

Which big league player, or players, did you most follow?

I was a fan of the New York Giants and Cleveland Indians. Of course, I knew all about the "Big Four" for Cleveland — García, Lemon, Feller, Wynn. Ironically, Herb Score, whom I played against, was one of my idols, too.

When did your baseball career begin in earnest?

In high school, at 18 years old, I played on three teams — American Legion, the Nimrod town team and a high school team. I went to high school in a town a little bigger than Nimrod. In my senior year, I pitched in a tournament and pitched against some larger towns and I did pretty well. There was a birddog scout named Mark Nutting. He was an insurance man, he just did scouting part-time. Nutting recommended me to a major league scout named Cy Slapnicka. He happened to have signed Bob Feller, Herb Score, Dick Brown, Gordie Coleman. A whole bunch of pretty famous ballplayers. Slapnicka was a wonderful man.

My first year in professional baseball was 1954. I was three days out of high school when I signed my contract. I went to Fargo, North Dakota, then Tifton, Georgia. My second year I was in Olean, New York, in the PONY League. In 1956, I was in Bedelia, Georgia. In 1957, I played in Hermosillo,

Mexico, but the food and water did not agree with me. I lost a whole bunch of weight and came home early.

But you gave playing outside the country another shot.

Nineteen fifty-nine was the year I ended up playing in Nicaragua. Cleveland wanted me to play winter ball and get a little more experience. It was really a good thing for me, because when I went to spring training, in the middle of February, I was in much better shape than most of the guys I was playing against. I was always kind of a slow starter, so playing winter ball helped me, and helped me to get confidence. Cleveland had a connection with one of the teams, the Boer. They were "The People's Team." Then there was the Five Stars team, Cinco Estrellas; it was the government's team. There was a pretty good rivalry between those two clubs. We also played León and another team [Oriental].

We lived in a hotel in Managua. I cannot remember the name. It had the "American Plan," where you received room and board, plus two meals a day. All the Americans stayed there, even the guys on the Five Stars team. We knew most of the players there from the minor leagues. Don Schaefer was a good friend of mine. He was there. He probably just had a cup of coffee in the majors. But Don and I played together in the minors, and were in the National Guard together. There was a casino next door to the hotel. Every night at midnight when they would close, they would play "*Granada*" with a trumpet or coronet. We could always tell what time it was by that horn playing. There was a pool in our hotel. We used to lay out in the sun, and we played a handball game against batwing doors and a wall that were all kind of together.

I hope I can ask you about the food.

The food was very good. Everything agreed with me. There was a dish I liked that looked like a banana [*platano relleno*]. They used to serve that in the afternoon. They had American food, too. It was a U.S.–friendly place. I remember Jim McManus jumped out of the balcony of the hotel into the pool, and that was the only time somebody ever did that and the hotel staff became pretty upset about it. McManus was just goofing around and jumped right into the pool.

You threw a few gems in your home stadium. Was it a pitcher's ballpark?

The stadium was very nice. The field was good. The hitters might complain about the lights. I do not recall that it had that poor lighting.

What about the clubhouse?

We dressed in the hotel. When we went on the road to a place like León, we did the same thing. Showered when we came back to our hotel.

León was your lengthiest road trip.

León was not a very friendly place. We would go there and their stadium had stands that were 20 feet from the first and third base lines. If you beat them, the fans were pretty calm. But if they beat you ... I remember we were driving out of town after a game we had lost. The roads were dirt roads. Every time there was an intersection, there was a big dip in the road. We [players] had to get on the floor of the bus because the fans were throwing rocks at the bus. There was glass flying around from the windows breaking. They liked to rub salt in the wounds, I guess. [Chuckles.]

Were there any native players that stood out to you?

The national players were really good players. Of course, nowadays there are so many Latin players playing in the major leagues.

Julio Moreno was a veteran on our team. This is kind of off the record. [Amused.] I remember Moreno did not wear any underwear under his uniform pants. I remember that distinctly. He was handsome guy. Dark hair. He never wore any underwear. *Nothing.* No cup, no supporter. Nothing. [Laughing.] He was a brave guy.

Very brave. And among the American players?

Maury Lerner was on our team. He played really well. But he was a high-strung guy. Wound up like a rubber band. An excellent hitter. I think Maury could have advanced in the pros. But Maury was so temperamental he could not handle his emotions. Maury actually called me a year or two ago and said he had spent some time in prison. I think he killed somebody. I do not know if it was second degree or first degree. Maury was very open about it. Said he had found religion. I never

Dick Stigman in spring training with the Cleveland Indians.

heard from Maury again. I cannot think right now who was the best pitcher, sorry.

Did you do anything away from the hotel?

It was when Somoza was president. You would see a military presence sometimes. There were a lot of people that were not happy with Somoza. We were in a movie theatre one time, and we heard this loud noise outside. Nobody paid a whole lot of attention to it. We went outside later and saw this vehicle sitting in front of the theatre all blown to bits. Somebody had put a bomb in it. At the movies, all the captions were in Spanish. Here we were foreigners and we were enjoying the movie in English.

Do you have any other lasting memory?

Opening Night, we played the Five Stars team in Managua. The place was packed. Somebody was shot. I do not think he was killed. The fans got pretty crazy, whooping it up with the rivalries. They would light a piece of cardboard and start flinging it around the stadium. They were fun-loving people. I really enjoyed the people we met. Everyone was nice to us—except in León. [Chuckles.] A lot of crazy things happened. I really enjoyed my time in Nicaragua. The people were wonderful.

What is occupying your time now?

I retired two years ago, in January. I am playing a little golf. We are going to ballgames and concerts and soccer games and things like that. We have flowers. That is actually what I am doing today. Planting flowers in our backyard. My health is real good. A few aches and pains. But generally very healthy. I am married, 48 years in June, to Patti. She was a flight attendant when we met. We have nine children, five biological, four adopted. The four adopted were older children. We have three Korean children and one mixed-race. I have 24 grandchildren.

There is a lot of life after baseball.

Jim Weaver

At 72 and three months, Jim Weaver was the second-youngest of the "boys of winter" that I interviewed. Still working part-time in a printing business ("and enjoying it") with his eldest son, Weaver discussed his experiences from three separate stints in Nicaragua, beginning in 1959 with Johnny Pesky's Cinco Estrellas team. During that first foray and few weeks shy of his 21st birthday, Weaver threw a no-hitter for Pesky's squad against the León Melenudos.

An injury to his pitching arm sustained in Managua and two years of military service staggered Weaver's progression to the baseball top. The left-hander reached the major leagues with the California Angels in 1967.

Weaver, a self-described "happy camper," was looking forward to celebrating his 50th wedding anniversary in the spring of 2012 with wife Barbara.

Your place of birth?

Lancaster, Pennsylvania.

How many in your family?

There were four children.

I played pick-up ball, and I went out for the high school team in my junior year. I played baseball and basketball. I did not think I could make the baseball team, but I did.

Which ballplayer did you most admire?

Mantle and Stan Musial were my biggest heroes.

When did you become serious about playing baseball?

I was scouted out of my senior year in high school. I signed in 1958 with the Cleveland Indians. After I retired, I went to college. So I did things kind of backward.

I started out in the Florida State League. I moved up to Class D ball in the Carolina League in 1959. Cleveland had an instructional league in Florida in the winter, where they sent all their, what they considered to be, phenoms. It was from there that I flew down to Managua, Nicaragua. I played three years in Nicaragua. The first was in 1959.

Do you remember your manager?

It was Johnny Pesky. He was in the Detroit organization at the time. Nicaragua's league had split seasons, and Pesky's team lost out the first time around on a playoff berth. So Pesky flew up to Tampa, where we were, and picked out four or five of the Cleveland players, and we went down and kicked butt [in the second half-season]. I was the best pitcher. I was 6–0 and had the lowest ERA.

How was that initial experience?

I lived at the Gran Hotel in Managua. Most of us stayed there. Jim Kaat was there. [Jack] Kubiszyn. Walt Bond. Dick Stigman. Duncan Campbell was a real good hitter, and a nice guy. I liked Nicaragua. I made a lot of friends. I met friends associated with the ball club, and others that were not. I tried to learn the language as best I could. At the movies, I would watch the subtitles. That is how I picked up Spanish. I enjoyed it. That is why I went back twice more. Jim McManus played for Leon, but he stayed at the hotel with us in Managua. We only went to León a couple of times, which I was happy about.

What was the average non-game day like?

We would probably get up around nine o' clock. We would stay up late. They had cantinas and bars that were open all night. We would go from one place to the next and talk to the fans. We would drink rum and coke and beer. We would have breakfast and go swimming. It was nice. We only played four days a week, so we did not have to grind that hard. All of us stayed in shape.

Guys played cards. We read. We took trips in jeeps. It helped if you knew some native families. And I did. So I traveled around the country pretty well. I met the native people at the hotel. I would walk around town and talk to people, and meet people. I think the natives liked that, because I was trying to learn their language. So I made a lot of friends. We went out on the lake. Lake Managua. It was the first time I had experienced fresh water sharks. One of the guys I met, I think, he owned an island on the lake. We would go out there and have a cook out. Just relax the whole off day.

We were paid in U.S. dollars. I would send most of my money home. I was on what they called the "American Plan."

What are your recollections of the stadium and fans?

The stadium was all concrete. We dressed at the hotel, and then we would take a taxi out to the stadium, or what they called a *microbus*. After the game, we would hustle out of the stadium and take the same transportation home. The only thing I did not like was when the fans would get so excited that the National Guard folks would have to hit them with rifle butts. I did not like that at all. It could get pretty rowdy. I remember later Clemente came over to Nicaragua to play in the Pan American Series, and a fan almost hit Clemente in the face with a rum bottle. Clemente was running over to make a catch down the right field line and he almost got cranked. That was bad. I remember later on in '64, Ferguson Jenkins pitched down there. Fergy pitched for León.

You said you were glad that you did not have to travel to León.

The worst road trip was always to León. Because if they beat you, we would have to put the windows down on the bus. We had iron bars across the windows. We would have to get down on the floor, because you would get hit with rocks the whole way out of town. I pitched a no-hitter against León. It was in Managua.

It was interesting to me that Pesky turned the team around with an upgraded roster of North American players.

Johnny Pesky was the most intense manager I ever played for in all my life. There was a guy who really hated to lose. And he hated the other ball club. Afterwards, Pesky would be okay—but, I mean, he was intense. You were never asleep on that bench. If you were not starting, Pesky had you in that ball game.

What were Pesky's tactics?

Well, a couple of things I remember, but it was pretty profane. I would rather not be quoted. Some of the things Pesky said to opposing players and umpires were pretty graphic.

[In the playoffs] I played first base for Pesky; I was not supposed to, and I suffered an injury. I was scheduled to pitch the second game, but could not after the injury. I could not lift my arm the next day. A guy pushed the ball up the first base line. Danny Hayling was pitching. He was a pretty good pitcher, but he shoveled the ball across the bag to me. I was nailed by the runner and dislocated my left shoulder. I eventually had to get it operated on. I was plagued by my arm kind of my whole career after that.

During the playoffs, half of our ball club went home when the team told us they could not guarantee us playoff money. I stayed and played first base for the rest of the playoffs. I liked playing first base. I could not pitch, because I had gotten hurt. I could barely lift my arm 12 to 14 inches from my thigh. I threw underhand. Almost all of the Cleveland guys left, but I stayed. I wanted to stay. I told John, I cannot throw. He asked me if I could still play first base. I was a good hitter. We did not want Cleveland to find out [about the injury], because I was on loan from them.

What did you think of the stadium?

I hit a home run off Julio Moreno in the playoffs, right down the right field line. It was 190 feet off the outhouse roof. Oh, Moreno was furious. It was in Managua. The wind usually blew out to right center. He threw me a high fastball and I ripped it. He was a good pitcher. He was an older guy. Dead center you had to crush the ball to get it out, but right center was pretty easy, I thought. It was not a pitcher's ballpark. Our team was beaten [in the playoffs] by León.

Although you spent three seasons in Nicaragua, you did not return until several years later.

After my two years of military service—I was drafted during the Cuban Missile Crisis—I returned to Nicaragua and played for Granada and lived in Granada. I was in Nicaragua again in '66, when they had the revolution.

Oh, did you favor the food at all?

I would say rice and beans with chicken. I loved that dish. I still do. I have a friend who makes that every Tuesday night. Every once in while my wife and I try and go over to his place and have it with him.

THE PANAMANIAN WINTER LEAGUE

Tony Bartirome

Tony Bartirome has had a Pittsburgh connection all of his life. Born in the Steel City, Bartirome was signed by and played for the Pirates; he stayed within the organization for decades, even retiring to the Pirates' long-time Florida spring training retreat.

Bartirome played four winter seasons in Panama, beginning in 1955, and all were with the Carta Vieja Yankees. Hitting .377, Bartirome won the league MVP in 1956-57, topping the loop in nearly every offensive category: average, hits, doubles, triples, RBI, stolen bases and tied for total bases. During the season, Bartirome went six-for-seven in an extra inning contest, scoring the winning run after tripling against Chesterfield reliever Jerry Davie.

The first sacker traveled to play in two Caribbean Series but only received the opportunity to participate in one, as his eligibility was revoked at the last minute by committee officials in Havana in 1957. Bartirome had been chosen as a reinforcement player by Cerveza Balboa, Panama's championship representative that year. In the 1958 Caribbean Series, Bartirome was one of only two Carta Vieja Yankees' batters to reach Caguas' pitcher Juan Pizarro for a hit, in Pizarro's dazzling 17-strikeout, 8–0 shutout of the Carta Vieja team.

What was it about baseball that first appealed to you and who on the Pirates most brought out that zeal in you?

I just loved the game. Paul Waner. Lloyd Waner. Pie Traynor.

You went to Forbes Field, I assume?

Only went to Forbes Field a few times. We really could not afford to go to games. We grew up in a poor neighborhood.

Who was the talent evaluator that recognized your baseball abilities?

Pie Traynor signed me to my first contract. I was playing sandlot ball. It was a great thrill [to be signed by Traynor]. He was a great man.

Some major leaguers become scouts or coaches or front office men after they retire. You realized another way of staying close to the game.

I was a trainer for 22 years. I was a trainer for three years with Columbus first, starting in 1964. I became a trainer for the Pirates in 1967, until 1985. I was the only ex–major league player that became a major league trainer. I worked in one of the physical therapy wards at one of the hospitals in Columbus, and in Pittsburgh I did the same thing.

Tell me about your time playing in the off-season.

I played four seasons in Panama in the late fifties.

That was a fairly long commitment.

Billy Shantz, the brother of Bobby Shantz, he contacted me. That is how it occurred. The first year I was there, Al Kubski was the manager, then Billy took over the team during my final three years. Kubski was great to play for.

What were your first impressions?

I will tell you what, Panama was one of the best experiences of my life. I played for the Carta Vieja club. That was the name of the rum company there. Our team were all white American players. We did not have any black or Hispanic or dark-skinned players. I really enjoyed it because the people down there rooted for us more than they did for their hometown guys. We did not have any rivalries where there was [bad blood] or fighting or anything like that. The fans were great, especially the boys. They knew baseball and they loved the game. Every young boy in Panama, it seemed, rooted for our team — the Yankees.

We stayed at the Roosevelt Hotel in Panama City. I was single. I played 14 years of professional baseball, I was single in all but one — my last. My first year, when we came off the plane, all the players went to the Roosevelt Hotel and headed to the dining room, which had American food. I did not feel comfortable eating what they had laid out. It did not look right to me. So I went outside and hailed a taxi. I asked the taxi driver, "Where do *you* eat lunch?" He said, "I go down to this place —" "Take me there." The driver took me there, and it was the first time in my life I had *arroz con pollo*. I ate at this same restaurant every day after that. Now that day, every player who flew down and ate at the Roosevelt got diarrhea, bad. I never became sick one day. I cannot remember the name of the restaurant, only that they called the lady who ran the place "Mama." It was diner-like.

You came into your own as player in your second winter season.

My second year in Panama I was named Most Valuable Player; I led the league in average. I was a lead-off hitter.

As a result of your outstanding season, you were chosen as a roster supplement to play with the league champion Cerveza Balboa in the 1957 Caribbean Series in Cuba.

I remember Leon Kellman; he was a catcher. A really nice man. He was manager of Cerveza Balboa, too. [At the 1957 Caribbean Series] In Havana,

I did not even stay because they made me ineligible for some reason. I did not get on the field. One of the officials of the club came to me and said you cannot play in this game. I was not very unhappy because I was going to come home. I flew right out of Havana.

Carta Vieja won the Panamanian pennant the following season, and this time around you did participate in the Caribbean Classic. What do you remember about that tournament?

I played in the [1958] Caribbean Series in San Juan, after we won the pennant in Panama. The ballpark was always packed, every game. The team stayed at a hotel very close to the ballpark, because we walked [to the games]. The fans were great fans, not rowdy or trouble-making. They knew their game, baseball. I remember we faced Juan Pizarro, he was a very hard thrower. Pizarro pitched a one or a two-hitter against us. Struck out, I don't know how many. I had one of the hits. What is funny, is, later on, we [Pirates] signed Pizarro. When Pizarro joined our club, I told him I was one of the guys that stroked a hit off him that day. He started laughing. Thought that was funny.

North American players lined up for a group shot following their arrival in Panama City. Tony Bartirome is in the front, wearing a jacket and dark tie with sunglasses. Evans Killeen is second from left. Fourth from left, holding jacket, is Dutch Romberger, next to Billy Schantz (dark jacket). Eli Grba, wearing a checkered short-sleeve shirt, is in the middle of the group (courtesy T. Baritrome).

Who were Panamanian League's best players?

What a player Héctor López was. All I did was play against him, except for that one Caribbean Series when we were teammates. I did not know him that well, but he could really play. Héctor López was the best player I saw there. Humberto Robinson. He was a side-winder. An under-armer, almost like Kent Tekulve. I was very lucky against him. I had success. I remember the Osorio brothers. Two brothers that played on different teams in the league. One was a power-hitting first baseman, Elías Osorio. The other, was a pitcher [Alberto]. There was a left-hander named Vibert Clarke, who was good. George Brunet was another good left-hander.

What did you do for fun in Panama?

We would go up to the Canal Zone. They had swimming pools and club-houses, that is how we spent our days off. There was great nightlife in Panama, especially for a kid my age. They had a place called the *Okay Amigo*, it was a nightclub. We used to go there quite often. That was in Panama City.

The national stadium in Panama, what do you remember about it?

The stadium was pretty typical of all the stadiums I had played in when I played in the International League. It was a big stadium. They used it for track meets and other kind of sports. The clubhouses of the stadium were like the minor leagues, except the plumbing was not as good. I remember the shower room. They had about three shower heads, and two of them did not work. Most of the time, we dressed in the hotel. Sometimes we would shower after the game, but most of the time we would hop on the bus and come back to the hotel and shower there. All our games were played in Panama City, except one game we would fly up — about three hundred miles from Panama City — to the city of Davíd. That is where Omar Moreno was from. He probably had not been born yet. But that is where he was scouted. I always wondered who the heck would go that far up and over the jungle to see a baseball game?

You had quite a game in one of those trips to Davíd. Enough to get you a citation in The Sporting News.

We went up to Davíd, once, it was on a Sunday. We were supposed to play at one o'clock in the afternoon. We left Panama City at about seven in the morning. The night before I had a couple of drinks too many. Our owner, a wonderful man named Gramas, he received word that I had been out drinking the previous night. He told me, "I am very disappointed in you. This is a very big game for us." I just said, "I am sorry." We started the game, and I led off and I hit a line drive down the right field line — I was an opposite field hitter so the right fielder had me shaded to left. He had a long way to run. The right fielder dove and made a sensational catch. I said, boy, am I in for a tough one today. It was hot. The game went extra innings and I came up six more times and went six-for-six, and we won.

The owner comes up to me after the game and says, "I want you to go out drinking every night before a game."

Jerry Davie

Jerry Davie manages a mobile home park in Central Florida with his wife of eleven years, Priscilla. More than half a century ago, he pitched in the winter leagues of Panama and Puerto Rico. Starting in the winter of 1955, Davie hurled three consecutive seasons from the mounds of the Isthmus country and then closed out his off-season playing in 1958-59 with the Mayagüez Indios. The right-hander pitched in the Caribbean Series of 1956 and 1958. In the latter series, Davie had the misfortune of pairing up against Juan Pizarro in the game in which the nearly unhittable Pizarro set a series' record for strikeouts.

In 1959, Davie realized his major league dream with the Detroit Tigers, his hometown team.

You are from the Midwest?

I am from Detroit. I was the youngest of nine children.

Was baseball always in your blood?

My parents told me I was playing baseball before I could walk.

Who were the players you most followed?

Ted Williams, George Kell.

You signed with your hometown team.

Lou D'Annunzio, Tigers' scout, he had talked to me. When I graduated from high school, he offered me a contract and I accepted. I played at Jamestown, New York, in the PONY League; my first year was 1952. I went to Korea with the Army in '53 and '54. I lost two years.

How did you end up playing in Panama?

In '55, I do not think I even knew there was winter ball. I received a telegram from Panama asking me if I wanted to play. It was from the Chesterfield club. It was from the general manager. I cannot think of his name. There were not any real jobs around, so I went down.

I had an attack of appendicitis. I cannot remember if the season had started. At the time, the president of the University of Panama, Díaz, I think his name was, operated on me. Chesterfield told me they were going to release me and send me back to the states. The manager of Spur Cola, Leon Kellman,

The Carta Vieja Yankees at the 1958 Caribbean Series in San Juan. Jerry Davie is kneeling fifth from left. On either side of Davie is a hatless Tony Bartirome and Humberto Robinson. Standing at the far right is Héctor López (courtesy T. Bartirome).

an old time black ballplayer, he asked me if I would play with them. They [team] were all black. I told him, yeah, I wanted to play ball. I was the only white person on that team. John Glenn was on our team, and Héctor López. I later played against Héctor the majors. I was treated well. There was no difference to us in our skin color.

Where did you stay?

We lived out in, they called it Chinatown. Bill Queen, from the Braves' organization, and his wife and myself shared a home. I remember the house being near the golf course. Sometime during that season I saw Arnold Palmer playing on that golf course. We would barbeque around the house. But I also liked the [native] food real well. I enjoyed living in Panama.

How were the Panamanian fans?

The fans were tremendous. We only played about three games a week, but we worked out almost every day at the stadium. We had to take a bus to get to the stadium. The fans were quite a ways from the field. Remember that song "Sherri Baby?" The natives used to sing it, "Jerry Davie." They would refer to me through that song. [Laughs.] I was kind of fortunate. I had a pretty good record. The fans were behind me one hundred per cent.

I remember we had a second baseman. A native player. He had gotten into trouble with the law, and had served some jail time. I cannot remember his name. But the fans did not trust him. He made an error once that cost us the ball game. He spent that night at the stadium. He was afraid to leave, because the fans were waiting for him.

And the stadium, the facilities inside?

The clubhouses were nothing to brag about. Kind of dark. Concrete or cement block.

What players do you recall from your first season?

Humberto Robinson had gone up with the Braves, part of 1955. He threw side arm. He had a reputation for being mean out there. Wally Burnette was in the Kansas City organization. Clyde Parris, sure. Earlier that year, Parris was tearing up the International League in hitting. Parris was a third baseman. Parris was a bad ball hitter; he loved the ball up around his eyes. We played some games at Colón in the Canal Zone. All I remember was that left field was far away.

When you returned to Panama, you played with another team.

That second year — I was with my wife — we stayed at a hotel. I remember it was hot. There was no air conditioning. We were near the army base and they would let us go in there and use the pool. I was with Carta Vieja that season. Bill Shantz was our manager.

I spoke with a teammate of yours, Tony Bartirome.

I played with Tony. He was on that team. Tony was a whale of a ballplayer. He was not that big, but he could do anything a big guy could. Tony became the trainer for the Pirates. Tony used to love my son. In Panama, Tony would take Brad all over, and to the movies.

Around that same time, the minor leagues also provided you with more international exposure.

I went to Cuba when I was in the International League with Buffalo. That stadium was excellent. There was a lot of talent there. They took their ball seriously in Cuba. The fans lived for the game. We stayed at a hotel — the Nacional? I was amazed at the hotel itself. It was fabulous. It was the best one I had ever stayed in.

You were able to compete in two Caribbean Series tournaments with Panamanian squads. Although you pitched sparingly in both, in the 1958 Series, you were on the losing end of one of the most dominating pitching exhibi-

tions in Series history when Juan Pizarro shut out Carta Vieja and struck out 17 batters.

I do not remember too much about the [Pizzaro] game. Puerto Rico had quite a team. I remember there was a bad call in one game. We were not playing. We were watching. An umpire made a bad call and the fans threw chairs on the field and everything else. I cannot remember the outcome, but I know it was a mess. I remember we kind of played above our ability. Because these other teams were really loaded. The big name players went to Cuba, Puerto Rico and Venezuela.

You spent your fourth and final winter season, playing in Puerto Rico.

The next winter, I played for Mayagüez in Puerto Rico. Bill Adair was our manager. Detroit had an affiliation with Mayagüez. The organization sent four players— myself, Charley Lau, Pete Burnside and Ken Walters. We lived at a hotel in Mayagüez. We were far from the rest of the league. The closest other team was in Ponce. San Juan and Caguas was an eight-hour bus ride, over the mountains, two-lane highway. It was an all-day affair when we went over there.

I remember we played in Caguas once and we beat them. The fans kicked dirt through small openings right outside the stadium area of the players' shower room. It became all muddy in that shower room.

Mayagüez lost a contentious playoff series against Santurce that year. One game, in particular, had plenty of fireworks.

We played Santurce in the playoffs on a Sunday afternoon in Mayagüez. Rubén Gómez did not ride the bus. Rubén drove his Corvette to away games. Our centerfielder, Joe Christopher, was hit in the head by a pitch thrown by Gómez. Christopher had to leave the game. Fortunately, Christopher had on one of the few helmets that they used back then. That beaning upset the fans. Later, Orlando Cepeda of Santurce, went over to catch a pop up near the first base stands. I was not playing that day. I was coaching at first base. Cepeda drifted over and he was bombarded with oranges and bottles, and he shied away and missed the ball. In anger, Cepeda picked up the ball that had dropped near him and he threw it into the stands. The ball ricocheted off a pole and hit a young boy and knocked out the boy's front teeth. The fans really got rowdy then. The umpires cleared the field. They tried to restart the game, but could not. The fans had gotten too far out of control. I think they [fans] totaled Gómez' Corvette. The police had to escort Santurce's players out of the park. There was only one road leading out of town. Jackie Brandt played for Santurce. Brandt snuck down among the baggage storage on the bus, and rode the bus out of town that way.

Who were the best winter league players you saw?

In Panama, it was Héctor López. The best pitcher was Humberto Robinson. He had the reputation of being hard to beat. In Puerto Rico, Roberto Clemente. It was between him and Orlando Cepeda. Cepeda was a hitter like the first baseman of Detroit now, Cabrera. Cepeda could hit to right with power; he could hit deep to left, depending on where the pitch was. Rubén Gómez was the best pitcher.

Do you have any parting remembrances?

When we visited San Juan, we would stay at a tremendous hotel. Right on the ocean. Very close to the ballpark. At night you could see the shark fins as they came in closer to shore, chasing bait. Beautiful beaches. I was in awe pretty much. I had never experienced the game the way it was in Latin America. Some of my better days were spent playing winter ball. It was quite a time.

We never made enough money in the minors where we could take the winter off. I had a couple of jobs that I quit just so I could play winter ball.

Dave Roberts

Dave Roberts shared the recollections of his young rise through the baseball ranks of his own country's amateur and professional winter leagues. Born in Panama City, Panama, Roberts played a handful of seasons in Panama, as well as one season in Puerto Rico and several in Venezuela during the 1960s. Roberts was a 19-year-old starry-eyed rookie for the 1952-53 Chesterfield Smokers, a team which eked out the pennant by one game (thanks to a game-winning hit by Roberts) and then traveled to Havana to play in the Caribbean Series — won by a star-studded Santurce Crabbers squad.

Roberts co-wrote an autobiography, A Baseball Odyssey, *published in 1999. It was aptly titled, for over a span of 22 years, Roberts showcased his baseball abilities in numerous leagues throughout two hemispheres. The father of four excelled in Japan for six and a half years, becoming the first North American player to smack forty homers in one season (1968). Including the minor leagues and Japan, Roberts belted over 420 home runs.*

The infielder/outfielder reached the big leagues in 1962 with the Houston Colt .45s, wrapping up his big league career a few seasons later with the Pittsburgh Pirates.

You are a native of Panama?

I was raised in the Panama Canal Zone. I went to school in the Canal Zone and lived in Panama City. There were nine of us in the family. My mom and dad were great parents. They brought us up to respect our elders. We had a very religious background.

How were you first introduced to the game?

My older brother played baseball. Everything he did I wanted to do. I started playing sandlot ball.

Was there any special player you looked up to?

Jackie Robinson was the whole scope growing up. When I saw him play with the Montreal team in Panama, I knew I wanted to be a ballplayer. I knew nothing about the job Jackie was being prepared for at the time. He was quite a ballplayer. He was my inspiration from the start.

Did anyone guide or instruct you on how to play the game when you were young?

The person who really showed me the way, whom I regard as my mentor, was Alonso Brathwaite. I saw him play. He did everything I thought a ballplayer should do. I just wish I could have thrown right-handed. I would have been a second baseman just like him.

You started out in amateur ball?

Chet Brewer saw me play in the amateur league in Panama and signed me to my first pro contract. The year Chet saw me I was a junior in high school, and I tore up the league. My mom signed the contract because I was too young.

You had a memorable a rookie season in the Panamanian Winter League.

Chesterfield was my first pro team [in Panama]. The manager was Sanford Graham. In the [pennant] clincher I hit a home run. That was the winning run. I think we won 1–0 or 2–0.

Tell me about the Caribbean Series.

We went to Cuba to play in the [1953] Caribbean Series. Oh, man, when I reached that Series, it was like, are you kidding me? I was seeing guys I had read about in *The Pittsburgh Courier* that we used to get when I was a kid that were weeks and months old.

I am talking about guys like Willard Brown, and Thurman and Rubén Gómez. These were big time ballplayers. Cuba had Amorós and Formental. Gee Willikers, it was quite a Series.

Of course, being a rookie, I did not start. Then I pinch-hit against Rubén Gómez and smacked a base hit. So that got me in the ballgame the next day, against Cuba. I hit two doubles off Mario Picone. Right after that, Joe Cambria tried to sign me, but I was already signed. I wish I had not been. I probably would have made it to the Senators in another couple of years. I had signed and played in Porterville, California in the Southwest International League that summer, my first year in North American ball. Chet Brewer had signed me to play there.

Those guys [Santurce] pounded us pretty good. I remember the stadium, El Cerro, or something like that, there was a clock in left center. In pregame meetings, they had said to be careful with Rubén Gómez, he is a pretty good hitter. And Gómez hit a ball out by the clock for a home run. [Chuckles.] That Puerto Rican team was very impressive. They had Victor Pellot Power, Junior Gilliam, Canena Márquez, Willard Brown and Bob Thurman. They were big time.

I was so taken by it all, I cannot remember any ceremonies from the Games. The biggest thrill I had was when we were in the hotel, and the players were all milling around the lobby. I remember talking with Piper Davis, he played with Venezuela. And then *El Inmortal* came in. And I said, my goodness, is that really him? The players got a kick out of me, the way I behaved. I was just a kid. But I knew who *he* was. I knew him from talking to Chet Brewer. Chet said he would pitch one day and beat you and then the next day he would play shortstop and kill you with a couple of triples. When he came in it was just a thrill to see that man. I just watched him. Are you kidding? I could not meet him. I just basked in his vapor trail. In his presence. Clyde Parris told me, hey Dave, you are a pro player now. You are just like everybody else. But I was a fan before I was a player.

Other guys were hitting nightclubs and other spots in Havana. But not me. I was, like I said, just a kid with religious feelings. I stayed close to home. Bobby Prescott was my roommate and we hung out together. Santurce won the Series. After that first year, reality would set in. It was not that easy [to win].

Leon Kellman was a well-known native player, who was also a successful manager.

I played two years for Leon Kellman and both years produced championship ball clubs. Kellman had a good sense of leadership. His presence was very commanding. A little bit on the no-nonsense side. Kellman's handling of the pitchers was his forte. That is probably where he will be remembered, because he had some pitchers that threw to him who were very successful: Vibert Clarke, Scantlebury, Andrés Alonso.

You have named three very good Panamanian pitchers. Scantlebury may be the most recognized outside of Panama.

Pat Scantlebury was an extraordinary pitcher. A good hitter, good fielder. He dominated the pro league when I was kid. Pat was one of the greats. He was among the reinforcements that we took to Havana.

There was also, of course, Humberto Robinson and Alberto Osorio.

Humberto Robinson was our best pitcher. We lost Humberto last year. He passed away. Humberto came from the side and his ball moved everywhere. Alberto Osorio was a fine pitcher. Very dependable. A great human being, and a very nice man. He threw just under 90. His control was extraordinary.

As far as everyday players, Clyde Parris was considered a star.

I spoke to Clyde about three days ago. He was by far the best third baseman Panama has produced. He should have been given a shot to play in the big leagues, but there were too many guys ahead of him in the Brooklyn minor league chain. Clyde did not get a shot, which was a shame. He was a .300 hitter and batting champion several times over. A very good teammate, and somebody that always showed up to play.

Three years after your first Caribbean Series, you received another opportunity to play under the same international spotlight.

We did not win again until 1955-56. The Caribbean Series was in Panama that year. We had no chance against Cienfuegos. They were a great ball club. I made several pinch-hitting appearances, that is all. I remember going up to try and hit against Camilo Pascual. And he threw me a couple of curveballs. Not having played much that winter, I was completely overmatched. Héctor López was on that team. You knew he was going to be something special. Héctor swung the bat real well. If he had a deficiency, it was, sometimes, lapses in the field. Héctor was going to be a big league ballplayer, given the chance.

Soon, you left Panama.

I moved away from that scene after the '56-57 season. I returned in '60-61 as an imported ballplayer.

After hitting a home run for Chesterfield, Dave Roberts trots home under the scrutinizing eye of the umpire (courtesy D. Roberts).

When I found out the players from America were making more money [than the natives], I wanted to play outside of Panama. It worked to my benefit. I was later able to command higher salaries as a result, in Venezuela and Puerto Rico and Mexico. Cerveza Balboa wanted me and they had to pay the extra money to get me. In Mexico, I played with Córdoba, in the winter league. I saw Roberto Ávila. Felipe Montemayor. Vinicio García. The food? Everything was hot.

Was the ownership in Panama committed to presenting a good product on the field?

The best owner in Panama was Carlos Eleta. He owned Chesterfield. Eleta was one of the greatest men I have ever met in my entire life. He owned all the tobacco concessions in Panama. Carlos Eleta was a player's owner, but the people around him discouraged him from being so. His subordinates would tell him, you do not have to pay the ballplayers this much, I will take care of it.

Tell me about your return in 1960.

The 1960-61 Cerveza Balboa team was probably the best team I played for in Panama. We had a great ball club. Héctor was on that team, Bob Perry. Milt Smith. Charlie White. Winston Brown. I played with Winston, also, in the Texas League; he was the ace of our staff. They said he had control problems. Winston was one of the great pitchers ever to play in Panama. He should have had a shot at the big leagues.

The Caribbean Series did not take place that season because of the political change in Cuba. A new tournament tried to keep the spirit of the international competition alive. It was held in Caracas.

Estadio Universitario in Venezuela. I came to know it much better after the [1961] Inter-American Series, because of the five years I spent playing winter ball for La Guaira, the Sharks. I played for them for three years and two years in Barquisimeto. People loved me in Venezuela. I played well. In Latin America, if you play well, they will bring you back. And they kept bringing me back to Venezuela every year. The stadium was built for baseball. It belonged to the University of Caracas. I loved the country. The people were great.

I have not inquired about the stadium in Panama.

Olympic Stadium in Panama was built for the Central American Games. It had a track. The track was always there. For baseball they would symmetrically partition the field. There was a fence before the regular stadium wall in right field. In my career, a Cuban guy, Eddie Filo and myself were the only players to hit a home run over that wall in right field. A pretty good poke. I did it my rookie year, I hit two that night and one of them went "out of the stadium." I cannot remember the pitcher's name, but I can still see him right now in my mind. I cannot put a name to his face, but he pitched for Cervecería.

The clubhouses were makeshift. The stadium was not designed with baseball totally in mind. That was one thing I thought should have been addressed during the years that I played. But you go along, and nobody says you can do this and nobody spends any money to make things any better. I thought they should have had better clubhouses.

Was there strong fan support?

We had a good following. We were a favorite team. We had players who were very popular. Frank Austin, our shortstop and captain, was probably the most popular player in the whole league at the time. The fan base, I think should have been a lot more. But for some reason, in Panama, it was a unique situation. It was a short season. By the time people developed an interest, the season was over.

It was a big deal when the season started. I remember the president [of the country] throwing out the first ball every year. It was a big thing. Like I said, it was a short season. So when the new season started, they would not have had baseball for seven or eight months; the fans were really ready to get things going again. They tried to enhance the economy and fan base of the Canal Zone with games over there. I remember Balboa Stadium because as a boy we used to shag balls there and pick up a couple of bucks. It was something my buddy and I did. The league even went into the interior later on. To David and Aguadulce.

Carta Vieja brought the white fans from the Canal Zone. Carta Vieja was as good as the Panamanian teams, Chesterfield and Spur Cola. There was a division because of the way the Panama Canal started out. There was a division between the laborers and those in charge of the jobs and job sites. It trickled down to living quarters, schooling, stores, commissaries, the whole bit. It divided communities. It was really a situation that deserves an extraordinary sociological study in itself, a great one. I knew as kid, when I moved to the Canal Zone that it was better than being in the city. But there were barriers that I had to adhere to. My folks made sure that I understood, that there were areas that we could go and areas we could not go. The Canal Zone was run like the southern part of the United States. The people were aware of who would go into their neighborhoods and for how long. If you were a laborer or tradesman, you got your job done and vacated. There were schools for whites and schools for kids whose parents worked in the Canal Zone. Panama

City was totally different. Everyone was the same, with the exception of those who had money. It was a money thing there. And there were quite a few people who had money, even some of color.

Did you encounter any problems?

The only problem I personally had was when I was a kid growing up in the community called Gamboa. The Armed Forces radio station sponsored an essay contest for all the kids in junior high — 100 words or less — and the topic was "Why I Like Baseball." I turned in the best essay, and then the radio station tried to say that the black community was not included. But the AFL-CIO got involved, and the radio station backed down and I was declared the winner of the contest. I won a $20 professional baseball glove. That was big time then.

Who was the best player and pitcher?

A tossup between Clyde Parris and Héctor López. Humberto was great. He was always up for the challenge. The game you had to win.

Any closing comments?

I used to get guff from Archie *"Terremoto"* Brathwaite, one of the best hitters Panama ever produced. But it was in a light manner. I think he just wanted me to do better. Archie provided me with guidance on things like my contract, on acting like a pro, dressing like a pro.

It was great time for a kid to break in.

Dick Tracewski

Dick Tracewski had two turns of winter league seasoning before establishing a major league career as a versatile infielder. The eight-year big league veteran and long-time coach of the Detroit Tigers spent the 1957-58 and 1960-61 off-seasons in Colombia and Panama, respectively.

A Brooklyn Dodgers draftee, Tracewski was part of three world championship squads during the 1960s — two in Los Angeles and one with the Tigers in Detroit.

Married to wife Dolores for 43 years, Tracewski is "living quietly and peacefully," in close proximity to his place of birth. A pleasant-sounding man, Tracewski is extremely proud of his more than three decades of accrued time on major league ball fields.

Where are you from originally?

It was a little town named Eynon, in northeastern Pennsylvania. I was one of five. I had two brothers and two sisters. I was the baby.

And baseball, when did it capture your fancy?

I just loved the game. I played in high school. I played it pretty well. Next thing I know professional people were scouting me, and I ended up signing with the Brooklyn Dodgers. [One scout] Every time he came to see me play it rained, so he ended up sending me and my father to Ebbets Field. And we stayed in Brooklyn and we worked out with the big club. I was 18. It was a thrill to see Jackie Robinson and Gil Hodges. Just to be in Ebbets Field and downtown Brooklyn, it was fun.

I spent seven years in the minors, and two years in the service.

You played in Colombia and Panama, one season, each.

Colombia and Panama were the lower classifications as far as winter ball was concerned. Puerto Rico, Cuba, Dominican Republic, that was where the major leaguers played. The guys that were on the cusp of major league-playing would go to Panama and to Colombia. Panama was very Americanized. Colombia was not. It was a fabulous country; I enjoyed Colombia very much, but it was not Americanized.

I would like to concentrate on Panama.

In Panama, I lived in the Canal Zone, at Fort Clayton, which was an army base. It was fun. We spent the holidays at Fort Clayton; it was different.

Dick Tracewski with the Dodgers, after their move west.

Of course, I had spent holidays in Colombia. But living at Fort Clayton, we had the run of the Fort. We would play golf there. We lived at the hospital on the top floor. We ate at the Officers' Club and the NCO clubs.

Tell me about your team.

Rube Walker was the manager. He came up with the Cubs and was traded to the Dodgers. He was Pee Wee Reese's roommate. Rube managed a long time in the Dodgers' organization. I played for Rube in Atlanta, in the minor leagues. That is pretty much how I ended up going to Panama. Rube was going to Panama, and asked if I would like to come and play shortstop for him? I said sure. And that is how it happened. And then I hurt my knee in Panama. I was lucky because it was a month before I had to report to the Dodgers. That was my first year on a major league roster. I had time to heal up. Not totally, but I was able to play afterward.

What about the players in the league?

We had Curt Roberts and Ken Roe. Jim Williams. Jim Koranda. They were all good high minor league talent. Bob Perry was a tall, thin, very talented player in the San Francisco Giants' organization. Curt Roberts played second base for us. He was a heavy-set player. He wore glasses. If you ever looked at Roberts, you would think he was a librarian. But he could really play. Bobby Prescott was a native player. Winston Brown. Though I cannot remember who Brown played for. The teams had sponsors. I played for Comercios. That was a group of businesses.

The main baseball venue was Estadio Nacional in Panama City.

We played in one ballpark, and we drew like hell. The playing surface was good. We played in a town on the other side of the Isthmus, Colón — that is where I was hurt, as matter of fact. We used to play Sunday games over there. There were a lot of Panamanian youths that played winter ball.

How did the fans treat you?

The fans were very rabid. They came on like gangbusters. When we played in Panama City, the stands were full. It was a good experience and I enjoyed it. I was there the better part of two months and then I hurt my knee and had to go home.

THE PUERTO RICAN WINTER LEAGUE

Pete Burnside

During the 1950s, chances for winter training were greater for a youthful property of the New York Giants than for that of most other teams. And that training was usually in Puerto Rico or the Dominican Republic. Pete Burnside experienced both countries as a Horace Stoneham protégé. Burnside received his Caribbean League indoctrination in 1954-55 with the storied Santurce Crabbers, a team for which Burnside, a left-handed pitcher, admittedly did not see much action.

A heavy minor league workload the following summer dissuaded Burnside to throw any more that year. But in the winter of 1956, a new tropic destination awaited the port-side hurler, playing in the Dominican Republic. Burnside was an integral pitching staff part of the championship-winning Escogido Lions, leading the league in ERA (1.77) and strikeouts (109).

By 1958, Burnside had seen brief action in the major leagues with the Giants and that winter he returned to Puerto Rico for the first of two final winter campaigns — both with the Mayagüez Indians. In February, 1959, after his Mayagüez team was eliminated in their contentious playoffs, the lefty was contracted by the Licey Tigres of the Dominican Winter League to pitch for its club in the island's post-season square-off. Burnside helped the Tigers engineer an upset championship victory over Escogido. The 28-year-old southpaw tossed the thrilling 3–2 Tigers' victory in the ninth and deciding game of the championship series. During our interview, the former hurler revealed an unsettling occurrence from earlier in that final series, involving Héctor Trujillo and a Licey player.

During his 21-year-long professional career, Burnside carved out eight seasons in the big leagues with four different franchises, and also pitched two years in Japan.

A married man of 46 years, Pete and wife Suzette have three offspring and eight grandchildren. Two of the children are school teachers, and the only girl is a doctor.

You are from a big baseball hub in Chicago, aren't you?

I was born just outside of Chicago, in Evanston, Illinois, in 1930. I had one brother. I loved playing anything with a ball in it. I played with the guys in the neighborhood — all the games, touch football, basketball. In those days, they did not have Little League. We had to wait until high school for any organized sports. We would take the "L" and go down to see the Cubs' games. Larry French was a left-handed pitcher I liked. We did not see a lot of games, but we saw some.

I had a fairly good high school record, and was noticed by some scouts. I played in a Chicago all-star game at Wrigley Field. It was the suburban kids against the city kids. The Cubs were in town, and later I received a chance to work out with the Cubs' team.

I attended college at Dartmouth in Hanover, New Hampshire. I signed with the New York Giants after my freshman year. That was 1949. I was assigned to St. Cloud, Minnesota. My contract said that I could stay in college and pitch in the minors when school was out in the summer. That is what I did. I graduated in four years from Dartmouth. It was a liberal arts school; I was a history and sociology major.

There were not many college graduates playing winter ball.

My first year playing winter ball was 1954-55. Santurce, Puerto Rico. They say that was one the best winter league teams ever assembled. Willie Mays and Clemente. George Crowe. Clarkson. Thurman. [Bill] Greason, Sad Sam Jones and Rubén Gómez. I did not play an awful lot.

I became friends with Rubén Gómez. He was an avid fisherman. We went fishing every chance we could. Gómez, Hal Jeffcoat and myself. We would take out a boat, or we would fish from the reefs along the shore. We caught pompano and tarpon, mostly. Yellowtail, too. Rubén was one of the best all-around athletes I saw. He was a good pitcher, a good hitter. If he took up golf, he became a great golfer. I think he set world records in fish size caught.

I lived at the Gallardo Apartments. It was great. Don Zimmer and I roomed together. I played with him when he came to the Senators, also. Zimmer is a wonderful guy. He spent a lot of years in baseball, and I consider

Pete Burnside in the uniform of the signature franchise of the Puerto Rican Winter League (courtesy Mrs. Pedrín Zorilla).

him a good friend. Zimmer did not fish. There was a casino at the Condado Beach Hotel, down the street from where we were staying. It was a Vegas-style place. Sometimes after the games, Don and I would go there. Don spent more time in there than I did—he was better at gambling than I was. Don was married; I was not. But Don's wife was not with him. We also spent afternoons by the pool.

I did not hang out too much with Willie. They quartered us in different places. There were several black players on the team. That is the way they did it in those days. We lived in different areas. I lived in Santurce; the black players lived in San Juan. I did visit their apartment a few times. We went out to dinner. I was young at the time. They were all well-known players in the black leagues. Mays was the best all-around player I ever played with.

I loved the food. There was a lobster dish, served as a rice stew. That was my favorite. The food was great.

Sixto Escobar Stadium was a quaint stadium. I think it was named after a boxer.

Santurce had to cut its roster down for the Caribbean Series in Caracas. I was a fringe player, but Pedrín Zorilla, the owner of the team, took me down as the batting practice pitcher. So I was able to travel with the team, but I could not play. I was on the bench when Willie Mays hit that game-winning home run off Ramon Monzant. Right, Sam Jones was the winning pitcher for Santurce in that game. Zimmer hit a big home run in another game. They won the Series. I say "they" because I was not really part of it. I was lucky to be on the team. I was lucky the Giants had sent me down there.

During that Series, there was a dictatorship at the time in Venezuela. In the stadium in Caracas, there were soldiers with rifles. But we were never bothered. It was a big stadium, with that beautiful highway you came in on.

I pitched a lot of innings with Dallas in the Texas League in 1955. I was called up to the Giants after the season ended in Dallas, and received two starts in the Polo Grounds. I won my first major league game at the end of the season. Because of all the innings, I did not pitch that winter.

I pitched quite a bit, though, the following year, in the Dominican Republic. For the Red team [Escogido]. That was a good team. That was 1956-'57.

We lived in a hotel in Ciudad Trujillo. Stan Williams was there and Bob Schmidt. I remember my nickname. I was not the only one that rode a bicycle. Stan had one. Schmidt, the catcher, had one. I did not ride it everywhere. You had to be careful along the streets because of traffic.

I never had trouble with the food anywhere, even when I played in Japan. I always liked the food from other countries. Well, in Santo Domingo, I loved flan for dessert. They had good fruit. The fish was great, too.

We did not travel around too much in the Dominican. Trujillo was pretty strict at that time. We stayed pretty close [to home]. We would go to the Jaragua Hotel. Sit around the pool. The Juaragua was the hotel where Batista stayed when he was pushed out of Cuba by Castro, before he was exiled to Spain. I did some fishing in the Dominican, but not much.

The Alous were making a name for themselves at that time, especially eldest brother Felipe.

What a wonderful guy Felipe Alou was. He was strong. As I remember, I was older than he was. I would see Felipe jogging from town to the ballpark. He did not have a car and did not have a lot of money. Just a fine guy. A good ballplayer. The Giants sent him to the deep south, which must have been hard for him.

I pitched against Felipe the next winter — or two winters later [1958-59]. I was on the Blue team [Licey]. He hit as long a home run as was ever hit off me.

It was two winters later when you pitched for Licey. I wanted to ask you about that, about the unexpected playoff series win you helped engineer.

I had pitched for Mayagüez in Puerto Rico. I believe three of us — Joe Christopher, Elmo Plaskett and myself — came from Puerto Rico to the Dominican at the end of the season. We all went to the Blue team, and we won that big series [against Escogido]. That was a thrilling championship series. The Red team had mostly Giants' players. Ozzie Virgil was on that team. Ozzie spoke Spanish, of course, and he helped a lot of the U.S. players. That series was the last time I saw Felipe, because after that I moved over to the American League and he stayed in the National.

There was an incident in one game in that final series that I do not think has been written about much. Andre Rodgers was hit by a pitch, and there was scuffle on the field — you know, how the dugouts empty. Héctor Trujillo came out from the stands onto the field and slapped Andre Rodgers. This is the brother Trujillo; he had armed guards with him. We were scared to death. I suppose Trujillo thought that Rogers had started the fracas because he had gone after the pitcher in retaliation. Héctor Trujillo was a little man; Andre Rodgers was a big man. Rodgers never touched Trujillo, did not retaliate. Rodgers was removed for a pinch runner and refused to play after that. He was going to leave the country, but they stopped him at the airport. Rodgers' team, the Red team, their players were going to go home, too. They were not going to continue after what happened. The series was delayed. Then the players were talked into staying and the series continued. Rodgers also played.

It was a nine-game series, and we won the final game. What an exciting night that was. Our team drove around the city, it could have been on a bus.

Then we went to the [presidential] palace. We met Trujillo's sister — she was a fan of the Blue team, a big fan. At the palace, someone would come up to you and stuff bills in your pocket. At the end of the night, I ended up with four to five hundred RDs in my pocket. That was what the Dominican currency was called: RD. It was close to a 1–1 [exchange rate] with the U.S. dollar.

My last year in winter ball was '59-'60 in Puerto Rico. I roomed with Charlie Lau. *He* was a fisherman. Charlie and I would take a fishing boat out from Boqueron, which was in the Mayagüez area. I was still single, and Charlie had his family with him. All the players were kind to me during the holidays. And the natives.

[Chuckles.] Going over the mountains, that is what I remember about traveling from Mayagüez. We went to Ponce and Caguas. San Juan, of course.

You know, hearing all those names you have mentioned, you have brought back such memories ... we were all young and healthy. It was a great, great experience. I sure would like to be young and do it all over again. I loved every minute of it.

Cot Deal

Ellis "Cot" Deal had celebrated his 88th birthday the month before I first contacted him. Deal owned an email account, which I found interesting for a person of his years. (Through that email, Deal sent me an interesting story about an incident that occurred during a three-game series in Havana, while he was the manager of Triple-A Rochester.) Deal was very agreeable about sharing his experiences in winter baseball, in which he famously won over a foreign legion of baseball followers — something difficult for any outsider to do without any kind of reputation preceding him. Deal's elevated nickname in his winter home-base of Puerto Rico grew from the quality of his play and the gained status as a special imported player: "Mr. Reinforcement."

Deal was a pitcher in the St. Louis Cardinals' organization when he was enticed to play winter ball in 1950. His first and most-beloved team was the San Juan Senators. In his second winter, he was traded to the Caguas Criollos. But Deal excelled enough with Caguas for league champion San Juan to add him as a roster supplement when the team traveled to Panama to play in the 1952 Caribbean Series. Deal's memory of that series was all but erased. Perhaps San Juan's 0–5–1 record in that Caribbean tournament had something subconsciously to do with it. The former pitcher's recollection of the Caribbean Series the following year was much better. The Santurce Crabbers (the team Deal reinforced) were

the Caribbean Series champion of 1953. Prior to his being added by San-
turce to play in his second Caribbean Classic, the sterling import had
finished an MVP season with the Senators, who had secured his services
for his third winter campaign. Deal's award was well deserved. An all-
purpose player in the winter league, Deal finished third in the league that
season in wins with 11, second in ERA at 1.85 and tied for fourth in strike-
outs (70). Cot also led the loop in RBIs with 49!

Shortly into his fourth winter season, the Cardinals pulled their player
back to the States to rest for spring training, months away. It was the end
of Cot Deal's winter playing career, though Deal would later return to
Puerto Rico to manage San Juan.

Throughout our interview, Deal's ever-present Oklahoma drawl never
failed to languish a bit more as it intoned with the genuine fondness he
felt for the people of Puerto Rico.

Where were you born?

I was born in Oklahoma and raised in Oklahoma and I live in Oklahoma today.

What about your family?

Growing up in our family there were three boys and a girl. It was tough growing up [during the Depression] but nobody else had any money, either. I have been married, it is going to be, 68 years to my childhood sweetheart Katie. We had two boys and a girl. They are not boys and girls anymore, but that is it.

Who or what were your baseball influences?

I played baseball because of my father.

How was your nickname derived?

When I was a little kid and I had hair, they called me Cotton Top. Somebody shortened it to Cot, and it stayed with me, through high school, with the teachers, even.

How did your winter league journey begin?

The manager that had been my manager at Columbus in the International League, was hired to be the manager of San Juan, and he wanted me to go with him, so I went with him. That was Rollie Hemsley. The winter league teams were allowed six imports at that time. They arranged for our kids to go to school down there and things worked out beautifully. It was good liberal education for them. In the schools, they taught in English and in Spanish. My kids picked up a little bit of Spanish. It was a great experience. I would not have gone without my family. That goes for all the years I played in Puerto Rico.

The day I arrived in San Juan, I was taken to the office of Mr. Cobián [San Juan team owner]. Rollie was there with me, of course, and there was the introduction and our meeting, and finally Mr. Cobián said to me, "You know, we play Santurce tonight, I do not suppose you can pitch?" I said, "Give me the ball." So I got the ball and Santurce beat me, I think, 2–1. But I immediately became a favorite of the fans because they knew I had arrived that very day. I became one of them. I became part of the family.

I know San Juan regretted moving you to Caguas the following winter, but at least they recognized their mistake and added you to their Caribbean Series roster. The 1952 CS produced the only no-hitter in its history, so far. Habana's Tommy Fine tossed it.

I do not know why I was traded to Caguas the following winter. I do not know how teams make trades, but they did. Luis Olmo was my manager, and a very good friend. I do not remember the [1952] Caribbean Series in Panama. Tommy Fine was also a good friend. I do not remember his no-hitter, I am sorry to say.

You hooked up once against Rubén Gómez in a 15-inning pitcher's duel.

I do not remember that game against Rubén Gómez. You say he and I *both* pitched 15 innings? I pitched a 20-inning game one time in Columbus. You see, they never had to take me out for a pinch-hitter. We kept playing, and finally we won it. Rubén had a nickname, like the rest of us did; he was Santurce's big gun, outside of Willard Brown.

That is a name not many winter league pitchers like to recall.

I remember facing Willard Brown. They called him, "*Ese Hombre*" and me, they called, "Mr. *Refuerzo*."

The San Juan club held a night in your honor.

How could I ever forget "Ellis Cot Deal Night?" My wife and children were there. The boy, Randy, had a uniform on, a St. Louis Cardinals uniform. Randy went to the games and he served as bat boy, and it was a very big thing for him. He is now a college professor, a speech pathologist. That night, the San Juan team gave me the Puerto Rican flag and they gave me a new car. And retired my number. I hope nobody is wearing old *numero ocho* now. The car was a DeSoto. I picked it up in New York. What a night that was...

Did playing in the off-season give you any type of edge when spring training came around?

Playing in the winter leagues did not help me as far as my big league career. The thing of it was that in my first big league spring training I hurt my arm and never fully recovered from it. I was able to get by with my arm, but not well enough to stay in the big leagues. I did play well in the winter leagues, but I was just not able to stay with it in the big leagues.

The San Juan Senators at the 1952 Caribbean Series in Panama City. The team had a disappointingly poor showing, failing to win a game. Cot Deal is shown bottom row, fourth from left. Other team notables: Luis Arroyo, bottom row, far left, followed by Charlie Gorin, who did not pitch in the Series due to injury. Middle row far left, Luis Olmo, next to Pantalones Santiago. Nino Escalera is fourth from left in the same row.

Santurce won the Caribbean Series of 1953 in Havana. You were added to the team from San Juan. The pivotal game in that Series occurred when Santurce rallied to score three runs in the bottom of the ninth inning to beat Habana, 6–5.

I do remember the [1953] Caribbean Series in Havana. Two guys that were instrumental in the game you mention were Rubén Gómez and Cot Deal. I will never forget the two-out double I hit to start the rally. I still have a picture of it in my mind today. The Cuban fans hooted and hollered and made fun of the Puerto Ricans because they had to use their pitcher to bat — me. A couple of our dear friends from Puerto Rico — we had a lot of good friends in Puerto Rico — the Carrións, owners of Banco Popular, flew to Havana for the Series. Joe and Lety. We went to the *Tropicana*, known to be the finest nightclub in the world. We loved our time in Havana. We were there one week. My wife accompanied me, of course. It was just great. We did not go back to Puerto Rico for all the hoopla. One of my brothers had flown to Puerto Rico and flew our two kids back home, and we had promised that as soon as we could we would come straight home. We still have such fond memories of it all.

I have a lot of memories of Havana Stadium because I managed Rochester in the International League and at that time a team from Havana was in the International League.

Your winter league career nearly ended after three seasons.

The only way the Cardinals would let me go back to winter ball in 1953 was if I would leave [at an appointed time] and that is what I had to do. I hit a home run off Bob Buhl in my last game. I faced Henry Aaron that season whenever we faced Caguas, and when I came back the next year in spring training, I said there is a kid that is going to be playing for the Braves this year that might lead the league in hitting. You could tell then that Aaron was a great one.

Puerto Rico had many fine players. Who would you rank at the top of the hitters and pitchers' lists?

The best hitter I saw was Willard Brown, "*Ese Hombre.*" He should have been in the big leagues, but he really did not go after it like he should have. Brown did not care that much about it. He was quite a guy, a likeable guy. He did not hustle like they [the fans] thought he should. Brown hardly got in and out to the outfield. But he was a good outfielder. Gómez was the best pitcher.

What did you like more, pitching or position playing?

I enjoyed pitching and playing the field. Did not have a preference. I enjoyed doing both. I just enjoyed the game.

Nino Escalera

A year before the Caribbean Series was conceived, Nino Escalera broke into professional baseball with the San Juan Senators. From that first 1947-48 season, Escalera played 16 consecutive campaigns with the same franchise and then one final season with Caguas. In Puerto Rico, Escalera was dubbed "El Caballero de la Inicial" ("The Gentleman of the Gateway"), because of his demeanor and because he had never been thrown out of a game. (That streak came to an end in 1960, when he suffered his first ever ejection.)

Like most all Caribbean players, Saturnino Escalera played baseball year-round. The first baseman/outfielder began his minor league career in 1949 in the Colonial League and, as a Cincinnati Reds' designate, played several seasons with the Cuban Sugar Kings during the following decade. In 1954, Escalera became the first black player to wear the uniform of the Cincinnati Reds. In his initial plate appearance, the rookie singled against Lew Burdette of the Milwaukee Braves at County Stadium.

After his playing days concluded, Escalera, a father of four, was a scout for nearly three decades, first for the New York Mets and then the San

Francisco Giants. Among Escalera's signees were major league veterans Jerry Morales, Ed Figueroa, Benny Ayala, José Oquendo and Juan Berenguer.

You are a native of San Juan.

I was born in Santurce, *calle Eloisa*, December 1, 1929. I had eleven brothers and sisters.

When was your first indoctrination to the game?

I started playing baseball on the streets with tennis balls and broom sticks. It was a poor neighborhood. There was at least one radio per family. We listened to league games.

Who were the players from those days that caught your attention?

I remember Satchel Paige, Leon Day. In the early fifties, white North American players started coming down.

Did baseball come naturally for you?

I played youth baseball, 8–14 years old, starting in 1940. Later, I played on the Miramar Lions, a sort of youth team of "future stars." I traveled to play in an amateur tournament in Cartagena, Colombia, and was named top player in the tournament. Right after that, in 1947, I signed my first pro contract with San Juan. An executive/scout with San Juan, he sold insurance, actually, signed me. I was signed to organized baseball on the recommendation of Pedrín Zorilla and a sportswriter, Santiago Llorens. That was 1949.

Pedrín Zorilla. That is a revered name in Puerto Rican baseball.

Zorilla treated everyone the same. His goal was to lift the entire league. If I needed something, I could go to him. If he could help, he would. He was a good man.

But you did not play for Zorilla.

I played for Rafael Ramos Cobián. He was the owner of all the theaters in Puerto Rico. He was a businessman. Cobián was the owner of San Juan for a few years, and when he saw a better situation arise, he left for Caguas, to become owner of that team. Bob Leith became owner of San Juan in 1960. He had connections in the United States, thanks to his business dealings. Leith had close ties to Baltimore, and he was able to bring down some of their young players. Leith is a current director of the Sports Hall of Fame — where they held my ceremony. He keeps his league championship trophy from 1960-61 there.

You enjoyed a long career. Did you ever have any problems with the manager of any of your teams?

I always respected the manager. I was there to play baseball, as the manager dictated. When I turned pro in Puerto Rico, you had to know how to play already. There was no one to teach you, to bring you along. I played for

San Juan but lived in Santurce. San Juan and Santurce are two inlets connected by the *Puente Dos Hermanos.*

As black player, did you feel any type of racial division between yourself and white players?

Well, I knew I was dark-skinned, but it was not an awareness like you had in the United States. It was different in Puerto Rico. The rich needed the poor as much as the poor needed the rich. The races got along. It was a different dynamic than the United States.

You had a chance to hit in all of Puerto Rico's ballparks. Did you have a favorite?

My preferred park was Sixto Escobar, even though the wind tended to blow in from the beach. I was a not a home run hitter, so it did not bother me. I was a line drive hitter.

Willie Mays was the star attraction of league in 1954-55.

I remember Mays' first game against us at Sixto Escobar. I smacked a ball to center that fell in, and I slid into second safely, stretching a single into

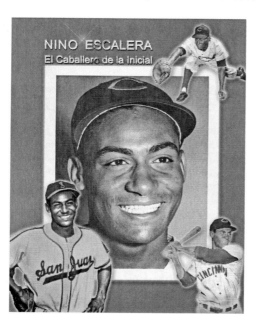

a double. Mays looked at me and gave me a signal saying that was the last time I was going to do that. And it was—I never tried to take an extra base on him again. I always tried to play the game like that. It is a mental attitude. In my opinion, Willie Mays was the best player of all time.

Another future Hall of Famer, Sandy Koufax, joined the league in the winter of 1956.

Sandy Koufax came to Puerto Rico to learn how to pitch. He did not have control of his pitches. I think I walked every time I faced him, at least the first five or six times. I was lead-off hitter, so I waited him out pretty easily. Sam Jones and Harvey Haddix were outstanding pitchers that season.

Nino Escalera was recognized by his native land for his many years of service and dedication to the game, in Puerto Rico and abroad (courtesy José A. Torres).

Henry Aaron preceded both Mays and Koufax.

Hank Aaron started as a second baseman and did not do well. Then they switched him to outfield and he tore up the league.

Another North American player who left a big imprint was Frank Howard.

Frank Howard was a giant. And so strong. He hit a *batazo* over a light tower at Sixto Escobar that they are still looking for. He did not care what direction the wind was blowing. He is a good guy, too.

I would like to hear about the San Juan and Santurce rivalry.

The fans of the rivalry slanted toward Santurce, as far as numbers. Santurce had more fans, even though San Juan was the capital's team. Santurce was the common people's team. They were Puerto Rico's team, you might say. Santurce had tremendous players over the years, Willard Brown, Rubén Gómez, Bob Thurman. Luis Rodríguez Olmo—a tremendous individual. A professional player.

You gained a reputation as an outstanding fielder.

The best first baseman I ever saw was Victor Pellot. There was running banter for years that said, "San Juan has the best first baseman in Puerto Rico—Nino Escalera, but Caguas has the best first baseman in the world—Victor Pellot."

You played in the Caribbean Series.

I played in three Caribbean championship tournaments. In Panama in 1952, with San Juan. We had a bad Series. I do not think we won a game. And we had a very good team. We had Canena Márquez, Luis Olmo, Cot Deal, a real good North American player. Buster Clarkson. Cot Deal stood at the plate exactly like Stan Musial. Deal had the same knock-kneed batting stance as Musial. Cuba won the Series; they had a good team. I only remember Formental. Maybe because he became a good friend of mine when we played together on the Cuban Sugar Kings. Formental was a man of extreme confidence in his abilities. I admired him for that.

As a member of the Sugar Kings, you obviously spent quite a bit of time in Havana.

With the Sugar Kings, I lived across from the United States embassy in Havana. It was close to *El Malecón*. Another Puerto Rican player was there at that time, José Enrique Montalvo. Yes, there was a rich nightlife. In fact, our home games with the Sugar Kings started at nine in the evening. I was married, but we traveled to the United States so much on road trips that my wife only came to visit me in Havana for a week at a time. I will tell you the truth, I went to Havana in 1984, managing a Puerto Rican amateur club. I did not see any change. I noticed more poverty then than I had 30 years earlier. The

Havana I first knew was a city of progress. There was a lot of capital investment. Havana was like any other Latin American city as far as treatment toward black players. I can not give you any negative particulars in this regard.

It took another seven years for you to make it back to the Caribbean Classic.

In 1959, I went to the Caribbean Series in Caracas as a reinforcement player for Santurce. Monchile Concepción was the manager. Again, we did not do well. Almendares won the championship, managed by Sungo Carreras. My last championship trip was with Bob Leith's team, also in Caracas [1961 Inter-American Series]. Cuba had withdrawn.

When you began managing, Jack Fisher was one of the pitchers that helped you get off to a good start from the bench.

Jack Fisher was part of the Baltimore group of players. In 1959-60, I was the player-manager for San Juan when Fisher first pitched. Fisher and others returned for the 1960-61 season, and they were part of our pennant-winning team that went to Caracas.

You were dubbed with an esteemed nickname.

A sportswriter in Puerto Rico, Emilio Huyke, gave me the nickname "*Caballero de la Inicial.*" I did get tossed, once, in a game on a controversial call at second base.

I know there were a lot of players to choose from, but who were the best?

I always thought Canena Márquez was a player with extraordinary ability. He hit home runs, he stole bases. I would say him. Pitchers, of the ones I saw, Tomás Quiñones and Pantalones Santiago were the best.

What do you consider your greatest achievement on the baseball field?

I led the league in three base hits three different times. That was one of my most satisfying accomplishments, if not most satisfying.

What will you always remember about being a baseball player?

When I was a kid, I managed to walk onto the field with my father during a team practice. We went up to Buck Leonard at first base and asked him the best way to handle short-hopped throws. My father translated.

Years later, when I was a scout with the Mets, in St. Petersburg, Leonard was visiting. He had been elected to the National Hall of Fame. I asked Leonard if he remembered a kid and his father years ago in Puerto Rico, asking him for tips on how to catch short-hopped throws. I am not sure if he did, but the advice he gave was the same. Leonard said the key was to keep your eyes wide open — not to blink — and follow the ball.

Jack Fisher

I spoke to Jack Fisher, a courteous man, a few days after he turned 72. A Maryland native, Fisher won 12 games as a 21-year-old rookie for the Baltimore Orioles in 1960. Something that can be credited, in good part, to his antecedent winter league campaign in Puerto Rico. The right-hander finished second in wins (13) to Earl Wilson (15), and recorded the fourth-most strikeouts and fifth-best ERA in the circuit. Fisher's two hibernal seasons in Puerto Rico wrought one league title. In 1960-61, when his San Juan Senators defeated the Caguas Criollos, 5 games to 3, in a best-of-nine championship series. (Sweet revenge for losing to the same team in the finals the prior season.) Fisher won twice in that series, including the final game clincher in Caguas. The other victory was a one-hit effort over Caguas, in which Frank Howard legged out an infield hit.

Fisher pitched in the Inter-American Series in Venezuela that island champion San Juan participated in after the 1960-61 season. The pitcher won the only game for San Juan in that series, a 5–2 triumph over Cerveza Balboa of Panama. Fisher was also on the losing side of a great pitcher's duel. He lost a 1–0 heartbreaker against Bob Gibson and Valencia later in the competition.

During his 11-year major league residency, Fisher had the misfortune of pitching several seasons for the expansion New York Mets. Fisher was also deliverer of two of the more noteworthy home runs in major league history.

What is your earliest baseball memory?

I always played baseball for as long as I can remember. I played in pick-up games with all the kids in the neighbor. When I was 12, that was the first year Frostburg [Md.] had a Little League, so I went out for Little League. That was the first organized ball I played.

You were which ballplayer's number one fan?

Bob Feller was the guy that I followed more than anybody in the big leagues.

You eventually relocated from Maryland.

My father was in the service, an army man, so I was an army brat. I was an only child. My father was stationed in Camp Gordon, Georgia, right outside of Augusta, so we moved to Augusta when I was 13. That is where I went to school, junior high, and high school. I played all the sports down there. All through school.

I guess baseball was the sport in which you showed the most promise prior to graduation?

I signed my first pro contract right out of high school with the Baltimore Orioles' organization and pitched in Class A baseball. The following year the Orioles sent me down to Class B, where I pitched my first full season. And then the following year, I actually broke camp with the big league club. That was in 1959. I played the first half of the year with Miami in the International League, and then I was recalled to major leagues. After the season, Paul Richards [manager] called me into his office and said that he would like me to pitch winter ball, down in Puerto Rico. I went down and pitched.

You spent back to back winters in Puerto Rico.

Both years, '59 and '60, I pitched with San Juan. I lived at the Darlington Hotel. Jerry Adair lived there. When you were not playing ball, you spent time out by the pool. I had my family with me. I was married.

What were the road trips like?

We traveled by bus, and to go to Mayagüez, that was quite a trip. All the way up over the mountains. I understand they have a tunnel going there now.

What do you remember about pitching in San Juan?

I remember Sixto Escobar Stadium, the park was practically filled every game.

And the paying customers?

They were absolutely great baseball fans. Especially when we were playing Santurce. Seemed like every time we played them, I would get hooked up with Juan Pizarro. He and I pitched many a game against each other. Usually the final score was 1–0. One way or the other. The fans, I can remember them "passing the hat." If I ended up winning a ball game there in San Juan, they would come and hand me, hell, I would have 150, 200 dollars cash from people chipping in.

All the parks in Puerto Rico were fair parks. Much like the parks I played in the minor leagues.

Do you remember your first manager there?

Nino Escalera was our manager. No communication problems. I cannot imagine him ever getting thrown out of a game. Nino was a gentleman. I played about 14 years in the major leagues. I was never thrown out of a game.

You did very well pitching for San Juan.

I can remember pitching a one-hitter against Caguas. Frank Howard hit a two-hopper down third base, and our third baseman bobbled the ball, picked it up, threw it to first, and somehow Frank got there before the ball and they gave him a base hit. Frank did hit some home runs down there. They talk about him hitting the longest home run at Sixto Escobar. Frank hit it over two centerfield fences, over some logs and barrels and out on the beach — and that was off me! I sure remember that one.

Frank was the type of player if you made a mistake, that was when he would really hurt you. If you made good pitches, normally, you had a chance to get him out. Howard hit a line drive back at me one day. The ball hit me on the heel of my spikes. It spun me around like a top on the mound. Luckily, the ball hit more on the bottom part of the shoe, and it really did not hurt me. I was able to continue pitching. If the ball had hit me on the ankle bone, I am sure it would have fractured it. That was about as scary as I ever was hit with a line drive. Frank was a nice guy, really was.

Your team won the championship during your second winter and earned a spot in the Inter-American Series in Caracas.

In Caguas, we beat them in the playoffs my second year. I won the clinching game in relief. I can remember coming back on the team bus. The bus pulled into downtown San Juan. I come out of the bus and I am being carried on fans' shoulders. We reached a bar. I walked into the bar. Reached back and my back pocket had been slit. [Laughs.] They took all of my money. I managed to get my wallet back, but no money.

I remember the trip to Venezuela well. We really had a great ball club. We went down there really thinking we were going [to do something].We won only one game. I remember the ballpark was a big, big, ballpark. Traveling in a taxi in Caracas was quite a feat. It was like whoever had the loudest horn was able to go through an intersection. I went shopping in Caracas. Everything you had to bargain to buy. Roberto Clemente and I went into one store. I was going to buy my wife a gold bracelet. Of course, they spoke only Spanish, and Robbie was my interpreter and negotiator. I ended up getting a very, very nice deal on a gold bracelet. It was all because of Clemente.

He was the best player I saw in the winter league. Playing against Clemente in the big leagues, you would appreciate him all right. But you did not understand what a really good ballplayer he was until you played with him. After seeing him play two full seasons in winter ball, there was not a thing the man could not do.

Following his Major League debut with the Baltimore Orioles in 1959, Jack Fisher pitched two successive winters with San Juan in the Puerto Rican Winter League.

Clemente was really a great ballplayer. Earl Wilson had a hell of a year, and like I said, I never saw Pizarro give up many runs.

Your two winter seasons were definitely well spent, it seems.

My experiences in Puerto Rico were positive overall. I was treated well. I enjoyed it. I had success. You know, there were a gang of scouts present. Probably kept me noticed. It certainly did not hurt me.

How are you spending your days now?

I highly recommend retirement to everyone. I am having a ball. I am playing a lot of golf. When the weather affords it. Other than that, I am doing a little bit of traveling, from time to time. Every once in a while, we will have a tournament with ex-ballplayers around. Family is all grown. I have three grandchildren. Two are in college, one is four years old.

Gene Freese

Gene Freese had much more success at the major league level than his brother George. Gene played 12 seasons with six different big league teams, and was the starting third baseman for the 1961 pennant-winning Cincinnati Reds. The infielder also experienced winter ball in three different countries. Freese first traveled to San Juan in 1954, then Mazatlán the following winter, and finally Havana in 1956. (Mazatlán was part of the six-team Pacific Coast League of Mexico.)

Freese, a father of three and grandfather of eight, exhibited a good sense of humor during our chat. He and his second wife Mary were making preparations to attend the 50th reunion of the 1961 Reds team in Cincinnati, complete with Great American Ball Park field ceremonies for the former players.

After speaking to your brother, I have a good idea of your background.

I was born in Wheeling, West Virginia. We were three boys and a girl. George, Elmer, and myself and my sister. Everybody in the family played every sport, depending on the season. My brother Elmer was bigger than both of us. My sister was quite an athlete, too.

Who was your sports hero?

More or less, it was my dad, because we did not get to see any ball games in Wheeling. Pittsburgh was close by, but we never went to go see a game.

But Pittsburgh went to see you, so to speak.

I was signed by the Pirates in 1953. Rex Bowen signed me. I was in college at West Liberty State College. Branch Rickey wanted to sign me for $200. My dad asked for $250, and Rickey said, okay. I said to Rickey, what if I had asked for $300? Rickey said, you would not have gotten it. So I signed a contract with Burlington, Class B. I did not do well with Burlington, so they sent me down to D-ball in Brunswick, Georgia. I won Rookie of the Year. They jumped me to Double A ball in New Orleans, the following year. That is when my brother came to the Pirates, in 1954; my brother was in the big Ralph Kiner trade.

That was your first winter baseball year, as well.

My brother played winter ball with Mayagüez. I played for San Juan. Harry Craft was the manager. Harry was good people. I lived in an apartment right by the ballpark, but I kept jumping into the pool from my second floor room and they threw me out. [Laughs.] As a result, I ended up living at the Darlington Apartments, and roomed with Arnie Portocarrero, and Arnie and I became really good friends. I am glad I roomed with him. Arnie was a big, good-looking guy. His aunt owned a used car agency in San Juan, and we would get cars anytime we wanted. If we wanted to ride around, find a girl somewhere, pick her up and go to the drive-in movies. It was a shame to hear Arnie died at such a young age.

How else did you occupy yourself away from the field?

There was a gambling place right by the ballpark. There was not a lot of entertainment. We played often, and there was a lot of traveling by bus. It was a good time for me. I was from a small town in West Virginia. In Puerto Rico, there was an American place, I would eat ham and cheese and ham and eggs. I am steak man, so I never acquired a taste for the [local] food.

Your bat provided one of the season's early highlights.

Branch Rickey told me to never be a hero in Puerto Rico. The fans will come and get you and carry you off the field. That is exactly what happened to me. Rubén Gómez was pitching against us. Gómez was a big league pitcher with the Giants. I was hitting in the last inning, and we were down a run. There were runners on second and third. Herman Franks was their manager, Santurce. He went to the mound. Franks asked Gómez if he wanted to walk me and pitch to the next guy. Gómez gave me that little look from the mound, *Nahhh, I'll pitch to him.* He saw I was young, never been to the big leagues. Gómez figured he could get me out easily. I hit a double off the fence in center and won the game. And here come the fans. They picked me up and wanted to take me to the church. [Laughs.] I was a big hit right after that. It was one of the first games of the season. I became friends with Gómez. Later on, I played with him in Philadelphia. Rubén was an okay guy.

I gather the media attention slanted toward Willie Mays that season.

Mays got there late. The season had already started. He and Clemente were in the same outfield. You just could not hit one between those guys. I did not know it, but Pittsburgh had picked up Clemente that winter. We ended up playing together with the Pirates.

Who were the league's best players?

Mays was, and Sad Sam Jones was the best pitcher. Jones was a great pitcher. He became friends with me. I made a deal with him. I said, look Sam, you don't hit me and I won't hit you. Let's just get along down here. We are in a strange country. [Laughs.] Jones was a West Virginia boy, too.

Every club took a back seat to Santurce that year.

We had a good ball club. Woodie Held at shortstop. I played second. Frank Kellert played first. Jim Rivera, third. Joe Montalvo was our catcher. Escalera was in right field. Elston Howard. Larry Jackson of the Cardinals was one of our pitchers.

There was an incident in a game between you and Tommy Lasorda.

We were playing in San Juan, and Lasorda was pitching for Mayagüez. Bob Cerv started the whole thing. He was at first base and he slid real hard into second base. Cerv took their second baseman out into left field. Lasorda said he was going to knock all of the San Juan hitters down, and all that jazz. Well, I am the next hitter. And I had been out gambling with Lasorda, my brother and Don Zimmer the night before. The first pitch Lasorda threw, sure enough, hit me in the back of my neck. I just walked to first base. I told Tommy, you had better watch it, the next guy is a real big guy. He will come out there and beat you. Frank Kellert was the next hitter. Frank was a first baseman behind Gil Hodges. Then a ruckus started. My brother is running in from right field. I never did get to Lasorda. Later, Lasorda came up with Brooklyn, and I was with the Pirates. First time I faced him, Lasorda hit me in the leg. I just flicked the bat away like the pitch did not hurt me, like I did not feel it. We all became good friends after all that.

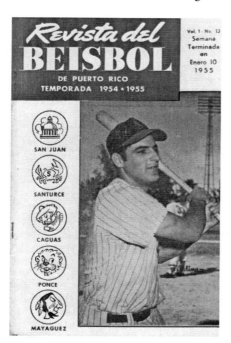

San Juan infielder Gene Freese graced the cover of *Revista del Beisbol,* a weekly periodical dedicated to Puerto Rican Winter League coverage.

Mayagüez was far from San Juan. So the only time I saw Zimmer and Lasorda and my brother was when we went there or they came over to play us. We had a good bus driver, which was good because it was not easy driving to Mayagüez. Someone said our driver only killed two or three people a year. [Joking.] Whoever used the horn first, that was it. They went first.

You changed leagues in each of the coming winters.

I was not invited back [to Puerto Rico]. The following winter, I ended up with Mazatlán in Mexico. It was a great resort town. Six of us stayed in one apartment. It was really nice down there. Dick Hall was on my team. He ended up being a pitcher with Baltimore. Like I said, I am a West Virginia boy, I just ate meat. I did not trust anything else.

The next winter [1956], I went to Cuba. I lived at Club Náutico. I was married that October. We did not go out much in Havana. Castro was bombing parts of the city all the time. They kind of warned us to stay off the streets, and we did. We would drive by places that were sandbagged. I was with Cienfuegos. We had a good club. We had Pete Ramos. Chico Fernández. Pascual. Ray Noble was the catcher.

We played four games a week. A doubleheader Sunday. We usually played the first game. It only took fifteen, twenty minutes to get to the ballpark. It was nice. They had good crowds. Of course, there was Miñoso. He was always a good player. I think he led the league down there. I played with him with the White Sox in 1960.

How are you spending your retirement?

I would not call it retirement. You retire when you have money. I just quit working. I am not doing anything now, and I am doing it well.

George Freese

George Freese and younger sibling Gene played baseball together at different professional levels, the highest of which was the major leagues. The Freese brothers were rookie teammates with the Pittsburgh Pirates in 1955.

A three-letter man in high school, George Freese grabbed his greatest baseball laurels in the Pacific Coast League with the Portland Beavers and with the Mayagüez and San Juan clubs in Puerto Rico. Freese played five consecutive winters in Puerto Rico, from 1952 to 1956. In each of his three latter years with the Senators, the slugging third baseman finished in the top five in home runs and RBIs in the league, including leading the circuit in runs knocked home (54) in 1956-57.

Hip problems have moved the 85-year-old Freese to rely on the use of a wheelchair for mobility, which according to him, will prevent him from ever visiting Puerto Rico again, a place that holds a most special place in his heart. A resident of Oregon for over 50 years, Freese was inducted into that state's athletic Hall of Fame in 2008.

Where were you born?

I was born September 12, 1926, and raised in Wheeling, West Virginia. My brother played baseball when he was young. I just followed him around and started to play it, too.

As a youngster, who was your favorite player?

Arky Vaughn was a shortstop a long time ago. I just liked his name.

Even though you were restricted on showcasing your baseball skills, the Dodgers saw enough in you to offer you a pro contract.

I was not allowed to play too much baseball in college because I was there on a football scholarship. The Dodgers watched me, I guess, and they were my original team.

How did you end up playing in the Tropics?

My first year playing winter ball was 1952. I was in Mobile, Alabama, and I received a letter wanting to know if I would be interested in playing winter ball in Mayagüez, Puerto Rico. The letter came right from the club. Naturally I was, because the money was good.

I remember Alfonso Valdés, the owner of Mayaguez. He really liked baseball. He would tell you what to do every once in a while. But he was good. We had a fellow that traveled with us all the time, Babel Pérez. He was like a general manager, he took care of all the ballplayers. In Mayagüez, we traveled in private cars to the ballpark. Away games, we had a driver that would take us to the towns and bring us back. We called the driver Humphrey. He was big [man]. It was four people in a car. Everything was provided by the team. On the road trips, we would buy and eat pork all along the way. It was great. Pork was my favorite.

With Mayagüez, you played in a game in which your brother was part of an altercation between your club and his.

Lasorda and I were on the same team. My brother [Gene] played down there for one season with San Juan. Lasorda hit him one time with a pitch. I thought there was going to be a fight, but there was not. When the inning was over, I come into our dugout and Tom says to me, "Hey you, SOB, if you want to stick up for your brother, I will meet you outside the ballpark." I said to him, "You don't have to wait that long." But nothing came of it.

Did you like living in Mayagüez?

In a Mayagüez store, they overcharged my wife once. The next day, the owner came to us and said, we overcharged your wife, here is your change. The people were so friendly, it made it feel like home. We would walk wherever we wanted to go. Everyone knew you.

My wife enjoyed it. My wife Betty and I met in college at West Virginia. We were married in Bayamón in 1952. My best man was Johnny Blatnik. He played on our team. We were engaged, and I was tired of waiting and I wanted to get married. My wife and her mother came down to Puerto Rico. It was a private wedding. We spent our honeymoon at the Normandie Hotel. That was right across the street from the ballpark in San Juan.

How about when you switched cities and moved over to play with your brother's old team.

In San Juan, the years I played with the Senators, we lived at the Gallardo Apartments. It was right across the street from the Condado Beach Hotel. All the ballplayers stayed at the Gallardo Apartments. It was real nice. Ralph Houk was the manager one year. Ralph was tough. You did not want to mess with him.

The league played in four different parks. How were they?

I enjoyed playing in the stadiums in Ponce, Mayagüez, Caguas, San Juan. They were all good ballparks. The fans knew everything about baseball. You would walk down the street and they would call out your name. If you were messing around, or having too much fun, they would let you know about it. I had a little problem with communication. The native ballplayers tried to teach me. They would always try and teach me the bad words.

How would you rate the talent?

They had good players. Louie Márquez, Carlos Bernier. Luke Easter. He beat me out for the home run title one year. Easter had 17 and I had 16. Rubén Gómez was the best pitcher.

A productive hitter in Puerto Rico, George Freese slugged for the Mayagüez and San Juan franchises (courtesy AC Archives).

How did you spend the holidays?

We would get together at Thanksgiving and Christmastime with the other players. The weather was great. We would go to the beach, play volleyball, picnic. It might rain for half an hour and then it would be dry.

I am still tickled over the fact that you were married in Puerto Rico.

I enjoyed every year in Puerto Rico. It really was a fabulous place to play. I loved it. The accommodations were great. My family was with me — we ended up having two kids, a boy and a girl. My expenses were paid. Puerto Rico was the best five years I spent in baseball.

Charlie Gorin

When Charlie Gorin was a teenager, America was fighting a world war on two vast global fronts. In 1945, at age 17, Charlie enlisted in the U.S. Navy. Gorin was discharged in 1946, and he was later recalled to active duty for the Korean War. In between, Gorin went to college on the GI Bill and reengaged his love for baseball, pitching in the U.S. minor leagues and several winters in Puerto Rico.

During his first season (1951-52) on the Island of Enchantment, Gorin tied for the league lead in wins with 14 and finished second in ERA (2.36) and third in strikeouts (112). The southpaw established a circuit record when he beat every team in the league, after being released early into the season by Mayagüez and then being picked up by San Juan. As a Senators' hurler, Gorin won the pennant-deciding game against Santurce and then followed that up with two more complete-game victories against the same team in the championship series. (Including those two triumphs, Gorin won an eye-popping 16 games.) Unfortunately, he was unable to pitch in the Caribbean Series due to an injury. Gorin, who briefly sniffed the rarified air of the major leagues, returned to Puerto Rico in 1956 with Santurce. While pitching for the Ponce Leones in 1957, the pitcher accrued ten victories, accounting for one-third of his team's total wins for the season.

Spending three seasons with the Austin Senators of the Texas League in the late '50s and early '60s, Gorin competed against Mexican League teams, when the two leagues engaged in interleague play. As an Austin Senator in 1960, Gorin threw a no-hitter in the Interleague Series' championship-winning game against the Mexico City Red Devils, missing out on a perfect game due to an error.

Ol' Charlie, with his cow-punching southeast Texas accent and impressive recall, was a most effectual interview.

Where were you born, and how big was your family?

Waco, Texas, February 6, 1928. My brother and I, and my mother and father.

Where did you learn to play baseball?

My father was a semi-pro player in Waco. We moved to Austin, following the stock market crash. My father's job — The FP Freight Depot — moved us. Thanks to my father's seniority, they "bumped him in" to Austin, after they closed his office in Waco. My father continued to play semi-pro ball in Austin. During the war, they had here what was called City Leagues and Midget Leagues. My father always took me to the ball games. He pushed baseball.

World War II put any baseball plans you might have had on hold.

During the war, you did not go anywhere. You had sugar rationing, tire rationing, gasoline rationing. Right out of high school — I graduated in May — six of us from the neighborhood went down and joined the Navy. Boy, we had guys who dropped out of high school to join. They were ready to go. Patriotism was a different thing then. I went off to boot camp and to a destroyer. It was not long thereafter that we dropped the bombs on Hiroshima and Nagasaki. When we came back to San Diego to decommission, I will bet there were 200 destroyers in the harbor.

After I came out of the Navy, I did not know what I was going to do, and one of the guys I had gone into the Navy with said that we could go over to the university in Austin — the University of Texas — and that they would pay for our books and tuition, which was $95.00 a month. That ol' boy and I jumped at that. The next spring, I tried out for baseball. Bibb Falk was the baseball coach at the university. He was a former major league player. Twelve, fourteen years. Falk had a lifetime batting average of .314.

We won the national championship in 1949 and '50, playing against Wichita in '49 and Omaha, Nebraska, in 1950. They had us back to Rosenblatt Stadium for the last NCAA Tournament to be held there. There were eleven of us left and nine came. They have built a real fine stadium in Omaha now. I signed right there in Omaha a Triple A contract with the Boston Braves. That took me to Milwaukee, in the American Association. I was optioned from there to Atlanta, in the Southern Association. I was a left-hand pitcher. Not too big. I was five-foot-ten, 150 pounds with rocks in my pockets. I went 10–1. But we got beat in the playoffs.

The following year, 1951, I went back to the Southern Association. I had a 12–9 record. We won the pennant, playoffs and Junior World Series. We played Montreal. Then ol' Louie Olmo got me to go down to Puerto Rico. Doggone, we won the pennant for San Juan down there, too. Olmo was well known in Puerto Rico. He was with the Braves at that time. San Juan had a good ball club. Sad Sam Jones was a pitcher for us. [José] Montalvo was the catcher. George Crowe was the first baseman. Jack Dittmer, second. Nino Escalera, remember him? Carlos Bernier in centerfield. He could run.

I started with Mayagüez, and they were going to send me home. I had pitched some good ball. But the team lost. I lost a 13-inning game, 5–3. Gorin, they said, you are going home. I said, oh kaaay ... I had my contract and it said they had to pay my way back. I hopped on a plane from Mayagüez and went to San Juan, getting ready to change planes [to come home]. Cobián, the owner of San Juan, and Roy Hughes, the manager, came to the airport. They asked me, "How would you like to come to play with us?" So I did. I will tell you what, you had to win in that league or you were gone. I pulled a muscle in my rib cage late in the season and could not pitch in the Caribbean Series. I had pitched a lot of ball in the states and then a lot in Puerto Rico. I probably overworked myself.

I lived at the Normandie Hotel, right across the street from the ballpark. The Caribe Hilton was right across from that. And Jack's Casino, I believe that was the name of it. Those were the three places.

Tell me, did you like the food in Puerto Rico?

I always fought a [reverse] weight problem. I would play in the states; it was hot, humid, I would drop weight. I was able to gain weight in Puerto Rico; I ate good there. At the hotel, you could eat continental or Puerto Rican. I learned to like avocados, and I ate the staple dish, *arroz con pollo con habichuelas.* It had a lot of protein. I liked it.

Then another military conflict interrupted your ball-playing career.

After that [season], I received my first major league contract. Two weeks later, I was called back to active duty for Korea. Boy, that was a kick in the butt. First time I joined the Navy during World War II, I could not wait to get there. Boy, this time I was not ready to go. I had a degree from UT then in Physical Education, so I ended up as an instructor in Naval School Preflight, for water survival — swimming, conditioning. We had cadets from England, France, Chile, and all of the states. When I came out, in '54, the Braves honored my contract and brought me to spring training. I stayed out of winter ball for the next two years. My father came down with cancer, and then died in 1955.

I went back to Puerto Rico in '56-57, with Santurce. Ol' Murray Wall and I were there. We were both from UT. We had José *Pantalones,* who was a pitcher for the Cleveland Indians. Rubén Gómez was pitching for the New York Giants. Valmy Thomas, who was a backup catcher for Wes Westrum. Cepeda was playing first. Junior Gilliam on second. Jose Pagán was at short. Clemente was in centerfield. Bob Thurman, and I forget the other outfielder's name.

I think we beat Koufax one time. He did not have good control. But could he throw. Boy, Koufax bounced a damned curveball over the plate. He threw overhand. That curve broke straight down. Koufax had the stuff. When Koufax put everything under control, he had quite a career. They had Ryne Duren down there, with Caguas. He not only could not get his pitches under control, he could not get his personal life under control. [Laughs.] One day, I remember, over in Caguas, you know, rain showers can come up real quick. You would sit in the dugout for twenty-odd minutes, waiting for the showers to pass, and then go at it again. During one rain shower, ol' Ryne came out of their dugout, ran across home plate, ran down to first base, dove into the bag. He jumped up, ran to second, slid in that rain and mud into second base. Did the same thing at third. Jumped up, ran home and slid across the plate on his belly. Ryne looked over to us in the dugout and said, "How do you

An exhilarated Charlie Gorin, after hurling San Juan to the pennant with an 18–3 triumph over hated Santurce, February 4, 1952. The lopsided win also crowned the Senators Campeónes de la Ciudad in the heated intercity rivalry (courtesy C. Gorin).

like that?" [Laughs again.] The fans were laughing like hell.

In San Juan, you had your own fans; the San Juan fan would sit on one side of the park, hollering and carrying on with the other fans on the other side. What I remember about San Juan is down the right field bleachers is where the gamblers stayed. Bet on fly balls, bet on ground balls. Then some of them would get into a fight. You would see a group of people just spread apart and then see two guys fighting. They would settle it and then the people would come back together and collapse the ring.

I will tell you a funny story — although it was not funny at the time. We [Santurce] went to play Mayagüez. Ol' Rubén Gómez, he never rode the bus. He had his Corvette. No top on it. Rubén used to like passing our bus on road trips. Rubén would have a buddy with him. He would come by on the road — *varoom* — and pass us, and all the natives on the bus would start hollering, *Rubén! Rubén!* Rubén was a character. He had a good screwball, and he threw pretty hard.

Well, we arrived in Mayagüez. They had an outfielder named Christopher. He was from the Virgin Islands, I think. He played with Pittsburgh. Christopher and Rubén did not like one another. We started playing, and Ruben downed Christopher with a bean ball. That got the fans all riled up, they did not like it. At Mayagüez, they had a new stadium, cantilever-type, with few poles. They had spiral staircases on each side, going to the roof. These Mayagüez fans grabbed hold of some big rocks and they fired those dang rocks on top of Rubén's Corvette and trashed the thing.

After the game, we dressed, hurried on the bus. Before we could move out, the fans swarmed the bus, lining up on each side, rocking. I thought they were going to overturn the bus. Well, a police jeep shows up just then. A police commander gets out, he had gold leafs on his shoulders and arms. He pulls out his pistol and fires two or three times into the air. Boy, those people moved back away from the bus. The police commander provided an escort for us out of the park and out of town. As soon as we reached the city limits of Mayagüez, the commander's jeep pulls off the escort. The native ballplayers on the bus start yelling to the bus driver, "*Más rapido! Más rapido!*" They wanted out of there fast. The bus took off back to San Juan. The fans, they were *fanaticos*. Look, in the fifties down there, you had baseball, boxing, cock fighting and horse racing. That was it.

That was great. Do you have anything from your time in Ponce that can match that?

I played two seasons with Ponce. George Scales was the manager. He was a manager in the Negro American league. We played in Caguas one night. Juan Pizarro was pitching for them. The score was 1–0, we were behind. Whenever somebody reached base, George would preach to the players, to move the runner up, to hit behind the runner. The Puerto Rican guys, they just wanted to hit the ball out of the park. Pizarro ended up beating us 1–0, and ol' Scales was hot. He told everybody — and his language was a little different than mine — to be at the park the next morning at ten thirty. Scales was a big guy. He meant it, and we were there. Luis Márquez would translate for the younger players. The older natives understood English well enough.

Scales walked out with a bat and showed everybody how to hit behind a runner. He said, I used to go to Cleveland every chance I could to watch the best line drive hitter in baseball — Bibb Falk. *Who did you say? Bibb Falk was my college coach. Take a level cut. That is what ol' Bibb was always telling us.* Good Night, I tell George, I played college ball for Bibb Falk, and ten, twelve years later I come down here to Puerto Rico and hear Coach Falk's name again. Yeah, George Scales. He was a good manager.

We had Leon Wagner on our team. He was *strong*. My gosh. He played with Cleveland some. Ol' George was saying once, if we did not get the signs, if we did not get the bunt down, it was going to cost us money. Ol' Leon says, "George, are you going to accept green stamps, too?" George looked at Leon like he was a dead man. Leon was not the brightest, but he was the strongest.

Ponce and Mayagüez and Caguas had new stadiums. Cantilever-type, not the old, wood kind. At Ponce, they had the outfield fence and outside the fence they had the big cement wall. The kids down there would get up on the wall, and with a signal — they would holler some command — would jump over into the park. Some would get through the police and into the stands, and the people would cheer them and let the kids get up under their legs so the police would not find them, until they could get up and watch the game. It was a show. Those kids wanted to see baseball, and that is what they had to do. All that is going on during the game. During Christmas and New Year's, the fans would shoot Roman Candles out onto the field.

One year, we went to Ramey Air Force Base for Christmas dinner. A lot of the men stationed there would come to the ball game. The Air Force food was pretty good at Christmas. Turkey and all the dressings. Ramey was out near Mayagüez.

Ponce's owner was a doctor. I cannot think of his name. He sponsored a lot of things there for the people. The owner in Santurce was [Pedrín] Zorrilla. Nice guy. Big guy. Friendly guy. Always had a nice smile on his face. The baseball offices for Santurce had life-size pictures of Josh Gibson. I cannot remember exactly where the offices were in Santurce. You would go to the ballpark, and they would say, Josh hit one there, hit one there. My gosh, it looked like it was a mile away. Gibson was a catcher that could throw to second without getting out of his crouch.

San Juan is an inlet, you had to cross a bridge. Santurce was on the perimeter of the bay. Caparra Heights. I lived there my last year in San Juan. My kids learned to walk there. Of course, they do not remember it much now.

You have identified many great players. Who were the best of the best?
I played against Clemente. It would be hard to pick anybody over him. Orlando Cepeda. Down there they called him Peruchín. The Baby One. Sad

Sam Jones was pretty good. He always had a runny nose, sniffling a lot. Boy, Jones, he had a curveball. Big breaking curve ball. Jones could throw a fastball. He really kept them honest.

The military had a swimming area behind the Sixto Escobar Stadium, and we would go swimming in San Juan bay. They had it screened to keep sharks out. When I was married, we rented a car and drove up into the rain forest. We would go to Manati, right on the coast, perfect sand. I really enjoyed Puerto Rico. It was not a bad deal for us. Playing winter ball, that is where I made money and saved money. I did that for a few years after I married.

Any last, parting thoughts about your time there?

The last time we returned home from Puerto Rico, we had a little airplane trouble. The youngest one was in my wife's lap. That was on a 707. The landing wheels would not lock. When we came in for a landing in Miami, we were circling around, because the cockpit light did not indicate all of the wheels were locked. They called out the ambulances and fire trucks. There was some scared people on that airplane. We were in seats in the first row. They carried up all the blankets and pillows, and they packed them inside the cockpit so the pilot and co-pilot could try and land without getting knocked around. That was in case we hit hard. One of the stewardesses, she sat down crying. I said, oh, my gosh. The other stewardesses were serving wine. I drank mine and my wife's.

It was the wheels on the right side of the plane that were indicating they were not locked. There are wheels on both sides of the plane. The pilot landed on the wheels that were locked and tilted the wing to bring down the plane on the other side, and those wheels would hit the pavement. The pilot did that two or three times. It showed the wheels were holding, and then he let the whole plane down easy. Rescue came and took all of the passengers off the runway. And we had a connecting flight to catch to Tampa! My wife is from Tampa, and we were going to visit her folks. We were real glad to finally get there.

I had some traveling experiences through Mexico from the Texas League.

I'm all ears.

I played for Austin in 1959 and 1960 and 1962. We arrived in Poza Rica one time, about two in the morning, and they would not let us into the hotel because of a glitch with the reservation or with some type of payment required. Finally, they let us into the second floor, but it was hot with no air conditioning.

When we played in Poza Rica, Veracruz, we did not go out, maybe just to get something to eat. I did get sick one time. It was in Poza Rica. They were supposed to have coolers with bottled water on the bench. Well, they did not. I was pitching and ol' Jim Callaway was catching. We were trying not to drink. I was so hot and dry my tongue began sticking to the roof of my mouth. So we began sipping water out of a nearby hydrant. Boy, that was not good. Ol' Jim and I both became sick.

I hope that was the only unpleasant experience you had.

Poza Rica had a double decker stadium. They were *fanaticos*. They [fans] threw rats at us, and snakes. Looking back, we were really having a time. There was an oil refinery right in the middle of town. You could smell that crude oil at the ballpark. It was something else.

What about the other parks in Mexico?

Mexico City had a nice stadium, big stadium. Veracruz was a nice city. Monterrey was good. I enjoyed the trips. We went to the bullfights in Mexico City. That was something.

I can remember one time we were coming back to Texas from Mexico City. We missed our regular flight. Ol' Allen Russell, president of the Austin club, got us a small plane that held all 27 of us, one kid and the hostess. Boy, that thing must have taxied a mile before we lifted into the air. We got up, just made it over the mountain tops. We looked around and here comes a girl with a tray of *Dos Equis* beer. They gave us all a beer. We followed the beer. They opened the cockpit door and gave the pilot and co-pilot a beer. [Laughs.] My gosh, well, that was one. We were going down to Matamoros. When we arrived there, here comes the girl again with another tray of beer. Opens the cockpit door. The pilot had his foot up on the dash like he was guiding a trotting horse. We were glad to be on the ground. We grabbed our bags ourselves. We took a bus and crossed the border.

That is some story. Where has your life after baseball taken you?

After baseball, I went back to school and obtained a master's degree in education. I went into High School Administration, the last 13 of them as an assistant principal. We have a group that plays golf two or three times a week. I do some volunteer work. Martha Rebecca, call her Becky, and I have been married since 1956. I have two daughters, married, and have two grandsons. One is playing ball.

Jack Harshman

Some players start their big league careers at one position and convert to another. But not many players start as a position player and then switch to pitching. That is what Jack Harshman did as a New York Giants' conscript. Helping him along the transitional way was a winter in San Juan, Puerto Rico, in 1953-54. Harshman excelled from the mound for the capital city Senators, leading the league in wins with 15. (Harshman also spent part of an earlier winter in Ponce as a first baseman/ pitcher.)

Having purchased Harshman from the Giants before the conclusion of the major league season, the Chicago White Sox hoped the pitcher's winter performance was a harbinger of things to come. It was. The top rookie pitcher in the American League in 1954, Harshman raked in 14 victories for the White Sox. That season, Harshman defeated Al Aber of the Detroit Tigers in a spectacular, 16-inning pitcher's duel, 1–0, on August 13. Both hurlers pitched to the game's conclusion. The winning run was driven home by a Minnie Miñoso triple in the bottom of the 16th. Incredibly, two days later, Harshman pitched two scoreless innings of relief for Chicago in one of the games of a Sunday doubleheader against the same opposition.

The left-hander retained a good deal of his prior hitting skills, socking 21 career home runs in eight American League seasons of work from the mound.

Harshman resides in Texas with Ginger, his bride of two decades.

You are from the West Coast?

I am from San Diego, California, and that is where I went through school. I am an only child.

A lot of ballplayers came from your area.

We could play twelve months a year in California. I developed early and it went on from there. I was a good high school player. In those days, the early forties, the only players you could see and watch were local. And the San Diego Padres of the Pacific Coast League had a first baseman by the name of George McDonald, who was a really fine fielder. I really enjoyed watching him play. So if there was a player I appreciated in my early years, before I reached high school, it was George McDonald.

Two prominent National League teams were after you.

I was scouted pretty thoroughly by the Brooklyn Dodgers and the St. Louis Cardinals. They both had scouts that lived in San Diego. I decided to go with the San Diego Padres, because if I signed with Brooklyn or St Louis, I might wind up behind somebody and might never have a chance to break in as a first baseman. San Diego was an independent team. If I made an impact, then any team in the major leagues could deal with me — and that is how it worked out for me. I was purchased by the New York Giants. The Giants made a deal with the Padres that was really unbelievable at the time. I led the league in home runs in the Washington International League in 1947. The Giants gave the Padres three players of Triple A quality plus $40,000, which was $10,000 over what was considered the "draft price" for the Coast League. It was really one heck of a deal.

In 1948, I went to the Giants' Triple A team in Jersey City, New Jersey. The next year, I went to Minneapolis and had a real good year, home run hitting, there. The next season, I opened the season for the New York Giants at first base at the Polo Grounds. I did not last there very long because the team was playing very poorly, or was not winning, and I was not hitting very well. They decided to make a change, and I was it. I made it to the major leagues in 1950 as a first baseman.

The Giants had a history of sending young players to play in Puerto Rico. You became one of them.

I went down to Ponce, Puerto Rico, in 1951. Ponce had scouted me when I played in Minneapolis. They offered me a pretty good contract to go down there and I took a chance. At that time, money meant a lot more to players. It was important for me, financially, to take advantage of the offer and so I

A happy Jack Harshman of the Chicago White Sox, center, following a late-season victory over the Cleveland Indians in 1955. Hitting stars of the game, Minnie Miñoso (left) and Bob Kennedy (right), are also all smiles. Harshman, the prior season, had authored a sensational 1–0, 16-inning victory over the Detroit Tigers.

went to Ponce. I did not stay there all season; I had to come home, but I was there for the first part of the year. My wife and I had an apartment in Ponce. I do not quite remember where it was. Benny [Huffman] was the manager. He was a nice man, and I enjoyed playing for him.

In the winter of 1953-54, I went back to Puerto Rico to play with San Juan. I was a pitcher then. I had pitched for Nashville and had an unbelievable season — I was 27-7. I led the league in almost everything you could think of, as far as pitching. I had a pretty good year hitting, too. I was voted Athlete of the Year by the sportswriters of Tennessee. That included all sports, amateur and professional. The owner of the Nashville team, in 1951, had come to me and said he thought I would be able to play first base in the majors, but because I would not have that high an average that I should try pitching. He asked me if he obtained permission from the New York Giants for me to try pitching, would it be okay with me? I said, sure. I did not care how I got to the big leagues. So my first full year as a pitcher was 1952.

I had a really good winter with San Juan. I do not recall that well where we stayed. It was a nice place, wherever it was. They did well by us. San Juan was a good city to play in. There was not a whole lot of entertainment that attracted me or my wife. I know they had gambling there, which did not appeal to me. We did occasionally go out for a meal. We stayed pretty close to our apartment. We spent time with some native families that were very kind to us.

You and Bob Turley were the top North American pitchers in the league.

I knew Bob real well. Bob had been with the New York Giants in 1953. The Puerto Rican owners would pay more for a major league player than they would for a minor leaguer. The salaries were kind of determined by where you played. So Bob was making more than I was making. Halfway through the year, I was pitching as well, if not better, than Bob. So I went to the owner of San Juan, and said, you know, it seems to me that maybe I should be paid as much as Bob, and you know what? The owner agreed with me and gave me the difference, which I thought was darn nice of him. We were paid by check, in U.S. money.

The schedule I remember was 80 games. I started, and completed 20 of them. That is really a lot of complete ball games. My record was 15 and 8. I might be wrong about this, but I think Santurce had a young 16-year-old boy that played the outfield named Roberto Clemente. I think that was his first year playing professional ball. Of course, he turned out to be one of the best players who ever lived.

I do know Henry Aaron played for one of the teams, Caguas, is that what it was? He was just getting started. I was pitching against Caguas in their ball park. Aaron came up to face me, and I worked the count to two strikes and no balls. The old adage was if you had them oh-and-two, you might brush them back or something. I threw a ball high and inside that Aaron could have gotten out of the way of. But instead, Aaron stepped back and went at it like swatting a fly and hit a line drive right over my head that went right over the centerfield fence. I have *never* ever seen anybody that made the bat move so quickly with what appeared to be a small effort. Aaron had great, great wrists. That home run was something I will never forget.

Do you recall Jack Cassini? He was the leading hitter for your team.

I grew to know Jack Cassini. He played second base for us. I had played against him in the American Association. We became be pretty close friends that winter in San Juan. I knew Cot Deal. I knew him well. He is a very nice man. Ellie was a good hitter. They had Eliie in the ball game as often as they could — either hitting or pitching. Those teams all had very good rosters.

Tell me what you remember about the travel, and the ballparks.

Mayagüez was way over on one end of the island, Ponce was down on the other end. Santurce and San Juan were on another, and Caguas was in the middle. You made about two trips a week from wherever you were head-quartered, so you got in a lot of roadwork. [Sixto Escobar] was a good ball park, and it was a fair one. If you hit the ball real hard, you could get it out there. If you pitched real good, you had a chance to win. They did not get any cheap home runs there. The clubhouses were nothing like they are nowa-days. They had lockers and a shower room, and that was about it. There was no problem there.

Did you grow accustomed to the food?

I liked the food. I have always been a Spanish-food enthusiast. I like Mexican food and I like Puerto Rican food. I enjoyed it very much. We visited a family there and the woman prepared, I guess one of her specialties, *arroz con pollo*. That was really good. It was a delicious meal. The husband worked for a bank there.

There was another family that owned a concrete factory, two of them, and it was busy 24 hours a week. Another family owned a Coca Cola franchise. Another, the White Trucking franchise. Frank Fullana was a big building con-tractor in Puerto Rico, and we grew to know him.

Then there was the Don Q Rum factory. People drank a whole lot of Don Q. [Chuckles.]

Earl Hersh

In most levels of organized baseball during the 1950s, if one was traded out of a league mid-season, it rarely required relocation to another country. But for players playing in the winter leagues, it was part of a potential occupational readjustment. Such was the case for Earl Hersh in the winter of 1957 when Puerto Rico's Caguas franchise sent him packing to Caracas, Venezuela, where he finished the season. Caguas had obtained Hersh's services, after watching the Milwaukee Braves' prospect, playing for Santurce the prior winter in Puerto Rico, come in second in home runs to Wes Covington. The two campaigns were Hersh's only seasons of winter ball.

In 1956, the annual fall roster expansion allowed Hersh an unrepeated absorption of the sights and sounds of the major leagues with the Milwaukee Braves.

Hersh and Janet, his wedded wife of sixty years, live happily in a southeastern Pennsylvania retirement home, their three children residing within a 30-mile radius.

Where did you originally call home?

I was born in Maryland, on a farm outside of a small town called Manchester. I had an older sister and a younger brother.

What made you turn to baseball?

My mother and father liked baseball. We used to go, one time a year, to see the old Washington Senators play. I can remember Washington had an outfielder named George Case, and another, Stan Spence, they were real good ballplayers. They had a Cuban ballplayer, I cannot remember his name anymore, he pitched in a doubleheader one Sunday afternoon. My mother liked Detroit, for some reason. We would always go and see Detroit in our summer trip; it was always in the afternoon, because we had dairy cows and we had to get back home to milk them.

How did you end up signing with a big league team?

I was lucky enough to go to college at West Chester State College in West Chester, Pennsylvania. A fellow by the name of Glenn Killinger was the football coach there and he convinced me to play football and baseball. I was pretty successful at both. Killinger knew a scout with the Boston Braves. I am sorry, I do not recall his name anymore. He signed me to a contract with a bonus of $500. That was 1953. I went to Hagerstown, D-ball. The next year, I moved up to Evansville, that was a Three-I team. Then I played with Atlanta in the Southern Association, Double A ball. Then I went up to Wichita, which was the Braves' Triple A team. That was 1956, and the Braves called me up to the big club toward the end of the season.

I would like tell you about my first major league experience. I am up there [major leagues], and I am a nobody, you know. Up there with Spahn and Burdette, and Matthews and Thomson and those guys. I really was scared, to be honest with you. Matthews, playing third base, sprained his ankle. Bobby Thomson, playing left field, was moved in to play third, and they put me in the line-up in left field. They put me in the batting order where Matthews was hitting, fourth. We were the home team, playing Cincinnati. A few of us jogged out to warm up in the outfield. The first warm-up ball I threw sailed over Billy Bruton's head.

Well, the game started and we come in to bat. Danny O'Connell was leading off, and then the second hitter was up. They made one, two outs. Hank Aaron was hitting third. I was wishing from the on-deck circle that Hank would make an out because I was too nervous to hit. He made an out. I am

Earl Hersh, pointing out something to Crabbers' teammate Bob Thurman and *Cincinnati Post* sports editor Pat Harmon.

leading off in the second inning and I am half-numb up there at the plate. I just swing and I hit a double over the right fielder's head. When I came into second base, Jocko Conlon, who was umpiring, he said, "Nice hit, rookie." And all the butterflies went away. And after that it was like old times, playing baseball.

You started out with Santurce. What was living in San Juan like?

The Braves had me go down to Puerto Rico that winter to get more experience, more playing time against good ballplayers. As you know, they had good ballplayers down there. We lived in an apartment building. My wife was with me and my two small children. It was like a wonderful vacation for them. The U.S. Army had a seaport down there, and we use to go there, to the beach, just about every day. We would play ball in the evening. Our lives were spent between the place where we lived, the ballpark, and the army station on the beach. We had great living quarters.

Did you have to adjust to the food?

The food was good, as far as we were concerned. Some of the dishes were different. It was pretty much all Spanish-speaking back then. A lot of times, you had to work on ordering your food, if you went to a restaurant.

I can tell by your voice it was an enjoyable time.

We really liked our experience down there. I was ultra-happy. The family was happy. They treated us special, for some reason. Every place we went, everybody liked us and helped us out. The people there liked baseball players. Going to Puerto Rico the first time, we did not know what to expect. We were overjoyed with the way were treated. We went back to Puerto Rico about ten years ago, for old times sake. It is a different place now. Back then it was kind of what you would expect Puerto Rico to be.

And the travel between cities?

We [team] had our own bus, and I will tell you one thing, when we went over to Ponce and went over that mountain, that was some trip. [Chuckling.] They did not have guard rails on the roads. It was quite an experience for me, I know that. We went to Ponce, and over to Mayagüez. Caguas was a short trip. Those were the three towns that I remember. Of course, San Juan and Santurce played in the same park. It was a pretty nice park. We always drew big crowds, and they were always into the ball game. The fans would yell and clap. I was impressed by the fans.

Do you remember a left-hander in the league by the name of Koufax?

I sure do. Koufax was tough *then*. I was a left-handed hitter, you know. Koufax was a left-handed pitcher. He was tough down there. He was tough anywhere. Gómez, yes. He was one of the stars [in the league]. Clemente played left field, and he was traded that year. I do not remember where. He was just a great ballplayer. Cepeda was young then. But Cepeda was big even then and could hit the long ball. You could tell he was going to be a good ballplayer.

You returned to Puerto Rico as member of a new team.

I played with Caguas the next winter. We lived in a house. The team made the living arrangements for you. I do not know what is involved, but it was somebody's home. It was a real nice place. I did not spend the whole year there. Halfway through the season, when it became clear that we were not going to win the pennant, I was traded, or sold, to a team over in Venezuela. We had to pack up and fly over to Venezuela. I finished the season there. It was not nearly as nice in Venezuela, but it was good baseball. The country was in the throes of an overthrow of government. You had to be in your apartment. They would take you to the ballpark in a car. Maybe not chaperoned, but the team guided us pretty well. It was for our protection. There was rioting sometimes in the streets. We were never in any trouble. They had a beautiful ballpark in Caracas.

Do you remember anything else about your short time in Venezuela?

We lived on the fourth floor of a building, my family and I. Venezuela was not quite as Americanized as Puerto Rico. My Spanish was not real good. Nobody spoke English. We went to the grocery store once to get food. I was in there, getting some bologna. They wanted to know how much I wanted, and I did not know how to tell them. I wanted a pound. They gave me a kilo, which is a lot more than a pound, I learned that. [Amused.] Again, we were treated well.

We flew over to where Aparicio played [Maracaibo]. That was a pretty good plane flight there, as I remember. Over the mountains. Aparicio invited a couple of us, not the whole team, just a couple of the ballplayers, to his home. We went one afternoon. We became pretty good friends later on.

Their ballpark was not as nice as the one in Caracas, but the field was good. The ballpark in Maracaibo had high screens around the field. Evidently some of the spectators liked to throw things. That was a little different.

I appreciate you contacting me. It brings back old times and good memories for me. We are all getting old now. These things are in the past. But it is nice to go back and recall.

Félix Mantilla

Historically speaking, Félix Mantilla's greatest baseball test was passed when he was a 19-year-old in the South Atlantic League. In 1953, Mantilla, Henry Aaron and Horace Garner, as Jacksonville Braves teammates, inte-

grated the racially intolerant league for the first time. (Fleming Reedy and Al Isreal, playing with Savannah the same year, also comprised for posterity the first men of color to play in the "Mother of the Minors.") That same winter, Mantilla and Aaron played together again, wearing the colors of the Caguas Criollos. It was the second of 12 seasons Mantilla spent on the professional diamonds of his native country. After ten campaigns with Caguas, Mantilla played his final two seasons with San Juan. His years with Caguas took Mantilla to four Caribbean Series, winning it all, once, in 1954, on home soil.

A versatile infielder who also played outfield, Mantilla spent 11 summers in the major leagues, more than half of them with the Milwaukee Braves. In 1959, it was Mantilla's 13th-inning, lead off ground ball hit to third baseman Don Hoak that Hoak misfired on to first base that initially ruined Harvey Haddix' "greatest game pitched." Five years later, the two-time World Series participant slugged 30 homers with the American League Red Sox.

Félix, who has lived in the United States for more than 50 years, resides in Wisconsin with second wife Kay. The father of two states his best spare time is spent fishing on Lake Winnebago.

Where in Puerto Rico are you from?

I was born in Isabella, Puerto Rico and I was raised in Isabella.

And how many were in your family?

My sister and my mother and father, who have long since passed away.

Who were your favorite players?

In high school, the players I admired were Luis Canena Márquez, *El Jibaro* Olmo— Luis Olmo, Victor Pellot, Rubén Gómez. There were a lot.

Was it in high school that you started playing baseball seriously?

I started in Isabella on a Police Athletic League team. I was about 14. I then played with the *Lobos* of Arecibo. That was a higher level than the P.A.L. After two years in Arecibo, we went to play in a tournament in Mexico and our team won it. I was then signed professionally by *El Jibaro* Olmo, who was player-manager with Caguas at that time. I played with Caguas for ten years. Olmo was also a coach with the Boston Braves. I also signed with the Braves. Hughie Wise, a Braves scout, signed me. The Braves sent me to Evansville, Class D ball. That was 1952.

That was your first winter season as well.

My first year with Caguas was not a good one. We finished last and I did not play very well at shortstop. Then Olmo switched me to the outfield. That is when I learned to play the outfield.

Henry Aaron became a teammate of yours in 1953 with Caguas.

The following year with Caguas, Aaron played second and I played shortstop. Aaron and I had played at Jacksonville earlier in the year. Then we played winter ball. When I first met Aaron he hit cross-handed. His left hand was above his right on the bat Handle. [Amused.] Aaron hit like that in batting practice. Buster Clarkson was the manager of Santurce, and he wanted to sign Aaron. But I spoke to Aaron and asked him to wait until I spoke to the Caguas' owners. I did, and the owners were interested in Aaron, so he signed with us instead of Santurce.

Aaron did not start well, and Caguas was going to cut him. I spoke on his behalf, and the team agreed to give him a little more time. The Márquez family owned the Caguas team, they were large furniture store owners. Aaron turned it around and went on to [nearly] lead the league in hitting. And Caguas was the champion of the league. Aaron did not participate in the Caribbean Series. We signed Canena Márquez as a reinforcement in his place. When we won the Caribbean Series, there was a caravan of cars and fans from San Juan to Caguas. A lot of people. Mickey Owen was our manager. I remember him [victoriously] riding our [mule] mascot after the Series. Owen was a catcher for the Dodgers. When he went to Puerto Rico, he had a dubious reputation. I guess from his time in Mexico, Owen had a reputation of being sort of a racist. But in Puerto Rico, he was a tremendous guy. There were never any problems with him. He treated everyone the same.

The team would rent us a house. I lived in Villa Turabo. Then, later, I lived in Villa Blanca. Pagán lived there. José Pagán, who died recently.

The following winter was also a memorable one in Puerto Rico with the arrival of Willie Mays.

The next year, Santurce won it all. They had Willie Mays and Bob Thur-

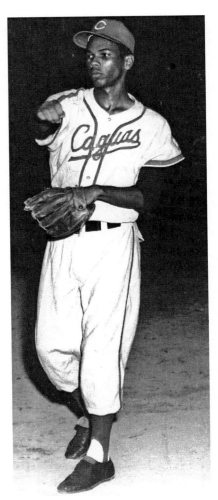

Félix Mantilla was an infield fixture with the Caguas Criollos for a decade (courtesy AGPR Archives).

man — Mays was like a god. The middle of Santurce's lineup [Mays, Thurman, Clemente, Clarkson and George Crowe] was called *El Escuadrón del Pánico* (Murderers Row). They also had Rubén Gómez and Sam Jones. It was a tremendous team. They beat us in the finals.

Tommy Lasorda was a teammate of yours with Caguas.

Lasorda played with us in Caguas. I cannot remember what year exactly. He pitched the first game of a doubleheader and wanted to pitch the second game, too. [Chuckles.] Lasorda was like that. He had a rubber arm. Lasorda started both games that day. He played several years in Puerto Rico. We were playing Mayagüez, once, and Lasorda was with Mayagüez. Something happened between Carlos Bernier and Victor Pellot at first base. Suddenly, there was fight, the fans got into it, the police came. It was quite a rhubarb. I remember Lasorda was not too involved. We sort of called him out for that. The people liked Lasorda because he spoke Spanish.

Caguas then won its second championship in three years. The team traveled to Panama City to compete in the Caribbean Series.

In 1955-56, we were champions of the league, again, but did not play well in the Caribbean Series. I think we were 2–4. The Cuban team won. They always had a great team. All I remember about the stadium in Panama was that the infield was pebbly. It was tough to play on that infield.

In the winter of 1956, Sandy Koufax pitched for Caguas.

Sandy, I remember. In one of the games of a doubleheader against Santurce, he barely gave up a hit, but lost, 2–0, because of walks. Incredible velocity but not much control. Pizarro and Clemente were traded to Caguas that season.

[In 1957] Pizzaro pitched for us the entire season. Pizarro pitched a no-hitter against Mayagüez, and he struck out 17 in another game against Ponce. Ted Norbert was our manager. His son played with us, too. Norbert was a nice guy. But a lot of the players did not agree with how he managed. But our team was so good, we won it all anyway. In the [1958] Caribbean Series, Pizarro struck out 17 against Panama. I played in that game. Nobody could even foul a pitch off him. It was strikeout after strikeout after strikeout. The next day we played Venezuela, and Chico Carrasquel asks me, where did we find that country boy? At that time Pizarro was young and he was a hard thrower. There was a game in that Series where there occurred another tremendous rhubarb. An umpire ruled an outfielder had not caught a ball, and the fans started throwing bottles on the field. We lost the Series to Cuba on the final day.

What was it like having to commute to the other cities and play in their ballparks?

We traveled by car. Five or six in a car. The natives would be in one car. The North American players were in another. It was about a five hour trip to Mayagüez from Caguas. San Juan and Santurce had their own buses.

Solá Morales [Caguas' ballpark] had a capacity of about 7,000. In all the parks the fences were far away. Down the line it was 340. I imagine that has been cut down now. The problem with Sixto [Escobar Stadium] was with high fly balls, the ocean breeze would carry the ball, sometimes over the fence. The stadium was right by the beach.

In Caguas, we used to say that we would play any team in the league with only our native players. We had Victor Pellot at first. I was at second. Pagán, short. Félix Torres played third. We had Luis St. Claire, who was *dominicano-boricua*, Pedro Alomar, Jim Rivera, in the outfield. We would play anybody with just that team of natives. Ponce had good native players but not the competitive caliber of our team. Pellot was the best first baseman in the big leagues and the best first baseman in Puerto Rico.

You finished your career with San Juan.

Later, when I played with San Juan, Clemente did not play much. He would play a few games and that was it. When San Juan played Santurce, it was war. There was a City Championship involved. The fans, when they bought their tickets, had to inform who they rooted for so they could be directed to one particular side of the field. The Santurce fans sat on one side and the San Juan fans sat on the other. But that did not keep the fans apart too often when one team took the lead.

What are your fondest winter league memories?

Rubén was a tremendous pitcher in the Puerto Rican League. He pitched, as I recall, 27 years in the league. Rubén and Pizarro and Tite Arroyo. Pantalones Santiago. Julio Navarro. All had long and great careers.

It was a great time for all of us players. The goal really was to play in the Puerto Rican League, where all the great Puerto Rican players had played. Like Canena Márquez, Carlos Bernier, [Francisco] Coimbre. And that is where I wanted to play. I never really dreamed of playing in the major leagues. I wanted to play in the Puerto Rican League.

Julio Navarro

A winner of 98 winter league games, Julio Navarro's career spanned San Juan's two main baseball venues. As a Santurce rookie in 1955-56, Navarro performed at Sixto Escobar Stadium over four campaigns. A trade to Caguas in 1959 saw Navarro continue his more than two decade-long career at Hiram Bithorn Stadium as a visiting pitcher, beginning in 1962.

A friendly fellow, Navarro, during our talk, placed his "biggest fan"— his wife of 53 years — on the line to say hello to me, a person she did not know from Adam. La negra, as Navarro fondly referred to her, told me all about their six grandchildren and four children, including former big league pitcher Jaime Navarro, current pitching coach for the Seattle Mariners.

The elder Navarro was a career relief pitcher in the major leagues with the California Angels, Detroit Tigers and Atlanta Braves.

Tell me about yourself and your early family history.

I was born in the district of Vieques in 1934 and was raised in St. Croix. In our family there were eight of us, I was the second. One of the children is now deceased.

How did baseball become part of your life?

I went to Catholic school. I played cricket and softball. The church in St. Croix formed a baseball team and that is how I began with baseball. I was 15 or 16.

What do you remember about breaking into the league as a young pitcher?

I was invited to participate in a tryout they had for a professional league made up of players that had played in Puerto Rico and players from St. Croix. Joe Christopher played in that league. He played for the Red Sox and Mets. Alfonso Gerard and Horace Clarke also played in that league. I made enough of an impression in an exhibition game that I ended up pitching for the St. Croix team against more or less an all-star team from Puerto Rico, made up of players mostly from San Juan and Santurce. Nino Escalera saw me pitch in the game, and he wanted to sign me. But Gerard came to me and said, "Don't sign with anybody. I have already talked to Santurce and they want to sign you. We are leaving for Puerto Rico tomorrow." And that is how I started my baseball career.

Santurce sent me to Florida, to an instructional camp. [Jose] Pagán was there. I was helped by the fact that I knew English, thanks to my St. Croix upbringing. I knew Creole, too. Pedrín Zorilla was the owner of Santurce. He had a connection with the New York Giants. I hurt my arm due to the cold weather. I was not use to that. A chiropractor in Puerto Rico, Dr. Sierra, helped me recover. After a year, I was able to pitch in my first game with Santurce. I pitched in relief at Sixto Escobar. It was 1955.

With Santurce, I met Roberto Clemente, Terin Pizarro, Rubén Gómez. Luis Rodríguez Olmo. I met Pantalones Santiago, who was my idol. I used to listen to games in St. Croix when Santiago pitched for Ponce. Buster Clarkson, Bob Thurman. Willard Brown I saw, but he was old, at the end of his career. Bill Greason and Marion Fricano, I spoke to about pitching. Santurce put me on a weight-gain regiment, because I weighed 150 pounds, soaking wet.

I lived with other rookies, young players in an apartment in Santurce at the *parada diecinueve*. I was single. I kid my wife, Ana, not to worry about the girlfriends I had when I first arrived in Puerto Rico, because they are all dead now. My wife is my biggest fan. When I first arrived in San Juan from St Croix, it was like arriving at 42nd Street in New York. It was so pretty. The people were so pleasant.

I used to take the bus for five cents from my apartment to San Juan, to Sixto Escobar. That was my favorite park. I guess because I met so many great players there, and players that would come from abroad. My favorite park to pitch in, though, was Hiram Bithorn. The wind blew in the pitcher's favor. I pitched in the quickest game ever at Bithorn Stadium, and my best pitching memories come from Bithorn. Later in my career, after I had been traded to Caguas, I pitched a playoff game against Santurce at Bithorn Stadium that set an attendance record — over 20,000 people. I was pleased because the effort was against Santurce, which had the best team, and that it was an elimination game.

Do you recall a playoff game incident between Santurce and Mayagüez a few years earlier?

Yes, I remember that playoff game in 1959 with Santurce. Afterwards, the Mayagüez fans pelted our bus with rocks. Rubén Gómez started that game and he beaned Joe Christopher, my former teammate in St. Croix. That is what started it. It was thanks to the Mayagüez police that our team was able to get out of there in one piece. The police escorted us out from the stadium and to the edge of town. We won the playoffs, and I played in my first Caribbean Series, in Caracas.

That was the 1959 Caribbean Series.

In my first Series start, I shut out the Panamanian team. I met Orlando Pena and Camilo Pascual in that Series. I also first met in Caracas Norman Cash, who I later played with in Detroit. The Caribbean Series was played at University Stadium. We were beaten in a game on a play that should not have counted. I asked Norman Cash about the ball they ruled that he caught in centerfield, which turned out to be the game-changing play, and Cash told me that he did not catch it. I asked Cash when we were with Detroit. "Tell me the truth. Did you catch the ball?" He told me, "No, I did not catch it."

The same thing had happened to another Puerto Rican team [Caguas] the year before [1958 Caribbean Series] in Puerto Rico. I did not participate, but I just so happened to be sitting near the right field bullpen when Canenita Allen caught the ball they [umpire] said he did not. I was there. I saw him catch it. It was a low liner he caught. He threw it back in for a double play, but the umpire ruled he had not caught it. Everybody saw it but the umpire.

You also participated in the last of the original Caribbean Series in 1960.

It was during the 1959-60 season that I became a starter, which I owe to Monchile Concepción [Santurce manager], who gave me the original opportunity. It came about after I was traded to Caguas. That same season, I went to my second Caribbean Series, in Panama, with Caguas. I met Pedro Ramos.

I will tell you how I ended up being traded to Caguas. Zorilla had sold the team [Santurce] to a man named Ramón Cuevas, who had sold off Terín Pizarro to Caguas. José Pagan and I were in a contract dispute. Santurce wanted to get Pizarro back, so they sent me and Pagan to Caguas for Pizarro. Pagan and I then played many years for Caguas. I pitched into the 1970s.

Julio Navarro as a major league rookie.

During your extended career, who were the best players to play in Puerto Rico?

I saw various. I never saw Willie Mays. I saw Roberto Clemente. He could hit, run, field and throw. Intelligent player. And he played to win. I remember hearing Clemente say that he always tried his best, so that he would never have any self-doubts about whether he gave it his all. I think the same words were attributed to Willie Mays or Joe DiMaggio. I saw Olmo, not a lot. But from what I saw, the way he played left field, you did not forget him. Olmo was elegant. It was Clemente and Olmo.

There were a lot of good pitchers. Terín Pizarro. A North American pitcher, Ellis "Cot" Deal, who played with the Cardinals. Tite Arroyo with Ponce. Pantalones Santiago. I remember Sandy Koufax. When I saw that lefty with that high leg lift, he let the ball go with such ease. Koufax was wild then, because he had not developed. I later saw him when I was with the Angels at Chávez Ravine. We shared the park with the Dodgers. Koufax told me what a great time he had in Puerto Rico. He commented how everyone was so nice to him. How blacks could move around everywhere.

What was the issue of race like for you?

White fans tended to root for San Juan. Santurce's followers were darker-skinned. But it was "*en familia.*" The divisiveness had more to do with geographic boundaries.

At that time, it was work and baseball. It was parties, with dancing. There were no drug problems or so much crime. The economy was good. They were great years. I thank God for having lived them and for the friendships I made throughout.

Luis Olmo

I met Luis Rodríguez Olmo during my trip to Puerto Rico. The Puerto Rican baseball icon invited me to his Santurce home, a yellow, two-story dwelling nestled between calles *Figueroa and Del Carmen. I interviewed him there on a late rainy afternoon. The Olmos, Luis and wife Emma, share the home with their daughter. The parents reside on the top floor, while the daughter occupies the ground level (Luis, Jr., Olmo's second child, passed away from an intestinal ailment more than a decade ago.) Olmo was exactly four weeks away from celebrating his 92nd birthday on the day we met and a few months away from celebrating his 71st wedding anniversary. I was impressed by Olmo's appearance, from his upright posture to the sinewy muscle strength I felt from the hand I placed behind his back and shoulders when we posed together for photographs.*

The Arecibo-born Olmo played for 15 seasons in his homeland, the major part with Caguas. Olmo retired as an active player during the 1956–57 campaign, and then managed for many years in Puerto Rico. (Olmo had been a player-manager with Caguas for several seasons.) Among a litany of Latin American league accomplishments accumulated from playing in Mexico, Cuba and Venezuela, the outfielder participated in four Caribbean Series and was named Most Valuable Player in the 1951 Caracas tournament. In that Series, Olmo became the first player to hit a home run in both the Caribbean and World Series. In 1949, as a fourth-year member of the Brooklyn Dodgers, Luis had connected against the New York Yankee's Joe Page in Game Three of the Fall Classic — becoming the first Hispanic player to achieve the grand post-season feat.

In all, Olmo played in six big league campaigns with two National League teams.

Where did it all begin for Puerto Rico's most venerable living baseball legend?

I was born in Arecibo, August 11, 1919. I was the third child in the family. There was José, Julio and myself, and then Gilberto was born. I was born with a baseball in my hand. Since I was very small, I have always liked baseball.

And which player did you favor most?

When I was young, I liked Billy Herman, second baseman for the Chicago Cubs. I later played with Billy in Brooklyn.

How did you begin your professional career?

I was signed by Caguas in 1938. I signed my first U.S. contract the following year, to play for the Richmond Colts. I made it to Brooklyn in 1943, and did well. Before the end of the season, I asked Branch Rickey for a raise on my salary for the 1944 season. Rickey called in his secretary and told her to get me an airplane ticket to go back home. I changed my mind about the raise.

In 1944, I had a so-so year with Brooklyn. In '45, I was hitting in the .300s, and the team decided to switch me from outfield to the infield. It was to try and disrupt my hitting. Brooklyn did not want me to do too good, so they would not have to pay me a higher salary. I still drove in over 100 runs. Rickey gave all the ballplayers that year a $500 bonus. He saved mine to give to me as a raise on my 1946 salary. The problem was I asked for a $3,000 increase. It so happened, I received a generous offer to play in Mexico. I told Rickey about it. Rickey told me, "Good bye and good luck." I wished him the same.

Jorge Pasquel treated me well. There were about 26 players that went down to Mexico to play. We were all suspended [by organized baseball]. I played for Mexico City. It was Pasquel's league. I saw him at the games, but I did not get a chance to get to know him. In Mexico, I lived in an apartment with two Canadian players, Roland Gladú was one. As a result of the suspension, I could not play ball here in Puerto Rico in the winter. I was injured in Mexico, my meniscus, and could not finish my first season. I was operated on, and returned to Mexico in 1947 and played well.

I went to Cuba that winter to play for the non-sanctioned league there. I played with the Santiago team, which folded half way through the season. I latched on with another league team, Leones, managed by Salvador Hernández. My wife and daughter, who was born in 1941, were with me. We lived in an apartment with Roberto Ortiz and his wife. Ortiz had recently married and he had a young daughter. Roberto was a great friend of mine, my best

friend in baseball. He and Gene Mauch. It was such a shame what happened
to Roberto. He was a saver. He passed up small treats for himself to save pennies. And Roberto saved, and he bought a three-story apartment building in
Havana. He was a contented man after that. But Castro came and took it
from him. Roberto left for Miami, and became a milkman. A *milkman*. This
great star of baseball. I saw him in Miami doing this. It was embarrassing.
Roberto died young, maybe of shame.

I was playing ball in Venezuela for Pastora, in the summer league, when
I was reinstated in 1949. All the players were. I rejoined Brooklyn in June or
July and we went to the World Series. We lost to the Yankees.

**During the 1950-51 campaign, you were involved in the most historic playoff
game in Puerto Rican baseball history.**

What can I say about 1950-51, the year of *"El Pepelucaso?"* Caguas, our
team, won the league by 12 games. But then we lost to Santurce in the playoffs
in seven games on a last-inning home run. I was in the outfield when that
ball sailed out of the park. We had just retired their two best hitters, Willard
Brown and Bob Thurman. Then Pepe Lucas comes up and hits a home run
to win the game. I walked home from the stadium, crying.

A welcoming committee of Crabbers' teammates prepare to greet Luis Olmo as
he pulls into home, following a fence-clearing blast.

Then Pedrin Zorilla asked me to join the Santurce squad as a reinforcement player for the Caribbean Series in Venezuela. Zorilla, he was a man who knew his baseball.

I know the way you played in that Series helped soften the crushing playoff loss. What can you tell me about the Caracas park and fans?

It was an older park, Caracas stadium was, I remember that. I hit three home runs and drove in nine runs, and was named Most Valuable Player. Puerto Rico won its first Caribbean Series championship. The fans in Venezuela were great. There were great fans all over. Everywhere I played. All the countries.

You were also chosen as a reinforcement player for the following year's Caribbean Series in Panama.

What I remember about the [1952] Caribbean Series, in Panama, the following year, was that Títa [wife] and I were wined and dined a lot by Mr. Cobián [team owner] and his son, and their wives. Again, I was chosen as a reinforcement player for the San Juan team. I think I did more eating and drinking than I did hitting. We [team] did not play well.

What was traveling like to the other ballparks?

We traveled by bus in those days. We met at the park. My favorite park to play in was Paquito Montaner Park in Ponce. It had a short left field, and there was a lot of terrain in right center. If you hit one in the gap there, you could run for days. I led the league in triples with 13 one year. I bet I recorded a majority of them in Ponce. On Sundays, we played a doubleheader at Sixto Escobar. I would play in the morning game. Come home and have lunch, and go back to play the second game in the afternoon. The food was good everywhere in Puerto Rico.

Do you remember Hank Aaron's season?

Of course, I remember Hank Aaron. He played with Caguas. I saw Aaron struggling on the infield and I suggested to [manager] Mickey Owen to try Aaron in the outfield...

So it was you. That is something. What about Willie Mays' arrival, and Sandy Koufax?

When Willie Mays came to play in Puerto Rico, he became the third outfielder in the league who used the "basket catch," after myself and Clemente. Sandy Koufax was a hard thrower, but wild. Fast and wild.

You were a playing-manager and then manager in the league after your retirement. Did you ever have problems with any players?

Victor Pellot. He was the only player I ever fined as a manager. For fielding with one hand. Pellot made me look stupid. Because he won eight gold gloves in the major leagues. Poor Victor. Died because he wanted to, or because he did not do enough to help himself. Rubén Gómez died from cancer; it was 15 days after Gómez had been operated on. Victor never forgot that. Never got over the closeness between the two things. Victor preferred not to undergo an operation on his prostrate right away. And he died from the complications sooner than he should have.

You have been married for more than seven decades. That is truly remarkable.

I met my wife while she was still in high school, which was pretty close to the stadium. One day she was buying ice cream at a stand, and I saw her. She was 17. I was 21. We married not long afterward.

You have so many great things to look back on in your career. Does any one thing stand out?

I was a six-time manager of the year recipient in Puerto Rico. I am the only player still alive from the league's inaugural season—1938. Millito Navarro and I were the only two remaining, but Millito died this year. He was 105 years old.

José Santiago

José Santiago was one of only a handful of pitchers to win 100 games in the Puerto Rican Winter League (the others were Luis Arroyo, Luis Cabrera, Rubén Gómez, and Juan Pizarro). Best known by his baseball nickname "Pantalones," Santiago hurled in all or parts of 16 P.R.W.L. campaigns. His most accredited mound work came during his nine seasons with Ponce, beginning in 1946-47. It was with Ponce that Santiago received his moniker, following a most impressive relief appearance. A sportswriter wrote that Santiago, with his performance, showed the other team who wore the pants that day—"Que pantalones!"

Santiago pitched in six of the first 12 Caribbean Series, tied with Rubén Gómez and Venezuela's Carrao Bracho for the most appearances by any one pitcher. Santiago's four victories in six decisions trails only Gómez, Bracho, Pedro Ramos and Camilo Pascual for the most Caribbean Series career wins.

In many ways a renaissance sportsman, Santiago was involved in boxing and horse racing promotions following his diamond retirement. Santiago worked with two of boxing's biggest promoters. The father of two daughters was also a television sports producer. In the early 1970s, Santiago purchased the live television rights to horse racing's Triple Crown and brought, via satellite, all the famed racing legs of the sport to an avid

Puerto Rican TV audience. Santiago also had ownership interests, at separate times, in the Caguas and Ponce franchises.

The right-hander pitched in the big leagues with the Cleveland Indians and Kansas City Athletics for short durations in the mid–1950s. In 1949, as a 21-year-old, Santiago threw a 5-hit, 16-inning complete game for the Dayton Indians of the Central League. His opposite number, Joe Nuxhall, also went the distance, suffering the 3–1 defeat.

Where are you from?

Coamo, Puerto Rico, but when I was 27 days old, I was brought to New York. I lived in New York until I was six. My father wanted me to learn Spanish well, so I came back to Puerto Rico and attended school here until ninth grade. Then I returned to the United States. I went to Seward Park High School in lower Manhattan, close to Chinatown and Little Italy. I have a brother, Arturo, who was in the Air Force; he lives in Tampa. Ted Williams was the ballplayer I most admired.

When did you come into your own as a baseball player?

At 17, I played with a Police Athletic League team against two semi-professional teams in Puerto Rico. We were beaten pretty badly. But I stayed over to pitch two other games. I matched up against the two best pitchers in the semi-pro league and beat them both — one by shutout. Martíano García, owner of Ponce, signed me on the advice of Pepe Ruíz, who worked for him. García was involved in the education system. I signed my contract in New York and then returned to play with Ponce. I received a $1,000 bonus. My first contract was for $35 a week. Pancho Coimbre, the best player in Puerto Rico, was making $50. Willard Brown and Thurman, great players, also made $50. The salaries became a little better once the new parks were built.

I began my career in 1946-47. I finished the season, 8–2, and was named Rookie of the Year. No one really showed me how to pitch. In those times, you fended for yourself. But I was fortunate enough that George Scales [Ponce manager] gave me an opportunity pitch. He had gone to high school in New York. I became one of the four starters on the Ponce team. We won the league championship that year.

With as an accomplished career as you had, you must have known Pedrín Zorilla.

Pedrín Zorilla was my closest friend in baseball. He added me to his championship club in 1951— Santurce — and we won the Caribbean Series. You could reinforce your Caribbean roster team with a few players in the league. It was the first time a team from Puerto Rico won the Caribbean Series. I was the top pitcher. I won two games in the tournament. I beat Hoyt

Wilhelm, Giants pitcher, and Clem Labine, who pitched for Brooklyn. I received a hero's welcome when I arrived back in Ponce. There were over a thousand people in the town square to honor me.

That was your first Caribbean Series, but certainly not your last.

In 1953, again with Santurce, I substituted for, you know who? Roberto Clemente. He was a rookie. The Series was held in Havana. I started on the mound in the famous comeback game against Habana. I was removed in the eighth inning, ahead 3–2. Roberto Vargas relieved me. I think they scored three runs against him. We were behind in the last of the ninth inning by two runs, and we made five straight hits and we won, 6–5. Formental, in right, could not play a ball hit by Cot

José "Pantalones" Santiago with the Mayagüez Indios, one of four Puerto Rican Winter League teams for whom he hurled during a 16-season career.

Deal. He was the winning pitcher, too, because he had relieved Vargas. There is a famous photo of me and Rubén Gómez with a Puerto Rican flag that was taken right after the game.

Zorilla always chose me for all of his Caribbean Series squads, except in 1955, when he decided to go with his team as it was. Pedrin convinced the Giants to let Willie Mays come to play in Puerto Rico. With Clemente and Mays, Santurce won the championship that year. In the Caribbean Series, Mays went 0-for-10 until he obtained his first hit. Don Zimmer was the outstanding hitter in that Series. I pitched in six Caribbean Series. I was a reinforcement player in all of them. Except in 1957, I was with Mayagüez. In the Caribbean Series, I seemed to pitch my best games against Cuba. The only game Marianao lost in the 1957 Series was the game I beat them, 6–0. That Series was also played in Havana.

In the 1958 Series, I was pitching against Bob Shaw, from the Chicago White Sox. Shaw was pitching for Marianao. I was ahead 4–3, but gave up a walk in the ninth and was replaced by [Marion] Fricano. The manager, Ted Norbert, told me I looked tired. I was not tired, I said, but he was the manager. Marianao loaded the bases on a hit and walk, and the next batter hit a fly to Canenita Allen in right field. Allen had trouble with it, but caught the ball at his shoe tops. The umpire called "safe," no catch, that Allen had trapped the ball. The fans went crazy. Everything was thrown out onto the field, including chairs. The game was suspended and finished the next day. Pizarro walked the first batter with the bases loaded and we lost.

My last Caribbean Series was 1960, in Panama. I remember Panama more from my boxing days. I was involved in the Esteban de Jesús fight.

You mentioned Cuba from a Caribbean Series perspective, but you also spent much more time there as a pitcher in the International League. Talk to me about that.

Cuba was Cuba. The cemetery in Havana was a city to itself. There were bigger plots that belonged to rich people there than most houses I had seen. I had the opportunity to play for the Sugar Kings in 1957 and 1958. In 1958, we traveled to Morón, and I pitched for the Sugar Kings in the first game played there. Against the Buffalo Bisons.

You must have seen all the great players.

People pick Willie Mays over Hank Aaron, but Aaron was the best major leaguer from my period. I saw all the great ones. Mays, Aaron, Clemente, [Frank] Robinson. Mays was a better fielder. I became a good friend of Mays.... Yes, Mays, played at Candlestick, where the wind blew in. But DiMaggio played at Yankee Stadium with that left field, and Ted Williams played at Fenway Park. Williams was a left-handed hitter.

Koufax played with Caguas. He was wild and did not pitch that much. Koufax became a friend and is one the best people I have ever met.

Pancho Coimbre was the best hitter in Puerto Rico. Clemente, also, although it is difficult to compare eras sometimes. Roberto was a good friend of mine. Terín Pizarro was the best pitcher. Pizarro threw harder than Herb Score. I told Hank Greenberg [Cleveland general manager] about Pizarro and he did not listen to me. Cleveland let Milwaukee sign Pizarro away. Willard Brown was the best foreign player. I understand he was the first black player to hit a home run in the American League, ahead of Larry Doby. Victor Pellot was the best first baseman in the world.

Frank Howard hit the longest home run ever at Sixto Escobar Stadium. Josh Gibson played when there was no outfield fencing at Sixto Escobar. Gibson's home run distances were helped by their bounces. Howard hit the longest home run. Howard's ball cleared the fence, the wall, the light tower, the beach and even the ocean. [Exaggerated laugh.]

You also must have logged a lot of miles on the road over all the years you played.

We used to travel by car at first, then in the fifties, by bus. The roads were not good. In 1948, they put in lights at Sixto Escobar. The league played three days a week — Thursday and Saturday and a doubleheader on Sunday. Later, three new parks were inaugurated at the same time — in Mayagüez, Caguas and Ponce. I won the first game at the new park in Ponce. We inaugurated the park on a Saturday and lost. The next day, Sunday, I pitched and we won.

What was your preferred ballpark?

I liked pitching in Ponce, my home park, because it was spacious.

It is interesting to note that you played abroad in the Negro Leagues before reaching the majors.

Believe it or not, the owner of the Harlem Globetrotters signed me to play in organized baseball. Abe Saperstein. I was playing with the New York Cubans in the United States. In 1947, we won the Negro League World Series. It was the only year the New York Cubans won the championship. I did not pitch much, I was young. I was 18. I roomed with Luis Tiant, Sr., who was a pitcher on our team. Tiant was already up there in age. He was at least 40, and his record that year was phenomenal. Tiant was a serious individual. Tiant did not have any vices; he did not smoke or drink. He did not speak to me too much about pitching. He was a left-hander and I was a right-hander. Tiant had an extraordinary screwball. And an extraordinary pick-off move to first base. Of course, there was the famous Tiant story from the Negro Leagues that Tiant picked off a runner at first base while the batter swung at the pick off move for strike three — double play. [Laughs.]

We were based in New York City. All of the players had their own apartments. I lived at home in New York. We played the Cleveland Buckeyes for the championship. I did not pitch in the series; I was too young.

The next season [1948] with the Cubans, I won six and lost two. Saperstein alerted a scout he knew with Cleveland, Bill Killefer. Saperstein was friends with Bill Veeck. I also recommended that Cleveland sign Minnie Miñoso, who played third base for us. [Team owner Alex] Pompez sold me to Cleveland for $10,000 and sold Miñoso for $5,000. Miñoso was 28 then; he is 91-years-old now and looks great.

Pitching for the Cubans that year, I defeated the Birmingham Black Barons and struck out 17. I struck out Willie Mays four times in that game. Willie never forgot that. In spring training later, he told me, "I have to get even with you. I have to get even with you." It was good-natured. Willie and I played pool. I was older than Willie at that time, and I beat him at pool, too. [Chuckles.] We did not play for money; it was just for fun.

Right after my 17 strikeout game, the Negro League All-Star Game was held at Yankee Stadium. I attended the game with Saperstein and Killefer. Miñoso had four hits in four at-bats. That is when they decided on Miñoso, too.

You carry a distinction among Puerto Rican major leaguers.

In 1949, I was the first black player from Puerto Rico to go to a big league spring training camp. It was the year after Cleveland had won the World Series. My roommate in spring training was Satchel Paige. Myself, Paige and Larry Doby were the only blacks on the team. We trained in Tuscon, Arizona. So did the Giants, in Phoenix. The Giants had Willie Mays and Hank Thompson as the only black players. As you can imagine, that Cleveland team would have been a hard one for anyone to make. I remember not many players wanting to take batting practice against me because I threw hard. Beto Ávila came up to me that spring — he was on the Indians — and said, "Hey, for a little guy you throw pretty hard." I told him, "I am not so little — you and I are the same height." [Chuckles.]

I went straight to the minors after camp. I won 17 games for Dayton in the Central League. Dayton's spring camp was in Marianna, Florida. It was a military base, with barracks, like Vero Beach.

We could not eat in the same places as the white players. We had to stay at the homes of clergyman, or in run-down motels. I was not used to that. In Puerto Rico, we had social problems as far as class but not race. But we survived. You cannot fight City Hall, as they say. My first year with Dayton I stayed at the YMCA. That is where I lived. The next year, I stayed at the home of the lady who cooked in the YMCA's kitchen. Her last name was Jeter. She lived on the other side of the tracks, as they say.

I will tell you the North American black players sometimes resented the black Hispanic players. In Spanish, the word *negro* is used with familiarity. We refer to our own loved ones using this word, in an endearing manner. But North American blacks would hear us speaking Spanish and using this word and wonder what we were saying and whether we were directing anything offensive at them. Also, there were Hispanic-owned restaurants that we would come across in Florida. We could go into these restaurants and eat, but the North American blacks could not. The black Hispanics were welcomed but not the North American blacks.

I also played in the Texas League a few years later, with Dave Hoskins, who was the first black player to play in the Texas League. He opened the season in April, I arrived the following month. The team had to expand the seating accommodations at the park for the additional black and Latin fans that came to see us.

I am really curious about your nickname.

Emilio Huyke was an admired figure in Puerto Rico. He was the one most responsible for forming the Puerto Rican Sports Hall of Fame. He was writing for the local Ponce newspaper, located on Isabella Street and which cost three cents. One game, against Caguas, with the score 2–1 in our favor, I was called in to relieve with the bases loaded in the ninth inning and no outs. I struck out the side and we won. Someone from the stands shouted at me, "*Ave María, que pantalones!*" Huyke heard it and used it in the next day's paper. It struck a chord. "Pantalones" took over for "José" after that.

You certainly have many things to look back on with pride.

One of my favorite memories from the league is winning both ends of a doubleheader. I pitched and won a morning game, then came into relieve in the nightcap, which we won in 19 innings. It was against Santurce. I also remember well the New York Yankees when they came to train in Puerto Rico in 1947. I faced six batters and struck out four. I received a great deal of publicity for that because I helped beat the Yankees in the game. I pitched a no-hitter at Paquito Montaner Stadium [Ponce]. Winning Rookie of The Year, and being enshrined in so many Halls of Fame are also great memories.

I am in eight different Sports Halls of Fame. In my hometown, in Ponce, in Puerto Rico's. I am in the Caribbean Series Hall of Fame, too.

You remained active in the sports world after your baseball retirement.

After I retired, I became a coach with San Juan. Then I entered into the boxing world, working with Puerto Rican fighters. I partnered with both Don King and Bob Arum. King told me to leave Arum and stay with him, which I did. But within the last year or so, I had to leave that completely to take care of my wife, Matilde. She has Alzheimer's. We have been married 63 years.

Bob Smith

Bob Smith was property of the Boston Red Sox when he was sent to pitch in Puerto Rico in 1956. Smith was owned by the Pittsburgh Pirates when he pitched in the Dominican Republic the following winter. Those were two of the four parent teams for whom Smith played in his four-year big league career.

In Smith's first winter campaign with island champion Mayagüez, the left-hander tied for the most wins (12) in the circuit and posted the league's best ERA (1.93). Smith had the privilege of initiating the Opening Game of the 1957 Caribbean Series in Havana. Smith, along with his team, did not provide a competitive showing in the tournament.

In the Dominican Republic, playing for Águilas Cibaeñas, Smith had a New Year's Day near no-hitter spoiled with two outs in the ninth. The pitcher was also a teammate of Dick Stuart, who was coming off a 66-home run campaign for the Western League's Lincoln Chiefs.

The 81-year-old Smith was getting over some health problems when we conversed. He was looking forward to picking up on his previous leisure activities of golfing and traveling with wife Anita.

Where were you born, and from where did your baseball background develop?

In a small town in New Hampshire, Woodsville, New Hampshire. I have a sister. Started off playing in sandlot baseball and playing in school, and stayed with it for a lot of years and a lot of places. They had what they called birddog scouts, guys that reported to a real scout. They went around to high school games. Somebody said we need to look at Bob Smith. In the summer, I played Legion ball, and that had some of the best players in the area. There were all kinds of scouts around. Joe Brawley was the scout that signed me. He was the actual Red Sox scout. I started at the lowest level. In those days they had D, C, B, A, Double A and Triple A.

When did you first play baseball outside the U.S.?

My first year playing winter ball was 1956-57. I played with Mayagüez. I was the leading pitcher in the league. Mickey [Owen], I think, attained a little bit of a bad rap for something that happened in the World Series. Mickey was a nice man. He had a lovely wife. They were so close. They did everything together. If you saw Mickey, you saw her. I cannot think of her name.

Living in Mayagüez, some of the time we traveled to San Juan with Mickey and his wife. We bussed it most of the times. Once in a while Mickey would take some of the wives. I thought he was real good manager. I liked him. I was doing well. Mickey liked me. He helped me a lot. He helped other guys. He got along with the native people down there. Mickey Owen helped me work on a sinker. But I never was able to throw it as well, afterwards, as I threw it in Puerto Rico. When we traveled on the bus, we would stop at these places called pig shacks, or something like that. They had live hogs. They sold cooked pork. The local guys loved it. They would stop to eat a lot of it and bring some on the bus.

They called us imports, there were seven or eight of us, we all lived in an apartment complex, a high rise. We had a good arrangement, spent a lot of time around the swimming pool. I believe everybody had their wives with them. I was not married. We would go out on boats. Fish a little bit. Did some night boating, and watched the fish in the water. A lot of swimming pool time and probably drank a few beers and things like that. We did not eat out. There were not a lot of places to eat. One thing I do remember was that there was a wonderful bakery. The product would come out late at night.

We would always be there to buy bread and things right out of the oven. Loaves, long loaves and pastries. We were at that bakery an awful lot. I remember Christmas shopping, having trouble finding what I wanted to buy. I went to a shirt factory and bought a lot of shirts.

What was the atmosphere like pitching at Isidoro García Park in Mayagüez?

I remember the stadium at Mayagüez being full of people, all waving white flags or towels. The fans were very excitable people and they really liked the ball team, and if we were doing well, they liked us even better. The ballpark was okay. Fine minor league quality. The facilities were average, not a lot of room, small lockers. Sixto Escobar Stadium was probably a little better than the others on the island. The fans there liked their baseball.

I beat Sandy Koufax one night, 1–0. Koufax was not quite then what he became later. I also stroked a base hit off him. I came to know Sandy afterward. We talked about our winter down there. He is a nice man. They had a lot of good players in Puerto Rico. Vic Power was a hard guy to get out. I remember Nino Escalera. I played a lot against Nino in the minor leagues. Juan Pizarro. Pete Wojey was on my team.

I would like to hear about your Caribbean Series experience.

I pitched the Opening Game of the [1957] Caribbean Series and lost. I do not remember the opening ceremonies, but that Series was a big deal down there. We did not play well at all over in Cuba. We went two and out. There was some kind of virus going around on our team, but that is not an excuse. We just did not play that well, and did not compete that long. I did not particularly like Cuba. I did buy some cigars. It was getting close to Castro. We were searched in and out of the ballpark, things like that. We did go out to a wonderful club, where I met Nat King Cole. He sang for us, sat with us a little bit. We had a whole table full of our team. I got Nat King Cole's autograph, and had a great time.

Bob Smith in his major league garb (courtesy B. Smith).

You made a return trip to the Caribbean the following winter, but detoured to the Dominican Republic.

In the Dominican Republic, we lived in a hotel, and I remember they had gambling and we did all we could to keep ourselves from gambling every day. Not that we had a lot of money, so we did not have to worry about doing *too* much gambling. The food was pretty good. We did a lot of sightseeing. We would walk around the markets and see the raw meat hanging with flies circling around. There was a lot of poverty. An awful lot of people walking with things on their heads.

The stadiums were fine, new stadiums. There was a big rivalry between two of the teams.

A teammate of yours was Dick Stuart.

Dick Stuart was on our team. He did hit some home runs. He was noted for his home runs and not his fielding. Dick was an okay guy. He was maybe a little misunderstood. He was a good teammate. Dick liked to be called "Sixty-six." He hit 66 home runs in a season somewhere. That is a big number.

You tossed a most memorable game against Estrellas Orientales.

I had a no-hitter going with two outs in the ninth inning, one game. This player that I knew from up here, [Manny] Jiménez, came up. He was a switch-hitter. I had gotten him out three times, hitting right-handed. He turned around and hit left-handed his fourth time up against me, and darned if he did not get a single. I pitched a one-hitter. We won the game, 1–0.

What did you take away from your off-season ball playing?

Playing winter ball really helped me a lot. I was playing at a high level. Almost at major league level, I thought. The native players were really good. It was a good brand of baseball. There were always representatives from the major leagues around.

I remember driving through the country in Puerto Rico, there were always lots of rainbows. The cars all tooted their horns, making lots of noise. The people liked us. You could feel that. They knew who we were.

Jim Stump

Perhaps no bigger change has befallen the game over the past few decades than the way starting pitching is viewed. For many a year, if a starter was pitching well he stayed in a close or tie game, until the game was decided —

in some cases, no matter the length. Jim Stump upheld this long-established pitching credo in November 1957, by throwing 27 innings, in two starts, four days apart, for the Caguas Criollos. The second start was an amazing 17-inning complete game home loss to Luis Arroyo and the San Juan Senators, 3–1. (Arroyo hurled 16 frames and received the win with relief help.) In Stump's case, the strenuous efforts resulted in a "dead arm," and curtailed his playing time in his first winter in Puerto Rico (and also a chance to participate in the Caribbean Series, as Caguas won the league championship).

Eventually, the right-hander from Michigan regained his arm strength and returned to Puerto Rico for three additional winter combines with the Mayagüez Indios.

Stump, now a widower, saw limited duty with the Detroit Tigers in 1957 and 1959, but had a long career after baseball with General Motors.

Where were you born?

Right here in Lansing, Michigan, February 10, 1932. It was just myself and my sister.

When did your professional baseball life begin?

In high school, I pitched. They did not have a draft back then. John McHale scouted me. I signed right out of high school with the Tigers in 1950, and '51 was my first [professional] year. I was a big George Kell fan.

An advancement through the ranks eventually landed you in Puerto Rico.

When I was called to the Tigers in 1957, from Birmingham, the Tigers wanted me to go play winter ball. I actually started in Mexico City, but they decided they would like me to go to Puerto Rico. I was only in Mexico a week or two. I stayed in San Juan but played for Caguas. It was not much of a problem. Caguas was not that far away, really. Ted Norbert was our manager. He was a manager in the Milwaukee Braves' organization.

What did you think of the food?

It was pretty good — is there a dish called chicken *asopao*? That was good. There was a restaurant in Mayagüez that served a goat fricassee. I liked that very well, it was real good.

I would think you had a similar opinion about the competition. Who were the real good players?

Vic Power and Juan Pizarro. Vic Power was darned good. Pizarro was the best pitcher. Ron Samford played second for us. Ramon Conde, I think, played short.

Those were all your teammates. What can you tell about the stadiums and fans?

It was a nice stadium in San Juan. The fans were rabid. You had to be very careful. I mean, they really enjoyed their baseball, I will tell you that. I remember, once, we were playing in Mayagüez. And we beat them. The fans in Mayagüez, you know, they peeled oranges, the skin in whole, and then they put rocks inside. They peppered our bus after the game. Travel was sometimes dangerous, too, to put it bluntly. Driving over the mountains.

You pitched an absolutely tremendous extra-inning game against San Juan.

The game I pitched 17 innings was supposed to be a seven-inning game, on a Sunday. I had joined the club earlier in the week, and I had pitched a ten-inning game before the 17-inning game. Jack Tighe was the manager of Detroit at that time, and he had wanted me to go down to Puerto Rico to work on my breaking stuff. Tighe was counting on me to be long man relief for Detroit in 1958. And I did not throw a ball in spring training, because my arm "went dead" in Puerto Rico.

They sent me home just before Christmas. The general manager, or owner, of the Caguas team, Cobián?— he owned the theatres down there — he called me into his office. Cobián gave me some money and sent me home. I could not throw. Oh yeah, it was the extra-inning games that did it. I had tried to work it out. I remember we were playing Santurce in San Juan, and I tried throwing on the sideline before the game. I became so dejected that I

Jim Stump wedged in two winter seasons in Puerto Rico during a two-season look-see with the Detroit Tigers.

went into the dugout, and there was a water fountain there. I kicked the fountain so hard that I thought I broke my foot. Anyway, I came home right before Christmas in 1957.

My arm recovered, and I played in Charleston in 1958 and went back to Puerto Rico that winter with Mayagüez. It was a small town. We had a good manager. Bill Adair. On our off days, we played basketball at one of the high schools. Phil Regan was there. Charley Lau. Bob Bruce.

It was good time all three years for me in Mayagüez. Our general manager in Mayagüez, during Christmas, he would have us over to his place. Charley Lau would go out and catch some lobster — he was a big fisherman.

We enjoyed the [hospitality] and the good food. I said Charley Lau was a good fisherman. One time in Mayagüez, Lau rented a powerboat. It had twin motors, and we went out fishing. I am telling you a storm came up so quickly, I did not think we were going to make it back. The waves were about 15 feet high. I thought we were goners.

How are things going for you now?

I never married until I was done playing baseball. I married my wife Carmen in 1963. We were married 25 years. Four days after our anniversary in 1988, she died. I never remarried. We had a good 25 years, and had three children, who all live around Lansing and that compensates pretty well.

The Venezuelan Winter League

Gary Blaylock

Gary Blaylock pitched a one-hit, 5–0 shutout the first time he took the mound for the Valencia Industrialists. Pompeyo Davalillo was the only Caracas Leones' player to reach Blaylock for a hit, a single leading off the ninth inning. Blaylock won nine more games for the Industrialists, in what was the best of his multiple winter league campaigns. Blaylock was a veteran of three Caribbean basin winter leagues. Prior to joining Valencia in 1958, Blaylock had spent all or part of three winters in the Dominican Republic and Puerto Rico.

In his third season in Venezuela, pitching for the Pampero Licoreros, the right-hander experienced an unpleasant incident in which he and two teammates were unjustly incarcerated by Caracas' authorities. To his credit, Blaylock did not let the occurrence cloud his view on his winter ball experience.

Blaylock reached the major leagues in 1959 with the organization that first signed him, the St. Louis Cardinals.

When we spoke, Gary was nearing his 80th anniversary of life. Sixty of those anniversaries have been spent married to Joy; together they raised three children.

Tell me about your early family life.

I was born and raised on a farm in Clarkton, Missouri. Three of us. I had two sisters.

When did baseball grab hold of you?

Like all kids, I started playing in school. I played Legion ball. I grew up listening to the Cardinals on the radio. I used to keep score lying on my stomach in the living room, listening to the games. Terry Moore was my idol. I went to a tryout camp in 1950, and I signed with the Cardinals. A scout named Buddy Lewis signed me.

I played in Johnson City, Texas, in 1950 and 1951. That was a Class D ball club. I progressed and played in Omaha the next year. In '53, I moved up to Columbus, Ohio. In '54, I played in Rochester, New York. I played there for about five years.

It was around then that you began, in Puerto Rico, what turned into a lengthy and varied winter league career.

My first year playing winter ball was 1955, with Mayagüez and Ponce. I was married. I had my wife and son with me. It took a little getting used to for everybody the first year. We could not speak Spanish, of course. But we went back, so we enjoyed it. The food took a little while to get used to. I am an old farm boy from here in the states, and we eat a lot of meat and potatoes. But I always liked to eat, so I adjusted quickly. Black beans and rice. They could cook it like we could not cook it here in the states. We could get good fresh bread everyday, too.

That was the year the Dodgers tried to make a first baseman out of Wally Moon. A few weeks into the season, Wally came down to Puerto Rico to play. Before he arrived on the island, I was traded to Ponce for Wally. Dixie Walker was the manager of Mayagüez, and he had all Dodgers' players at Mayagüez, so the trade made sense. Plus Mayagüez had good pitching but could not score any runs. Ponce was not going to make the playoffs, so, a short time later, they traded me, or sold me, to San Juan. But apparently it was past the trading deadline. Eventually, the deal was not allowed to go through. I had to stay with Ponce—but I had already moved to San Juan. So, living in San Juan, I pitched for Ponce against San Juan and Santurce, and against Caguas,

Gary Blaylock as a St. Louis Cardinals' rookie in 1959.

when Ponce came over to play against those teams. I was traded "twice" during my first season in Puerto Rico. [Chuckles.]

We traveled to other towns on what they called *públicos*, taxis, that you would share with three or four other people. The taxis did not have air conditioning, though. Mayagüez to San Juan was the longest. Mayagüez to Ponce took only a couple of hours.

What I remember about Sixto Escobar Stadium was that the infield was hard. You know a player named Nino Escalera? He wore me out there. Nino would hit the ball into the ground. The ball would bounce so high that he would beat it out for a hit. Nino must have gotten 10 or 12 hits off me just because of those high chops. [Amused.] Ponce's stadium was larger than San Juan's. I am talking about dimensions, not capacity. The dimensions in Ponce were almost of equal distance from the foul poles to right center and left center. It was fair to both hitters and pitchers as far as distance was concerned. Mayagüez' park was similar to Ponce's.

When I was with Ponce, our third baseman was Ramon [Luis] Conde. His father was a coach on Ponce. Ramon's father had all of the American players to his house for Thanksgiving dinner. It was a small house; he had a large family. It was a real good meal. It was not turkey that they served, it was pork. It was a full Spanish meal. Conde's family was great. Mickey Owen and his wife were there. Mickey was the player-manager for Ponce. Faye Throneberry was there, he played for us.

Roberto was just starting. Clemente was the best ballplayer I ever saw. Pizarro was starting out about that time. I remember Pizarro more from the states. Sandy could not get the ball over the plate. He had great stuff but could not throw strikes. It was always amazing to me how Koufax could have been that wild as a youngster and then develop the kind of control he did later on in his career. Koufax was one of the top three pitchers I ever saw, by the way.

I played with San Juan the following winter. In San Juan, we stayed in a little apartment complex right near the stadium. Right near the beach. At these apartments, they closed off a place where you could swim in the ocean. We had access to the beach right there, and we went swimming. It was quite convenient, being so close to the stadium.

Ralph Houk was the manager. [Laughs.] I can remember that second year in Puerto Rico, I had brought packages of chewing tobacco with me. You could not find chewing tobacco in Puerto Rico. Ralph kept eyeing that chew. Finally, he said to me, "Why don't you spread some of that chew around? Some of the guys would like some. I will get you some more." I said, "Are you sure about that?" I only had packages of chew, not a carton. Ralph said, "Yeah, yeah, I will get you more." Well, the chew ran out, and Ralph contacted someone at the air force base in Mayagüez, who was able to provide some chew for Ralph. Just in time for he and I and Karl Drews to go fishing. Karl played with one of the other teams. The three of us were fishing, right off the shore near our apartment, and Ralph pulls out a pack of this chewing tobacco. Karl reached in and took some. Karl looked at Ralph and said, "Ralph do you realize this chew has worms in it?" Ralph looked at the chew and said, "By golly, it has." Ralph picked through the chew with his fingers and threw out a little dab, then another little dab more. Then Ralph reached in and pulled a big wad out and stuck it in his mouth and said, "Naw, it will be alright." [Laughs.] You had to be there to really appreciate it. [Laughs more.]

Ralph was great. He was good people. Even though he released me. It really was not Ralph. The San Juan team was not doing well and they wanted to cut one of the imports. It was around Christmas. Houk had all the Yankee players with him at San Juan. I was the only one of the foreign players with San Juan that was not with the Yankees. Ralph explained to me that he had to stay loyal to his players. Ralph felt bad, but he also told me that he had gotten me a job in the Dominican, playing for one of the teams there. Well, the Cardinals would not let me go.

But the Cardinals did let me go there the following winter [1957–58] — to play for Licey. The Cardinals had a working agreement with the Licey team in the Dominican League. Every time I pitched against the Red team that year, I would get beat — 2–1, 3–2. I just could not beat them.

We stayed in a pretty nice hotel, there in the capital. I think it was the hotel La Paz. Most of the foreign players stayed there. The hotel was only a few blocks from Trujillo's palace. Trujillo would come out for a walk every afternoon around four o'clock. They had all these guards posted along the street.

I remember a race at Trujillo Stadium involving Felipe Alou. Felipe and Julián Javier and a Dominican sprinter — the Dominican Republic's best sprinter. This sprinter was an Olympic sprinter. The race was really hyped. There was a full house at the stadium. The three of them raced along one of the foul lines to home plate — 110 meters, they marked it off. And who do you think won that race...? Felipe. By almost 10 yards. The last 30 yards Felipe separated himself from the other two. I thought Felipe had the most beautiful strides I had ever seen on a human.

I do not have a strong opinion on who was the best pitcher or best player in the Dominican. I did not spend a full season there. I was released at the end of the calendar year. Maybe my record had something to do with it.

By 1958, I had been in the minors for quite a few years and did not know if I would make the majors. I told myself I was going to milk this right arm for all its worth. I decided to keep playing winter ball, especially since I was making pretty good money. Venezuela was the best place I could find. I played for Valencia. Otero. Reggie Otero was the manager. I had a good year for Valencia. I won 10 ball games, and I pinch-hit a lot. I hit 10 home runs. It was my best year playing in Latin America. It was kind of a long year because I missed my family. I was not sure of the political situation in Venezuela, so I did not take my wife with me. You hear things, you know.

There was a colony of Americans there. There was a Firestone plant and Goodyear plant. I was able to meet quite a few people, nice people associated with the businesses. I stayed at a hotel called the Hotel Four Hundred.

You lost a no-hitter in the ninth inning in your first start for Valencia. Pompeyo Davilillo spoiled it.

I do not remember that game [one-hitter], but I do remember Pompeyo Davilillo. He was a little second baseman. Earl Battey and Lenny Green were players I came to know real well.

The next winter my family was with me. My boy went to school in Valencia, in that American colony I mentioned. He had just reached school age, and he was able attend the American school because, about three times a week, I would teach phys ed for all the kids at the school.

Every Christmas at the Firestone plant, they would bring out 50 or 60 orphan kids for a party. The kids would go crazy with that piñata. They also gave each of the kids a pair of shoes. The Firestone people did all of that, out of their own pockets.

I do not remember the players' strike in 1959. I remember leaving before the end of the season. Maybe that had something to do with it.

I remember there were student riots one year. That was 1960; I was with Pampero. Don Thompson was my roommate. I was by myself again that year. We stayed in an apartment, hearing gunshots and sounds of a disturbance. Don and I made ourselves kind of scarce for a few days.

You were involved, along with two teammates, in an unfortunate incident in Caracas that season.

I was not going to mention that; it was not a pleasant experience. We lived close enough to the park there in Caracas where we could walk to our hotel. Babe Birrer, a pitcher, and Don Thompson and I were walking home after the game one night. We got to a dark spot on the street. Three guys walked out of the shadows, you might say, on the sidewalk. One of the guys asked me for a match. "*Dame fósforo.*" I told him, "*Yo no tengo fósforo.*" I spoke a little Spanish by that time.

We kept walking and the same guy comes back around me, asking me for a match again. I repeated I did not have a match. I turned around and walked away again, and now he started pulling on my jacket. When the guy did that I turned around and shoved him. I told the guy, "Go home, go home." Then a car pulls up with some of the Latin players from the ballpark, and those kids, or guys, scatter.

Everything broke up and we started walking down the street, when another young man walked up to me — he had a black leather jacket on — and asked me for my *cédula*. A *cédula* is your identification card. When I went to hand him the card, he pulled a gun on me. He said he was a policeman. He could not have been more than 19. He took the card and started walking down the street. The three of us looked at each other, asking me what I wanted to do? Well, I said that I wanted to get my ID back. I was not sure this guy was a policeman. So, we followed the guy with the leather jacket and he headed to a police sub-station not far away. Turns out, the guy with the leather jacket was a policeman. Then a police car pulled up with the three kids from earlier. They are all talking Spanish very fast and I do not know what they are saying. So the police put us in a car and drive us off to somewhere, I do not know where. But we land in jail. They put us in a cell with six other people. These people eventually told us they were police trainees, and that they had done something wrong. That is why they were in there.

I called the owner of the team, and he did not do a thing for us. I do know his name, but I will not tell you. He spoke better English than I did. He wanted us to play hard for him, but when we needed help, he was not there for us.

We contacted the American consulate and the man in charge said that there was nothing he could do for us now. That we would not be released until 8 o'clock in the morning. This was Saturday night. He told us that the authorities could hold us for 72 hours, whether we did anything wrong or not. We spent the night in jail. They never gave a reason why. Disturbing the peace, I guess. Come 8 o'clock the next morning, the guard comes in. We get our watches and wallets back, and anything else they had made us surrender. They release us, and we went outside. That is when we realized that we had not been in jail. We had been in prison. We were about 15 miles from Caracas. No one offered to take us into town.

That is the end of that story, but not the real end of the story for me. But I will not tell you the rest of what happened.

I played winter ball for seven consecutive years. It was an experience; I will never forget it.

Billy DeMars

Billy DeMars played for a pennant-winning team during his one winter season in Venezuela. That team, the Caracas Leones, was managed by Cuban legend Martín Dihigo and participated in the 1953 Caribbean Series. However, DeMars opted to return home after the campaign to be with his pregnant wife and missed out on the Caribbean Classic. DeMars and his Lions' teammates helped inaugurate the first Winter League game played at new University Stadium in Caracas. On Opening Day, DeMars, an infielder, set a Venezuelan League record by registering ten putouts and four assists in the Lions' 9 to 5 win over team Venezuela.

The Brooklyn-born DeMars broke in with the Philadelphia Athletics in 1948 as a shortstop, and had an 80-game major league career over three seasons. DeMars had an extended tenure as coach of the Philadelphia Phillies during the 1970s, before moving on to Montreal and Cincinnati in the same capacities.

You are a native New Yorker.

Brooklyn, New York. I had a brother and a sister. I lived near the schoolyard. I was born in 1925, and when we were kids, everything was done outside on the streets near the schoolyard. We played stickball, punchball, boxball, any kind of ball. So my whole life as a kid I spent playing a kind of baseball.

You had a lot of great players locally to cheer on. Who did you cheer on the loudest?

Living in Brooklyn, you rooted for the Dodgers. Pee Wee Reese. Mostly him. Duke Snyder was a favorite. I ended up as a shortstop in baseball, so Pee Wee Reese was, more or less, my idol. Back in those days, we had a thing called the Knothole Gang. On certain days, they allotted tickets to kids and we could go to Ebbets Field and watch the baseball game.

Champions of the 1952-53 Venezuelan Winter League, the Caracas Leones. Gale Wade is in the top row, far right. Also in the top row, fourth from left, is Pompeyo Davalillo. In the middle row is team owner Pablo Morales (wearing white hat). Also in that row is manager Martín Dihigo, *el Inmortal* (sixth from left). Next in that row is legendary Venezuelan pitcher José Bracho, then Dick Starr and Lorenzo "Piper" Davis. In the bottom row, Chico Carrasquel, fourth from right, sits beside the team's trainer. Carl Erskine is seated at the far right. Billy DeMars had apparently already left the team when this photograph was taken (The Sporting News Archive).

You ended up signing with the occupants of Ebbets Field.

I made All-City in high school. My senior year in high school, I started playing with the Dodger rookies. Different kids from all around New York City. Then I met Branch Rickey, and Brooklyn asked me to sign a contract. I signed a contract in 1943. Me and Ralph Branca, who later pitched for the Dodgers, signed together, and we both went up on the train with the scout that signed us to Olean, New York. Rickey was a great general manager. One thing he insisted upon was that you had to be able to run and you had to be able to throw.

Of course the war was on, and I ended up in the Navy. But I was lucky enough to play baseball at Jacksonville Naval Air Station. I was the shortstop. The second baseman was Charlie Gehringer, who ended up in the Hall of Fame. Our left fielder was Ted Williams. So we had a good baseball team. When I came out of the service, I went to Nashua, New Hampshire, which was Dodger farm team. I played with them in 1947.

But it was a connection to a different team that acquainted you with winter baseball.

I was drafted by the Philadelphia A's in 1948. They sent me to Triple A. I eventually ended up in Toronto in 1952. I played there in '52, '53, '54 and '55. Four years. After the first year, Ferrell Anderson, who was one of the catchers on the team, asked me to go down to Caracas, Venezuela, because he was playing down there in the wintertime.

I played with the Caracas team. We played a team called Magallanes. Well, that was like the Dodgers and Giants. Big rivalry. The stadium was always packed. I tied a record for either putouts or assists, I cannot remember which. I played second, short, third and left field, wherever they needed somebody. I hit pretty well, too, .289, I think. There were four teams in the league at that time and all the games were played at one stadium. We did not have to travel. Our manager was Martín Dihigo. He was a big, popular player in Cuba. He was a pitcher and an outfielder. What I remember about him was that he was a big man. He was quite big. I am sure whatever he did, he was an excellent player. He could explain things well, his English was pretty good.

Chico Carrasquel was on the team. He was a great player. When Chico wanted the night off, I would play shortstop. When he played shortstop, then I played second or third. Gale Wade, our centerfielder, he could fly. Gale could really run, and the people loved him. We were pretty close friends and when we were walking up town, he was taller than me and he was balding, so he was easily recognizable to the natives. Dick Starr was on our team, a right-handed pitcher.

It was a great stadium to play in. It was a brand new place. We played the first game ever in the history of the stadium. Everything was great, the clubhouses, showers. That first game we were beating Magallanes in the seventh inning, about 8–2. You know, they sort of searched the fans before they went into the stadium. You could only have a paper and scorecard. So about the seventh inning, I am out at second base and I see the whole place is ablaze. On fire. The whole stadium! I could not believe it. The fans were lighting up these things and it was like a funeral pyre. It was meant to symbolize a burial for the other team. I said to myself, wait till I get home and tell everybody what happened in this game, they will never believe me. It was the Caracas fans "creamating" the Magallanes team.

The fans were wild down there. At Christmastime, the fans would throw cherry bombs down on the field. I was playing third base one time and one of those cherry bombs went off right in back of me. The people in the stands thought it was funny. I did not think it was too damn funny myself. But they were allowed to do it. It was crazy.

[Outside the stadium] I remember the cars, they used to have brooms and straw sticking out from the bumpers, because fans would throw nails and tacks on the road. These things kept the cars from getting a flat tire. I saw these cars with the brooms and straw on the front bumpers and I did not know what was going on. So I asked somebody, and they told me, the opposing fans throw the nails and tacks to stir up trouble. The brooms helped to push the tacks and things out of the way.

On Sundays we would play one game that started at nine A.M., the other one started at 11:30 or so. We only played two or three times a week. On off-days, sometimes we would go to the stadium and take batting practice in the morning. I cannot even remember taking batting practice before a game. In fact, they did not even turn the lights on until about 15 minutes before the game.

All the guys from our team lived in the same hotel. I do not remember the name. I had my wife and two kids with me. I had to send them back after about a month. The kids were having a tough, tough time. They could not eat the food, they were passing out. It was not very good. I survived on ice cream and bread and soup. We were stuck in the hotel. Once in a while, a couple of us guys would go to the movies. We were not able to do anything, really. The political climate was not good, and it was not the best idea to be out roaming around the streets. Sometimes when you were out walking around, you would run into a soldier with full military gear. In fact, when we landed and came off the plane, there were 13 soldiers with rifles and bayonets that rounded us up and took us into a building. When I saw that, I said, oh my God, what the hell am I doing here?

Sometimes when it would come to be pay day, we would go to one place [to collect], they would tell us no, you have to go to another place, and we would go there and they would tell us no, to go to another place.

We had a very good team. Good Triple A players. We started getting a big lead, and the people who ran the team came to us and told us not to play so hard. Because they wanted to keep the race close, instead of us running away with the league. Fan interest would die, they said. They wanted to keep it close for the fans. We were never taught to do that. We were always taught to play hard. What would happen is when we would go out to play, some of our best native players would not show up. Like they were told to stay home. Our lead dropped down to three or four games, and everybody came back, and we finally did win it.

You said the political climate was not good.

It was a dictatorship at that time. Jiménez was the dictator. There was a strike once, and they made us play the game, even though there were only 50 people in the ballpark. They did not want to call the game, because then the people would think something really bad was going on. It was not the best place. The baseball was good, the money was great, but it was not very much fun. We were stuck in the hotel. I had no problems whatsoever. I played the games. I liked playing the games. Everything was great, except the living conditions were not that great and the food was not that great. I made friends down there, the fans I met on the street were great. I was lucky and had a good year myself. They wanted me to come back, but I never wanted to go back.

You did not accompany your pennant-winning team into post-season play.

I did not go to the Caribbean Series because my wife was at home, she was expecting and she was having trouble. I said, I cannot [go], we have two kids and my wife is expecting the third. I had to get home.

How do you occupy your days now?

I play golf twice a week. I am still in decent condition. I work out, ride a bicycle. I was a hitting coach in the major leagues for 19 years. Every once in a while I work with some young kids I know. I take them over to the ballpark and have them hit off the tee.

And what does your current family consist of?

Three children and six grandchildren. My wife's name is Catherine, and today happens to be our 65th wedding anniversary. So we have had a great day.

Ed Mickelson

Ed Mickelson's biggest thrill in baseball came during the first game of the 1972 World Series, watching Oakland A's starter Ken Holtzman, whom Mickelson had coached in high school. "The first pitch Kenny threw was to Pete Rose," Ed told me with pride. "It was a strike, and a chill went up my back and neck."

Mickelson was also another former player-turned author that I encountered. His recent autobiography, Out of the Park, *was published in 2010. Mickelson had a successful winter round of play in Venezuela with the Valencia Industrialists in 1956, though his team was eliminated in the championship playoffs by the Caracas Leones. A city about 70 miles from Caracas, Valencia was part of the four-club circuit that battled for the Venezuelan Winter League pennant. Mickelson generously relayed some interesting and amusing tales that appeared in his book.*

A tragic airplane crash that took the life of Charley Peete, a promising minor league ball player, affected all North American players in Venezuela that season. Mickelson poignantly expressed how the plane's crash site on the side of a mountain was visible from the field of University Stadium in Caracas.

An outfielder and first baseman, Mickelson spent 11 years toiling in the minor leagues. He sparsely and intermittently reached the promised land of the majors during the decade of the 1950s.

Mickelson's first wife and "best buddy" Jo Ann passed away in 1999. Ed, a father of two, with three grandchildren, married his current life companion, Mary, in 2002.

Ed Mickelson drove in the last run for the St. Louis Browns franchise (courtesy E. Mickelson).

I would like to know about your young baseball life, starting with your place of birth.

Ottawa, Illinois, but I lived in Marseilles, just like in France, until I was nine. Then my family moved to Chicago. From there we moved to University City in St Louis. I have been in the St. Louis area most of my life. Just me, I am a spoiled only child. I never played Little League or baseball in high school until my senior year. The Cardinals and Browns had what they called a Knothole Gang, and we could get into games for about 15 cents, 10 cents. I saw the Gashouse Gang, with Terry Moore and that group of guys. Johnny Mize, Pepper Martin. I saw Dizzy Dean pitch. I saw the Yankees when they came in. I do not know if I had a favorite.

When I became older I played with Stan Musial. I would say he was my favorite player. Favorite player and favorite person. He is quite a gentleman. I went into the service in 1945 for two years.

How did making the same team as Stan Musial come about?

The corner druggist lived right across the street from Leo Ward, who was the traveling secretary for the Cardinals. That druggist told Ward about me as an athlete. I had received a football scholarship to Missouri University and I also played basketball, which was my best sport. I received a tryout at Sportsman's Park. Del Wilbur, a third-string catcher, pitched batting practice. He was laying them in there at about 75 miles an hour. I hit some balls over the fence and into the bleachers. The Cardinals signed me the next day. This was 1948. I had to learn baseball, sort of, on the job. I played with Decatur in the Three-I League — Iowa, Illinois, Indiana. They had some good pitchers there, Carl Erskine and Howie Judson and Kenny Lehman, who pitched for the Brooklyn Dodgers.

In 1950, I hit over .400 in the minors in just over 360 times up, and the Cardinals called me up. I sat on the bench for about a week, and I wondered, why in the hell did they bring me up? Then we were playing Boston and the Cardinals' manager, Eddie Dyer, said to me, "Hey kid, you're in there today. Musial's back at the hotel with a 103 fever. By the way, Warren Spahn is pitching." Spahn pitched a two-hitter that day, he beat us, 5–0. But I had one of the two hits; my first hit in the majors was off Warren Spahn, in the first game I started.

It was not until several years later that you made it across international borders to play.

I played in Venezuela in 1956. I had played with Louie Márquez in Portland and he tried to hook me up with the team he played on in the Puerto Rican League. But that team signed Bill White to play first base for them. So, I went to Venezuela and played for the Valencia team. I had a pretty good year. I know I was in the top ten in hitting.

Reggie Otero was our manager. He was a good manager. Fiery. We were playing in the playoffs against Caracas. Their shortstop, Chico Carrasquel, who played with the White Sox, was involved in some big hullabaloo on a play that ended the inning, and Reggie rushed into it. Our dugout was on the third base side. Reggie ran across the field from his third base coaching box and into the visitor's dugout. All hell broke loose. The first base side had an iron railing and concrete, and the fans in the stands all came down bunched together and their weight pushed that railing over. The first group of fans landed down on the field, and more people fell on top of them. I think a couple of people were hurt. One guy had his chest crushed. The soldiers, in the khaki uniforms, they had machetes and they started hitting the people on the butt with the flat side of the machete, to get them back into the stands.

The soldiers finally scurried them back up there, and the ambulances came out for a few people. This happened at Valencia.

The first game I played in Venezuela, I hit a home run with the bases loaded in the third inning. And a torrential rain comes along and rained the goddam thing out.

My wife was with me and she enjoyed it. It was a great experience. We stayed at the Hotel Cuatrocientos. The American players stayed there. It had a swimming pool — if we took care of it, drained it, filled it up, kept it clean, we could use it. Earl Battey was there. Chris Van Kuyk, left-handed pitcher. Ed Burtschy, he pitched for the Philadelphia Athletics. Ronnie Plaza. He was a coach for the Reds when Pete Rose had that consecutive game hitting streak.

Even though there was sometimes extensive travel, it was not a taxing schedule.

We played in various places. We took a lot of trips, of course, to Caracas. We never went to Maracaibo. I wanted to go there. We went Barquisimeto, that was one of the places we traveled to. We went to Isla de Margarita. To Carúpano. That was a beautiful place. Oh, we played down at Ciudad Bolívar. [Chuckles.] They had taxis to take us there. We drove there from Valencia. But we had to cross the river, the Orinoco River. By the time we reached the crossing, the big steel boat that carried cars and people over to the other side, to Ciudad Bolívar, was sailing away. We saw it, a double decker ferry, pulling out just as we arrived at the crossing. It was not going to come back again until the next day. They had told us there were piranhas in the river. Ronnie Plaza could speak Spanish pretty good. Ronnie talked to this kid who came up to us, and the kid found some old guy — he was about 70 years old — in a rickety boat to take us across. The taxi drivers stayed with their cars. As we were crossing, the guy's boat starts leaking! We all reached for some cans and started bailing out the boat. We were scared to death that we were going to go under and the piranhas would get us. A piranha can take a person's finger clean off with one bite. And here we are crossing that damn river in a leaky boat. You would not want to be in that boat on a safe river. It was not very comfortable to ride in, or sturdy. It is laughable, really. It is a lot of fun when you are young and you do not mind those things.

We made it across and played ball that night. The next morning, I looked out and saw these guys ankle and waist deep in the river. I asked somebody — I could speak a little Spanish — what the hell are those guys doing out there, aren't they afraid the piranhas will get them? He answered, no, that once a month they dynamite, and that drives the piranhas away for a month. Then they dynamite a second time, to keep the piranhas away from the hotel.

We played ball in a town called Maturín. Ronnie Plaza and I were in the hotel there. Early in the morning on Sundays you could hear the church bells all over town. We woke up one Sunday and took a taxi to the ballpark. At the park, we were working out a bit when we saw a big dust cloud coming toward us from the town of Maturín. The dust cloud was trailing the cars and trucks, one after the other on the same road, following all the vehicles to the ballpark. [Chuckles.] That was quite a site.

I saw that big Angels Falls when we were flying to play somewhere. Boy, that is beautiful. It is much bigger than Niagara Falls.

A terrible thing happened while we were in Venezuela, to one of the players who was coming to join us. Charley Peete. He had led the American Association in hitting. Peete was going to be the first black ballplayer for the St. Louis Cardinals. The city of Caracas is like in a bird's nest, nestled in between mountains. Peete was flying in, a commercial flight, he, his wife, mother-in-law, and a child or two. It was a French plane. There was a fog over Caracas, and the French plane was told to circle the airport for half an hour and it would probably clear up. You know, Caracas is surrounded by seven mountains and they are not real tall mountains, but they are pretty big. There was a landing strip on the side of one of the mountains. Rather than do as instructed, the French pilot decided to bring the plane in anyway, and it crashed into the mountainside and everybody on the plane died. Charley Peete was 26. I had ordered some baseball bats, other guys, too. Those bats survived the crash. The owner of our team, Mr. [Raúl] Branger, said, no, there is no way you can have those bats, or use those bats. I told him, I would like to have them, hit with them. Mr. Branger said, no, that they have death on them. You cannot have them.

Mr. Branger took us out on his boat in Puerto Valencia. We had a great time, fishing and swimming. Mr. Branger let us have his English car to drive on the autobahn. It was about six lanes across and you could really fly on that autobahn.

The road we took from Valencia to Caracas and back was two lanes. It was very slow. It was hard to pass. The drivers disconnected their horns, they were afraid they would run their batteries down. The way cars passed one another on that road was to pound on the side of their car doors as hard as they could and holler, and then pass. All the Americans were down in the car on their hands and knees, crossing ourselves, whenever this happened. Félix García was our driver, and he had a big station wagon. Félix drove us back and forth to places we were going to play, primarily to Caracas.

One night we were coming back from Caracas, and Ronnie Plaza talked Félix into letting him drive. If you were in Venezuela with a visa, you were not allowed to drive an automobile. Ronnie was driving and this guy pulls up on a motorcycle alongside of us. He did not have the soldier's khaki-type uniform on; he had the green uniform and cap. Those guys were like the SS there. He pulled us over, and Félix just about crapped in his pants, because he knew he was not supposed to let anyone else drive. They took us all to *la chota,* jail, about ten miles outside of Caracas. It was the town of Los Teques. We were in *la chota* in Los Teques. [Laughs.] They did not put us *in* jail. But they kept us there for about two hours.

They were in the back grilling Félix, giving him a hard time. Finally, Ronnie Plaza, who spoke Spanish fluently, and I, went over to the sergeant at the desk. Ronnie starts talking, and the sergeant looks up at me and points, "Ed Mickelson, *primera base.*" The sergeant looks at Ronnie. "Ronnie Plaza, *segunda base.*" That is when I knew we were going to get out. It turns out the sergeant had listened to the game we had played against Caracas. The country was ruled by Jiménez, the dictator. He had people he did not like imprisoned everywhere. I sure did not want to get put in any jail down there.

We played Wednesday, Saturday afternoon and Sundays. Three days a week. That is pretty good, isn't it? When we went to downtown Valencia, the wives shopped. We would occasionally eat out in Valencia. We did not spend any time in Caracas. It was go there and play, and come back. Go there and play, come back. It was a beautiful city, from what I saw. I think they had an American section there. I think it was a very cosmopolitan city and very nice. We stayed near our hotel. We had that swimming pool deal, we used that a lot. We ate at the hotel most all the time. The eight American guys would be there at five-thirty, ready to eat and the restaurant had not even opened for dinner yet. [Laughs.] The people at the hotel, the natives, they did not eat dinner until eight or nine. It was good food. I did get sick when I first arrived. Montezuma's Revenge got me. They warned me not to drink the water, drink beer. So I drank a lot of beer down there. They had a bar at the hotel, so it was *cervezas, cervezas, cervezas.*

What are your recollections of the players in Venezuela?

There was John Roseboro, who took over for Campanella when Campy was hurt. Tom Burgess. Mike Goliat, second baseman for the Phillies, Lou Limmer and Rus Rac were with Pampero. Bobby Balcena. He was one of the best centerfielders I ever played with. Mo Mozzali came later. Mo Mozzali was always playing somewhere in the winter. I guess the best player at the time and the biggest name of all was Chico Carrasquel. He was pretty much in his prime then. I hit pretty good in Venezuela. I cannot think of anybody right now, but from our side, Valencia, the best pitcher was Cueche. Emilio Cueche. He pitched for us in one of our playoff games that we won.

New stadiums had been built in Valencia, as well as in Caracas. What do you remember about them?

Our clubhouses had showers and toilets. You could not put the toilet paper down the toilet, you had to put it in the basket on the side of the toilet.

I thought that was kind of different. University Stadium was a big, beautiful stadium; it seated about 35,000. Across the street, there was a soccer stadium that seated more.

What do you remember about the fans?

One time we were losing a game in Valencia, it was the eighth inning and we were done for. We played a terrible game. Down the right field line in that concrete stadium, I see a fire. What the hell is going on there? Some fans were drinking that white lightning, Tequila, or whatever they drank down there. A bunch of guys were gathered around the fire, and it was supposed to be a symbol of the death of the team. One of those white lightning bottles whizzed onto the field between me and Ronnie Plaza, and toward the pitcher's mound. That was kind of interesting.

Did any other "interesting" or" different" things happen?

In the playoffs, I hit one with the bases loaded to right centerfield at Valenica Stadium. The top of the wall, concrete wall, was not flat on top; it was like a pyramid, it came up to a point. The damn ball hit on that point and instead of bouncing out, the ball bounced back into the field. I pulled up with a triple, and they gave me a bunch of money for it. I received 810 bolívars ($270), because it was station 810 that was broadcasting the playoffs. The prize was for whoever hit a grand slam, but no one did, so they gave it to me for coming closest.

Jack Spring

Jack Spring made his mark in the major leagues as a left-handed relief pitcher. Spring saw the bulk of his big league playing time with the Los Angeles Angels, during the first years of that franchise's existence.

In the mid–1950s, Spring developed some of his pitching aptitude as a two-year member of the Syracuse Chiefs and one-year recruit with the Miami Marlins. As a result, the young Spring was first able to savor the international flavor of baseball with road trips to Cuba when his International League teams faced Havana's Sugar Kings. In 1956, the 23-year-old ventured to Venezuela for the first of three consecutive seasons. Midway through his second winter, Spring changed leagues from the Caracas-Eastern League to the Western League, headquartered in Maracaibo.

Nowadays, with his wife of nearly six decades at his side and all of his children residing close by, the 78-year-old Spring continues to count his blessings, even after being diagnosed with a degenerative illness a few years ago.

You are from the Great Northwest. What did your young family life entail?

I'm from Spokane. My parents divorced when I was three. We lived in Idaho for a time. That marriage did not last either, and we moved back to Spokane. I was really raised by my grandparents. I went to Lewis and Clark High School. We were three boys. One died tragically while I was in high school.

When did baseball start making its impact on you?

I played in what was called a Park League. That was my first organized ball playing. In high school, I pitched pretty well. After high school, I went to Washington State University. I then signed with the Spokane Indians. They were an independent franchise. The Phillies came in and took me away from them. That was 1952. I progressed from there, and got my cup of coffee with the Phillies in 1955.

Playing in the International League first gave you a taste of Caribbean baseball.

I played two years with Syracuse and had a chance to travel to Cuba. Havana was great. The food was great. My favorite dish was black beans and rice.

The fans were rabid. The stadium was always full. I remember one game, someone hit a long drive to right. Right field had about an eight foot wall that separated the bleachers right behind. Our right fielder jumped up to try and catch the ball and when he came down, his foot stuck at the bottom of the wall. We were down the line in the right field bullpen and went right out to help. One of the guys brought out a baseball and stuck it in our right fielder's glove. He did not realize it, he just wanted to get his foot loose. The right fielder opened his glove just as the umpire arrived, and the ball was inside. The umpire called the batter "out." Meanwhile, there was a guy in the front row of the bleachers with the ball that had been hit out. The fans started throwing things on the field, but the call stood and the game continued.

We stayed at the Hotel Nacional whenever we went to Havana. That was something. Everything was great.

Another time, our manager, Skeeter Newsome, called us into his room right before a big series. Skeeter had just met with somebody and he told us that he had reason to believe that the Havana team had hired "professional women," you know what I mean, to, ah, distract the players. To keep us out late, whatever. They were planted, supposedly, in and around our hotel lobby. We had three players on our team — we called them the Dalton Gang — Dick Farrell, Seth Morehead and Jim Owens. They just about knocked over everybody to get out of the room and downstairs to the lobby. [Laughs.] They were good guys. They were just ... young and athletic.

I was married, but I never took my family with me during my three years playing winter ball. I went alone, unfortunately. I had two girls at that time. One year the girls could not get their vaccinations on time, because they had the flu or something, and it was a necessary thing, and they just never came with me after that.

How did you break into winter ball finally?

I was playing with Miami, again, in the International League, when it was suggested I go to Caracas to play winter ball. I went for the money more than anything else, because I was having trouble finding work over the winter in Spokane. That was 1956.

I played with Pampero. Now that you say his name [Fermin Guerra], I remember. He must have been a good manager. I do not remember any problems. That first year I lived in a rather nice hotel; it was small but nice. One thing I remember about it was that the hotel had a nightclub in the basement. The reverberations of the drums and music would echo up through the rooms most of the night.

Caracas is in the mountains. I remember we took a tramway that went

Jack Spring (left) and Don Leppert in front of the upscale Hotel Humboldt, located high above the city of Caracas (courtesy J. Spring).

up alongside one of the mountains. We did that a couple of times, for the views. We took a trip down to the coastline, to the beach, a few times.

I started out with Caracas the next year, but, yeah, they probably released me and I ended up signing with a team in Maracaibo, where the other winter league in Venezuela was based. So I spent a season and a half in Caracas and a season and a half over in Maracaibo.

I have to relate this story — it is a tragic one, and in your research you probably ran into it. It happened my second year in winter ball. I had gone over to Sandpoint, Idaho. My dad had a little lumber mill, and I was working there. Anyway, I received a call, and somebody wanted me to go to Caracas again, and I agreed to go. The team put quite a lot of heat on me to be in New York at a certain date to depart for Caracas. The trips that I made to Venezuela, I went to New York City first and then flew directly to Caracas. But there was no way I could make it when the team wanted. Turns out the date the team wanted me to go, another player went, with his wife and family. That flight crashed into a mountain on its approach to Caracas. There were no survivors. Charley Peete was a highly-rated prospect. Charley, his wife and two children, as I recall, were on board. The sad part of it was when I did get to New York, I went to the Venezuelan embassy to get my visa, which you needed to get into Venezuela. And this lady that I dealt with, that issued the visa, started crying. She said, standing right there where you are standing, three days ago, was the Peete family, getting their visas for their trip. And she had these big tears in her eyes, and just broke up. Some people said I was lucky. Fate. But I had stated from the beginning that there was no way I could make it on that date. I never considered taking that flight. I had some personal matters to take care of before I could get to New York. But that was a very sad occurrence.

Chico [Carrasquel] I remember, he played in Caracas. I remember him more when he played with the White Sox.

Much like in Caracas, there were four teams in Maracaibo. It was a similar situation where everybody played in one stadium, except for one team. In the Caracas league, it was the Valencia team — they had their own park. In Maracaibo, there was one team, where we had to take a boat ride across the lake there, Lake Maracaibo ... Cabimas?

The third year, in Maracaibo, I lived in a house with my teammates. We had a maid that took care of our house and cooked our meals. It was first class. A couple of times a week, we went fishing out on the lake, Lake Maracaibo. I still have some pictures. This same guy in this little boat, a pointy ended boat with a Briggs and Stratton engine, he would squat up there in the back-end of the boat all day long and drag us around the lake. We did pretty good and had a lot of fun. It was a group of three, mostly. Don Leppert and Duke Carmel were the others.

Besides photos, do you have any keepsakes from your time in Venezuela?

I have one article, newspaper clipping. I do not know what kind of picture of me you can get from it. I made the headlines in Caracas with a game I pitched. I threw nine innings and allowed 18 hits, and won the game! [Laughs out loud.] That was the only time my name made it into the papers my whole time down in Venezuela—for pitching an 18-hitter and *winning* it.

What is you family life like now?

I ended up with five kids. I came down with Parkinson's about three years ago, and it is affecting my left side, my left hand. It is hard for me to write. So I have learned to print with my right hand, which was my weak hand. That is the bad news. The good news is that the disease is progressing slowly, so I am doing quite well.

I was married in 1952. Vona and I, we are coming up on 60 years. I consider myself fortunate. I have five kids and they all live in Spokane. Seven grandkids, a couple are at college. A lot of people have their kids grow up and they live here and there. It is a real joy to have my family right here with me.

Gale Wade

One of the more pleasing aspects of this project was the occasional and unexpected occurrence of reconnecting old teammates. Cot Deal told me that if I ever spoke to his "good friend, Louie Olmo," to give him a big hello from his part. I did, along with Deal's contact information. I gladly helped Dick Schofield reach out to Ron Negray, and likewise, provided Gale Wade assistance in contacting Billy DeMars. Wade and DeMars were teammates on the Caracas Leones in the winter of 1952, and experienced the inaugural season of state-of-the-art Estadio Universitario in Caracas.

Gale Wade, a speedy outfielder purchased by the Cleveland Indians out of the Brooklyn Dodgers' organization before being traded to the Chicago Cubs, made several winter sojourns to Venezuela, following his initial one in 1952. The Washington state-reared ballplayer saw limited major league action in two seasons with the Cubs.

Wade accompanied his pennant-winning Caracas team to Havana for the 1953 Caribbean Series, where he hit .353. (The Caracas team won only one game in the tournament, a one-hitter pitched by Charlie Bishop.) In 1955-56, Wade, as a magallanero flychaser, led the Venezuelan League in hits (75), runs (44), stolen bases (11) and finished second in batting to Norm Larker (.344 to .346).

Wade's first wife, Billie, passed away from cancer in 1961. They had three children. Gale and second wife, Barbara, married for 49 years, have retired to their North Carolina farm. They spend the winter months at their second residence in central Florida.

Where were you born?

In the Ozarks, six miles south of Branson, on a farm on a high ridge. There is a golf course there now called Murder's Rock. There were four boys and one girl, five of us. If you lived on a farm in the Ozarks, you did not have electricity or water in the house. We did not even have an outhouse. We went out behind the smoke house. My mom and dad divorced. My mom took me and my sister to Bremerton, Washington. I went to high school there.

When did baseball cross your path?

Football was my premier sport. I did not play high school baseball. I played Legion ball. A Brooklyn scout saw me. I should have gone on to college and played football. I always regretted it. Football was natural to me, baseball was not. That was February 1947.

And how did you arrive in Venezuela?

In 1952, I had a good year with Elmira in the Eastern League. I was invited to go to Venezuela that winter. My gosh, the offer was heaven in itself. Because when I played you had to get a job after the season was over. Somebody on the Caracas team wanted me. Chico Carrasquel played on that team.

There were four teams in the league. We only played three days a week. Martín Dihigo. I will tell you what, he was really a nice person. He was a big fella. He was a good six-two. At that time, I did not know the history behind Martín. He was a wonderful guy, a good manager. In later years, I read and learned Martín was star in his own right.

I lived at an old hotel called El Comercio Hotel. I roomed with an old knuckleballer in the Dodgers' organization, I am trying to think of his name ... well, what I remember about him was, my goodness, he had a liquor jug. The first thing he would do in the morning was take a big old shot of that liquor jug.

We could not speak Spanish, of course, and the waiters there could not speak English. They were all male waiters. So when we sat down to eat, you would point at what someone else was eating and that is what they would bring you. I remember, when I first arrived, one breakfast. Everybody would drink coffee out of little demitasse cups. I did not realize why. I just thought, well, those cups are awful small. The waiter asked me what I wanted to drink, indicating, you know, with his hand. I pointed over to one of those demitasse cups—but I said, bigger, demonstrating, using my hands. Well, the waiter brought me over a big old cup, kind of jar-like. I did not how strong that coffee was. *My God.* Then I realized why those people drank out of those small cups. That stuff was unbelievably strong.

The year we were there they had, what do you call it, an uprising. At one point we were confined to our hotel. The soldiers were chasing these outlaws down, right outside on the street, and shooting at them.

What stood out was the ballpark [University Stadium]. It was a beautiful, new concrete stadium with bleachers all around. Real modernistic. The crowd was split. The fans of the team in the first base dugout would sit from home plate on over in that direction, and the fans for the third base dugout team, sat on that side. And then they had soldiers standing on the field all the way around. No one got out of line.

Caracas is up there in the valley, a beautiful setting, up above the airport. I did not have any problems playing in the altitude. The toughest thing we had to do was learn to speak some Spanish. A lot of the American players thought those people should learn our language. That was wrong. You are in their country, you have to learn theirs. I was fortunate and obtained a little book — one I still have — and I learned to speak the language. That helped me out as far as the fans were concerned, because they gave me a nickname of *el Galgo*— the Greyhound. The fans were wonderful, and what won me over with them was that I was one of the very few players that attempted to speak Spanish.

I cannot recall their names, but, oh yeah, you knew the owners as well as you knew the manager.

They paid all of your

Gale Wade and Chico Carrasqeul show there were no hard feelings in the aftermath of their violent on-field encounter (courtesy G. Wade).

expenses, your lodgings and food. They gave you this much to live on, but you could live on less. We could send our total paycheck home — we would send it to Chase Manhattan Bank. The United States Government said we did not have to pay taxes on the money because we were considered goodwill ambassadors. I have told people over the years the only money I ever made in baseball was from the years I spent in Venezuela. [Chuckles.]

One of the things I would do is, I would get a *carro*— the taxicabs down there, they called them *carros*. I would go into the interior of the country and get acquainted. I would have the taxicabs stop at farms, and I stayed overnight with families back in the interior. I learned a lot. All those people would listen to the games, so they were real happy to have me. A baseball player was kind of like a celebrity. The only thing I missed as far as comfort was that nobody had any beds. The people did not sleep in beds in the interior. They had, what we called, hammocks, stretched across the corners of the rooms. I learned how to sleep on those things.

I will mention they built a new hotel, Tamanaco; somebody told me it still exists. It was brand new in the early fifties. That is where the airline

Sitting a spell on Havana's famed Malecón seawall are Charlie Bishop, left, Gale Wade, center, and an unidentified person. The four-century-old Morro Castle, built by the Spanish to protect Havana's harbor, can be seen in the background (courtesy G. Wade).

people stayed, business people coming into Caracas, everybody stayed at the Tamanaco. But that was too high class for us.

My first child was born in June of 1953. We went back down to Venezuela, again, in the winter of '54. We lived in an apartment right next door to Jack Lohrke and his wife. Jack played for the Giants. My first wife, Billie, and my little daughter — who is going to turn 58 this week — could use the pool at the Hotel Tamanaco. In fact, we pierced my little girl's ears down there. And she actually played with Venezuelan kids, and she started speaking Spanish. Yeah, you would talk to her, and she would come back at you in Spanish. It was really interesting. My wife liked it. They furnished a cleaning lady. Our wives did not have to clean the house. The fact that the Lohrkes lived next door, really helped. They spent their time up at the Tamanaco's pool, Billie and Jack Lohrke's wife.

As league champs, the Caracas squad represented Venezuela in the Caribbean Series. It was played in Havana. Do you recall the opening ceremonies, at all?

I do not remember the opening ceremonies [of the 1953 Caribbean Series] in Havana. What I remember about Havana was that there were restaurants and bars that were American-owned. But we were placed in a hotel — oh gosh, it was not a high class place, I do remember that. It was old. What I saw of Havana was no more than I could walk [from the hotel]. I do remember going out to that cove, I cannot remember the name [*El Malecón*]; it had a military barricade, or something [*El Castillo del Morro*]. I do not remember moving around a lot, because we did not have any way of getting around.

In Havana, Charlie Bishop pitched the first one-hitter in Caribbean Series history.

I am glad you mentioned that name — Bishop. Charlie Bishop. I remember him, a big right-hander. Billy [DeMars] was a wonderful guy; he was our second baseman. If I had to pick one, I would have to say Chico Carrasquel. No pitchers, really, that were outstanding.

You then played for Magallanes, which competed against Caracas for the most fans in the league.

In 1955, my third winter in Venezuela, I played with Magallanes. I remember [mgr.] Lázaro Salazar. He was a smaller individual compared to Dihigo. And Salazar was more outspoken. Salazar was a nice person. Treated us all well.

We traveled and that was some of the worst travel. We went to some little island over there. Then we traveled way west across the mountains. It was not good. We traveled by plane, but the accommodations were horrible. That would have been 1957, my last year there. The stadium in Caracas was so immaculate, and then the stadiums in these other places were so bad, it was like going from the majors to Class D. The places we stayed, it was like being back in the bush. Some of these stadiums did not even have bathrooms. But I made some great contacts and saw a change in governments.

How did you spend your off-days?

On the nights we did not play, some of us would go and watch the other teams play. One game I was sitting behind the owner and general manager, so to speak, of the Caracas team. They should have noticed me. I understood enough Spanish by then to know what was going on. I was on a hot hitting streak. I was leading the league in home runs, which was unusual for me. The following night, or two nights later, we were going to be playing Caracas. I had overheard the Caracas owner and general manager talking about making sure that the pitchers knocked me down. I took that information to our manager, and he went to the Caracas manager and told him that I had heard this. We thought everything was ironed out before the game started.

Now Chico and I were good friends. We played together. I thought the world of him. The first time I came up, this big right-hander, I cannot think of his name — I used to call his name all the time — well, his first pitch went right by my head. I turned around to the catcher and told him — I spoke enough Spanish to where they could at least understand me — I told him, *no más,* and so forth. By golly, the next pitch made me go down to the ground. I then made an out. I come up for the third time and for the third time in the game I go down to the ground. I had told the guys in the dugout, I said, now boys, if they throw at me again and I get on first base, somebody is going to pay the price.

Well, I singled. Norm Larker followed me, a left-handed hitter. I did not even think about it being Chico. I just wanted to make someone pay. Larker hit the ball on the infield and I caught Chico — he is covering second — with a rolling block and took him half way into left field. And he was out. Well the crowd on the third base side was the Caracas bunch, and boy, they got on their feet, and the only thing that kept them off the field was those army guards. I stood up and came back to the dugout. They carried Chico off the field. I apologized later on to Chico. All I was thinking was that you guys wanted to take me out. I just wanted to make sure somebody paid the freight.

The game went on and about two innings later, I am in the dugout, and one of our guys hits the ball. I turn my head to watch it, when out of the corner of my eye I caught a glimpse of Chico. He had come to, gotten dressed, and come into our dugout. Chico was getting ready to bust me right on the side of the head. I turned just in time and pulled back and his fist went beside my face, and then I took him down right into the bottom of the dugout. I am on top of him, I was a little stronger than Chico and had the advantage a bit, although he was a good size boy. The players from the other side came over. I could feel people pulling on my uniform. I was on top of Chico. I was afraid to come up because I thought the guys on the other team were going to hit me. And by golly, Norm Larker, and I have always remembered and talked about it, how Norm Larker and I raised up, and we stood back to back, while these guys are threatening us with bats. What I did not appreciate was that the American guys down in the bullpen did not come out of there to help us.

After the game was over, I was the last one to shower and get ready to get out of there. And again, it was Norm Larker who asks me if I wanted him to wait to go out with me. I said, nope, you go ahead, I will be all right. I waited about twenty minutes, because I had heard there was a crowd of fans outside — waiting for me. Before I left the clubhouse I took a fungo bat with me. If I was going to get attacked, by golly, I was going to take one or two with me.

So I walked out. I remember I had one of these shirts, you wear not inside the belt because it hung on the outside [guayabera]. It had a pocket up there on the left hand side. As I walked out of the clubhouse the main gate opened up and there was a tremendous crowd out there and they made a big, threatening noise. And then all at once there was no noise at all. You could have heard a pin drop. That gate opened and there was a guy with brass from the top of his head to his toes, flanked on each side by two people. He had four guys, and he comes walking straight towards me. And I thought, oh my god, I have really had it. The army is here to get me. Well, this guy comes walking up, looking straight at me, and he gets to about 15 feet from me and he starts to smile. And he comes up and, in perfect English, says, "It seems like you are in trouble." I said, "Yes sir, I am in trouble." And without shaking hands or anything, he puts something into that shirt pocket. It was a little pistol. When I saw what it was I reached for it and said, "No sir, no, no," and I handed it back to him. Then he said, "I think you need to come with us. We will take care of you."

I walked out of there through that many fans on the outside of that ballpark — and I am not exaggerating when I say there were 10,000 of them — through the gates and into this big limousine. We walked out and climbed into that limousine, and there was not one murmur from the crowd. And the army man took me home and gave me his card; it was a gold-plated card. He said, "If you run into any more trouble while you are in Venezuela, simply show this card." That man's name was Lieutenant Colonel Benjamin Maldonado, in effect, the vice-president of the country. He was in charge of *all* the military. And you know, in later years, he and his family visited us right here on our farm in North Carolina.

That was the most memorable moment I had in all my years in Venezuela.

PASSING OF AN ERA: DON LEPPERT

*Don Leppert performed three separate seasons in three different coun-
tries, starting with the Mexico City Aztecas in the Veracruz Winter League
in 1956-57. Leppert, a Milwaukee Braves' find, also played in Venezuela's
Occidental League and then in Puerto Rico.*

*A catcher, Leppert reached the major leagues in 1961 with the Pittsburgh
Pirates. The following winter, at the behest of the Pirates, the backstop
suited up for Ponce. Leppert and his Leones' teammates helped inaugurate
Hiram Bithorm Stadium, the new home of professional baseball in San
Juan. Leppert made a name for himself in Puerto Rican baseball history
by hitting the first home run in the Bithorm Stadium inaugural.*

*A four-year major league player, Leppert spent a decade in winter ball,
the majority as a manager in the Dominican Republic and Venezuela,
where he was a two-time manager of the year (1976 and 1977). Don was
generous with his time. He stressed during our protracted talk how enrich-
ing he felt the time he spent in the various foreign countries had been for
him. He mentioned how grounding it was for his growing children to compare their lives at home with children of similar age in the Dominican
Republic.*

*Leppert's last job was with the Minnesota Twins as director of player
development in Fort Myers, Florida. He and wife Daphine have retired
to an area not far there.*

**Can you tell me your place of birth and your earliest childhood baseball
memories?**

In Indianapolis, Indiana on October 19, 1931. Mom, dad and one brother.
Cincinnati and Chicago were the teams in closest proximity. With travel
restrictions in those days, I never was able to attend a major league game. I
lived across the street from a public park. In the summer, it was just routine
to get up in the morning, eat your breakfast, and take off for the park to play
baseball. Those pick up games went on all day, until night fall. Of course
during the game, you might have to come home and cut the grass, or something like that. But you cut the grass, and went back over to the park and the
games would still be going on.

I played in high school, but I attended college on an academic scholarship. I left college when the Korean War broke out. My hero was Ted Williams.
Not only because he was such an outstanding player, but because I admired

his service in the Marine Corps. I was in Korea when Williams was flying his missions. Williams is still my hero.

You began playing professionally after your hitch in the service?

When I returned from overseas, I had a few months remaining to finish out my enlistment. I played baseball for a base team in Fort Worth, Texas. While I was playing there, Roxy Middleton, who was a scout for the Milwaukee Braves, saw me play. There were other scouts interested in me, but I signed with the Braves in December, 1954. I had a tough sell there with my mom. I promised her I would go back and finish college later.

My first minor league season was with Evansville in the old Three-I League. Then I was promoted to Corpus Christi in the Big State League.

In the military, I was in the MPs. Master Sergeant Ernest Davis, I can remember, made a comment to us that I have lived with all my adult life. The army is what you make of it. If you hate the army, and treat it that way, you will be miserable. If you look for things to bitch about, you will find a lot of things to bitch about. But if you take the bad with the good, you will have a good term of enlistment. I took that with me to the winter leagues. I went down there with a positive attitude, thinking I could have all the fun in the world, and I did. Some of my best memories are from playing winter ball. I still get Christmas cards from people I met in the Dominican.

My first winter league season was in Mexico City in 1956-57. I played for the Aztecas. It was wonderful. It was all new to me. I loved it. Of course, you are going to have some difficult times when you are in foreign countries. Customs are different. The food in Mexico. I did not have any problems. It was an advantage over what I had been eating in the army. Anything is better than K-rations.

I lived in a hotel, right in the middle of Mexico City. Not far from the *Paseo de la Reforma*. I cannot remember the name of it, but it was a nice hotel. I think all the players from the U.S. lived there. Maybe about three or four players had their wives with them. Another three or four of us were single players. What I remember about the stadium in Mexico City was that they were building on to it. We played all day games for a good portion of the season, because the lights had not been fully installed.

We went fishing and duck hunting. Dove hunting. I really liked Mexico. Of course, they have gorgeous resorts around Acapulco and Veracruz. I remember we played in a town called Córdoba. There were wildflowers growing all over the side of the mountain. These wildflowers were very aromatic. The workers at the hotel we stayed in would pick the wildflowers, and then would fill the swimming pool with them. The wildflowers would float in the pool. There was just a spectacular aroma when you woke up every morning.

Don Leppert, with cap, a domestic named Margaret, Duke Carmel and Jack Spring — and a soon-to-be consumed pair of sea bass.

I have heard travel by bus at that time in Mexico could be somewhat demanding.

Well, it was not like the superhighways we have today. A couple of the towns we traveled through, you could not take a bus, because the bus could not make some of the turns on the mountain roads. The main roads were paved okay, but others were poor.

Johnny Riddle was our manager. Unfortunately, I was injured with about two or three weeks of the season remaining. There was a play at home plate. The throw came in from the outfield. I was ready to block the plate, and make the tag on the runner when the ball skipped up and went over my glove and hit my jaw, and broke my jaw. I had to come home. At that time, as I recall, it was three-team race, between Veracruz and the other Mexico City team and ourselves. I think the other Mexico City team won it, although I cannot be sure. I was back in the states.

The fans were pretty rowdy fans. My most memorable experience in Mexico had to do with the fans in Puebla. We were involved in a close game. I was hitting in the top of the ninth. I hit a two-run home run with two outs. It tied up the game. When I came up again in extra innings, the same pitcher I hit the home run against, drilled me. I charged the mound and there was a big fight. I was ejected from the game, and as I was walking back to the dugout, some fans started throwing things at me. Just as I reached the dugout, a bottle hit me in the chest. I was adjacent to the bat rack and grabbed a bat out of the bat rack and fired it at the fan that threw the bottle at me. It was a fungo bat, as matter of fact. I was arrested and went to jail. [Chuckles.]

That was a Saturday afternoon. We had another game on Sunday. I stayed overnight in jail. Apparently, it was custom for a priest to come to the jails on Sunday morning and ask if anyone wanted to attend mass. Being Catholic, I said, yes, I do. They took me from my cell, which was pretty primitive, and brought me to church. I was still in my baseball uniform, pretty well tore up, and metal spikes. [Amused.] If you can just imagine what those other Mexican churchgoers thought when they saw me walking down the center aisle of that cathedral with a guard, in my tattered uniform and spikes... [Laughs.]

The pitcher who hit me was an American pitcher. I cannot think of his name, right now. I did not think I would ever forget it, but I have. He pitched for the Detroit Tigers in the major leagues. I only faced him again in Triple A. The fan I threw the bat at, ducked. No one was hurt. It was a bad choice on my part. I was the one hit — with the bottle. I do not know if there was a legitimate reason for my arrest.

I was able to play in the game that Sunday afternoon, and the story of me walking into the church spread pretty well throughout the small town, so that was some debut for me in winter ball.

I was set to go back and play with the Aztecas the following winter, but the Braves' medical staff told me that I needed a knee operation. So I had the knee surgery.

Your next sampling of international baseball occurred in Venezuela's occidental winter league.

[In 1958-59] Jim Fanning was named the manager of Gavilánes of Maracaibo. He was a manager in the American Association; I had played for Fanning in the minor leagues for one year. He asked me to come down to Venezuela with him, which I did. I was married then. My wife was pregnant; she stayed home. My daughter was born right after I returned home, toward the end of the spring training. I lived at the Detroit Hotel in Maracaibo. Most of the residents were Americans who worked in the oil industry down there.

The stadium in Maracaibo was similar to all the other stadiums we played in. The stadium itself was pretty well maintained. The clubhouses were not always up to standard to the minor league parks in the U.S. In Maracaibo, they had some problems with the water. Most of the times, we dressed in the hotel and headed to the ballpark in uniform.

We went fishing every day. Oh, that Lake Maracaibo was something. They call it a lake, but it is really a bay. A salt water bay, like Tampa Bay. At that time, the world record tarpon and the world record snook came from that lake. There was another ballclub down there called Rapiños. Louie Aparicio played for them. Some of his family members were big fisherman. They hooked us up with commercial fisherman, and we rented boats from them. It was really enjoyable.

We would take the fish we caught and bring them to the fisheries and trade them for whatever particular kind of fish they were featuring that day. We ate different types of fish, twice a day, for the whole winter. It was great. We had a Jamaican maid; she was probably the best cook on the planet. Margaret was her name. Billy Muffett's wife used to come to her, and she would teach Billy Muffett's wife how to cook fish. We had a ball. It was probably the best year I ever spent in winter ball. We never went out to eat, because there were no better cooks in Maracaibo than our own Margaret.

Fanning fished, Billy Muffet fished. Tracy Stallard. Jack Spring. Oh, Duke Carmel. There were some Rapiños players every now and then that we would run into. Sometimes we would join them or sometimes they would join us. One of Aparicio's cousins, Aurelio, maybe? was in one of those fishing groups. It was great fun.

When we went out on the road, we stopped at some restaurants. Barbeque places, where they would cook the steaks for you right there at your table. They would take the fillet off the grill with a pair of thongs and slap it on your plate. It does not get any better than that. Venezuela was a big cattle producer. The produce was very fresh. I remember the strawberries.

One of the more unique towns in that league was a town called Cabimas. We had to take a ferry to get to where we played. There is probably a bridge there now. We played games on Sunday at 11:00 A.M. The reason being was that they used the same stadium for bullfights in the afternoon. Win, lose or draw, the game had to be over at the appointed time to make way for the bullfights.

Caracas was in the other division, or league. Traveling from Maracaibo to Caracas was a little tough. We needed an off day for travel...

Do you remember visiting the Hotel Humboldt in the capital?

Oh yeah—I remember that. In Caracas, Jack Spring and I took a tram that went across that ravine, I do not remember the name now, up to that hotel. I must have the same photo you are talking about. That was quite a spectacular view. That tram was made in Germany. It was fairly new, state-of-the-art, in those days. Caracas was probably one of the more modern cities in South America, one of the more inspiring cities, as far as places that had baseball. Of course, I had never been to Rio De Janeiro, or any other big city in South America. Caracas was fine once you entered the city. Transportation was good. You could do some sightseeing. The ballpark, the facilities, were all up to date.

Any clashes with the fans in Venezuela like you had in Mexico?

No particular incidents with the fans there, that I can recall. Just the normal stuff, throwing things at the umpire. The language was not a problem. Most of the people we came in contact with were bilingual. Most of the managers were, what they called "imports." Joe Schultz took over our club the following winter. I was on my way down there again to play. I had signed my contract, and my father had a heart attack and died. So I did not go. I went back later to manage in Venezuela in the 1970s.

Before that, you took part in one last winter league campaign.

I played winter ball, once more, in Puerto Rico in 1962. In Ponce. We lived at the Darlington Hotel. I was with the Pittsburgh organization. Bob Veale, Dave Cash, a longtime major league player, were on our team. We had one trip where the road across the top of the mountain left a lot to be desired. We took station wagons. It was pretty spooky.

They opened a new Stadium in San Juan that was called Hiram Bithorn Stadium. As a matter of fact, I hit the first home run ever hit in that stadium. I have a story about that, too. I homered against Denny LeMaster, pitching for San Juan. The next time we came into San Juan to play, the president of the league called me out to home plate before the game and gave me a plaque, designating that I hit the first home run at Hiram Bithorn Stadium, with the date on it and all. I gave the plaque to the clubhouse guy, and he put it in my locker. I played the game, and when I came back to the clubhouse someone had stolen the plaque right out of my locker. [Laugh of consternation.]

A few years later, I was coaching with Pittsburgh, and we had a staff get-together at my house. José Pagan was there. The subject came up, and I told him the story about how someone stole my plaque. Well, we went to Puerto Rico when the Clemente sports complex opened. The Pirates played the Cincinnati Reds in an exhibition game. Before that game, they gave me a replacement plaque. I still have it. I am looking at it on my wall. "Don Leppert ... first home run ... Hiram Bithorn Stadium ... October 24, 1962." Here is another one... "Venezuelan Winter League ... Don Leppert ... MVP of the 1959 All-Star Game."

In Puerto Rico, what did you do when you were not playing?

Oh, same thing—I fished all the time in Ponce. There was an army base not far away. Bill Adair, who I replaced as manager that season when he was fired, he had some connections with an army officer who gave us permission

Opposite: Sixto Escobar Stadium in 1962, the year the PRWL abandoned it in favor of new Hiram Bithorn Stadium. The Normandie Hotel can be seen in the background to the left (The Sporting News Archive).

to fish on a lake. Lake Guayabal. That was fresh water fishing, mostly large-mouth bass. We had quite a winter there fishing. The places we went to eat were just like the restaurants in the United States.

Did anything else occur during the season that could match hitting the stadium's inaugural home run?

The one big incident in Puerto Rico happened during the Cuban Missile Crisis. President Kennedy had the Fifth Fleet armada stationed right off the coast of Puerto Rico. From the roof of the Darlington Hotel, we could see practically our whole navy. One funny thing about it. My wife's mother, who was living in Kentucky, my wife's former home, she called Daphine. *My God, there is going to be a nuclear war, come right home. Take the next plane back home.* I had to calm Daphine down by telling her that I was no expert on nuclear bombs, but I did not think anyone was going to drop one on Ponce, Puerto Rico. I think we are safer here, I told her. That became a joke in our family later on, that Khrushchev was going to attack Ponce, Puerto Rico.

What's a day-in-the-life like for you now?

I have been married 54 years. We have five children, nine grandchildren. I celebrated my 80th birthday the day before yesterday. It has been a good run. And I am still fishing!

The winter leagues were great fun. I would go back tomorrow, if somebody would call me up and hire me.

BIBLIOGRAPHY

Books

Antero Nuñez, José. *Series del Caribe*. Caracas, Venezuela: Impresos Urbina, C.A., 1987.

Crescioni Benítez, José A. *El Béisbol Profesional Boricua*. First Book Publishing of Puerto Rico, 1997.

Figueredo, Jorge S. *Beisbol Cubano: An un Paso de las Grandes Ligas, 1878–1961*. Jefferson, NC: McFarland, 2005.

_____. *Cuban Baseball: A Statistical History, 1878–1961*. Jefferson, NC: McFarland, 2003.

_____. *Who's Who in Cuban Baseball*. Jefferson, NC: McFarland, 2003.

Mickelson, Ed. *Out of the Park: Memoir of a Minor League Baseball All-Star*. Jefferson, NC: McFarland, 2005.

Roberts, Dave. *A Baseball Odyssey*. Sacramento, CA: Embarcadero Press, 1999.

Stallworth Kubiszyn, Lucy. *When a Star Fell on Alabama: The Jack Kubiszyn Story*. Tuscaloosa, AL: Word Way Press, 2009.

Treto Cisneros, Pedro. *Enciclopedia del Beisbol Mexicano*. Segunda edición. Revistas Deportivas, S.A. de C.V. Mexico D.F., 1994.

Van Hyning, Thomas E. *Puerto Rico's Winter Leagues: A History of Major League Baseball's Launching Pad*. Jefferson, NC: McFarland, 1995.

Articles

Gabcik, John. "Jack Harshman." SABR Baseball Biography Project.

Kahrl, Christina. "Minnie Miñoso's Still Not in the HOF?" December 5, 2011. ESPN.com.

Web References

baseballalmanac.com
baseball-reference.com
blackacesblogspot.com
cubanball.com
retrosheet.org
rickswaine.com
wikipedia.org

INDEX